Colorado's
Canyon Country

**A Guide to
Hiking & Floating
BLM Wildlands**

Text by **Mark Pearson**

Photography by **John Fielder**

WESTCLIFFE PUBLISHERS

www.westcliffepublishers.com

For more information about other fine books and calendars from Westcliffe Publishers, please contact your local bookstore, call us at 1-800-523-3692, write for our free color catalog, or visit us on the Web at www.westcliffepublishers.com.

INTERNATIONAL STANDARD BOOK NUMBER:
1-56579-387-0

TEXT COPYRIGHT:
Mark Pearson. 2001. All rights reserved.
PHOTOGRAPHY COPYRIGHT:
John Fielder. 2001. All rights reserved.

EDITOR:
Kelly Kordes Anton
DESIGN AND PRODUCTION:
Rebecca Finkel, F + P Graphic Design, Inc.
PRODUCTION MANAGER:
Craig Keyzer

PUBLISHED BY:
Westcliffe Publishers, Inc.
P.O. Box 1261
Englewood, Colorado 80150
www.westcliffepublishers.com

Printed in Hong Kong
by H & Y Printing, Ltd.

PLEASE NOTE:
Risk is always a factor in backcountry and high-mountain travel. Many of the activities described in this book can be dangerous, especially when weather is adverse or unpredictable, and when unforeseen events or conditions create a hazardous situation. The author has done his best to provide the reader with accurate information about backcountry travel, as well as to point out some of its potential hazards. It is the responsibility of the users of this guide to learn the necessary skills for safe backcountry travel, and to exercise caution in potentially hazardous areas, especially on glaciers and avalanche-prone terrain. The author and publisher disclaim any liability for injury or other damage caused by backcountry traveling, mountain biking, or performing any other activity described in this book.

COVER PHOTO:
Dolores River Canyon Wilderness Study Area.

TITLE PAGE: Sunset, Squaw/Papoose Canyon Wilderness Study Area.

Photos by John Fielder.

LIBRARY OF CONGRESS CATALOGING-IN-PUBLICATION DATA:
Pearson, Mark, 1959–
    Colorado's canyon country : a guide to hiking & floating BLM Wildlands / by Mark Pearson ; photography by John Fielder.—2nd ed.
        p.   cm.
    Rev. ed. of: Colorado BLM wildlands. c1992.
    Includes bibliographical references (p.) and index.
    ISBN: 1-56579-387-0
    1. Hiking—Colorado—Guidebooks. 2. Canoes and canoeing—Colorado—Guidebooks, 3. Colorado—Guidebooks. 4. Wilderness areas—Colorado—Guidebooks. I. Fielder, John. II. Pearson, Mark, 1959– Colorado BLM wildlands. III. Title

GV199.42.C6 P43 2001
796.51'099788—dc21   00-047233

Acknowledgments

Recreational use of Colorado's Bureau of Land Management (BLM) lands has grown exponentially in the last 20 years. Due to the booming demand for outdoor recreation, in 1976 Congress directed the BLM to undertake a thorough evaluation of its roadless lands for wilderness suitability. Conservationists actively participated in the BLM's wilderness inventory, even pre-dating the BLM's efforts in several cases. This citizen involvement was coordinated by the Colorado Open Space Council (now the Colorado Environmental Coalition, or CEC). One of the tools developed by CEC to better educate and involve the public was a hiking guide to Colorado BLM wildlands: *Finding Freedom: A Guide to Colorado's Unknown Wildlands.*

The guide, published in 1983 by CEC, is now out of print. As one of the original contributors to this guide, I want to thank the editor, Sharyl Kinnear, and several other contributors, including Norm Mullen, Dick Guadagno, and John Stansfield, for their permission to occasionally borrow from *Finding Freedom* in the preparation of this more extensive hiking guide to BLM lands in Colorado.

Many BLM employees greatly assisted in the preparation of this guide as well. Although my more than 20 years of exploration in these areas alone and being a leader of CEC and Sierra Club outings provided me with a solid foundation for preparing the guidebook, my experience was bolstered by conversations with BLM field staff about alternate routes and their help nailing down legal public access. In particular, Dave Cooper in the Craig office, Carlos Sauvage in Grand Junction, and Eric Finstick in the state office gave valuable comments and advice. The many BLM employees who participated in the preparation of the numerous wilderness environmental impact statements and associated plan-ning documents deserve thanks, for these documents contained a wealth of information and physical data about the areas. Finally, the BLM's assistance in obtaining the base maps used for the initial production of this guide was invaluable.

—MARK PEARSON, *Durango, Colorado*

High in a sandstone seep, Dolores River Canyon Wilderness Study Area.

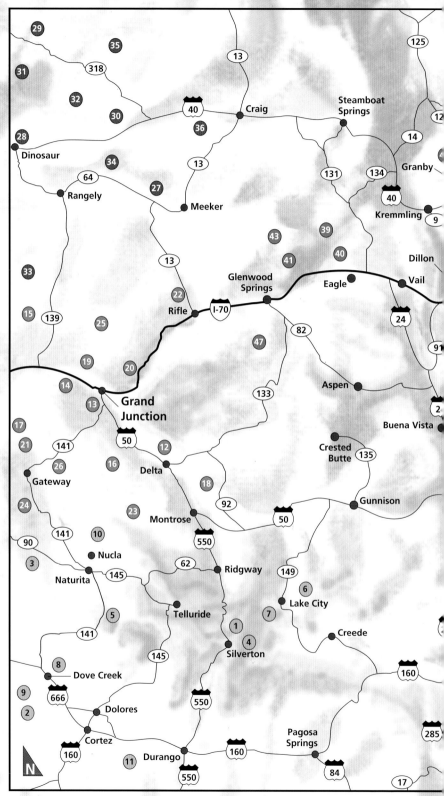

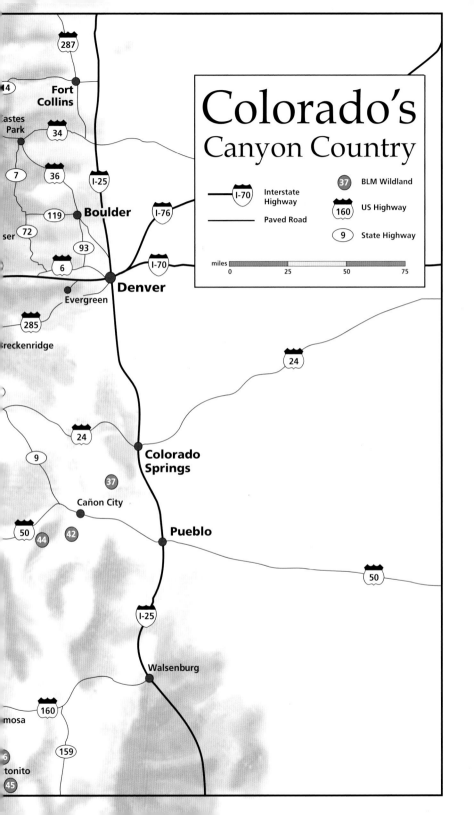

Colorado's
Canyon Country

Legend

- **I-70** Interstate Highway
- Paved Road
- **37** BLM Wildland
- **160** US Highway
- **9** State Highway

miles
0   25   50   75

287

4

Fort
Collins

astes
Park

34

7

36

I-25

119 **Boulder**

I-76

ser 72

93

6

I-70

Denver

Evergreen

285

Breckenridge

24

24

9

37

Cañon City

50 44 42

Pueblo

50

I-25

Walsenburg

160

mosa

159

6

tonito

45

Table of Contents

Foreword

My earliest dreams of Colorado conjured views of lofty snowcapped peaks, fields of wildflowers covering the colors of the spectrum, and cool crystalline waters cascading over moss-covered boulders. Those were the dreams of a 13-year-old North Carolinian. As a 21-year-old fresh out of college, I decided to check the accuracy of those dreams. I came to Colorado to seek my fortune.

I may not have found my fortune, at least not right away, but I did learn that my dreams were accurate—almost. Not only did I discover those mountains, flowers, and creeks, but ultimately much more. Though the central Rocky Mountains run through the middle of Colorado, to the east lie the Great Plains of eastern Colorado and to the west the deep canyons of the Dolores, the Colorado, the Yampa, and the Green Rivers.

Often overlooked by recreationists, many of these non-mountain places are under the jurisdiction of the Bureau of Land Management (BLM). What most of us consider to be boring grazing lands are actually some of Colorado's most scenic areas— and they are virtually undiscovered! Many of these BLM lands are roadless, affording the hiker or rafter a chance to see Colorado as it existed a thousand years ago, and most are being studied for inclusion in the National Wilderness Preservation System.

In southwestern Colorado, Cross Canyon Wilderness Study Area, near the town of Cortez, contains many unrestored Anasazi ruins. Whether you seek ancient Indian artwork on rock walls (petroglyphs and pictographs) or just solitude in a sweet-smelling piñon-juniper forest, you are guaranteed a unique experience. The Dolores River Canyon Wilderness Study Area hides scenery and wildlife enjoyed by relatively few people.

The BLM wildlands of southwestern Colorado are not unlike those in the midwestern and northwestern sectors of the state. Most are dominated by deep sandstone canyons replete with waterfalls, plunge pools, and Indian artifacts. The Grand Junction area offers the world's second greatest accumulation of natural arches, and BLM wildlands in the Craig area contain acclaimed eagle habitat as well as sandstone formations the envy of any sculptor.

In addition, some very special alpine and subalpine mountain lands have slipped through the National Forest system. As a result, the BLM manages the columbine wildflowers, black bears, and elk that overrun places such as American Flats, Powderhorn, and Castle Peak Wilderness Study Areas. Two BLM wildlands actually contain a pair of 14,000-foot peaks: Handies and Redcloud!

When you visit, tread lightly—Mother Nature is quite fragile, both in high and desert country. Vehicles are prohibited by law from entering wilderness study areas. Always pack out your trash from the backcountry, but don't pack out Indian pottery or other antiquities—it's also against the law. Leave things the way they are, so the next person who comes along can imagine he or she is the first to discover that hidden spot!

Author Mark Pearson has written a marvelous guide, with not so much information that it spoils the surprises you will encounter, but enough to get you safely in and out. Here, we present 48 of Colorado's most spectacular—yet unknown—wildlands. I hope you have the opportunity to enjoy them all!

—JOHN FIELDER, *Englewood, Colorado*

Opposite: Black Rocks and the Colorado River, Ruby Canyon,
Ruby Ridge Canyons Wilderness Study Area. Photo by John Fielder.

Preface

The Bureau of Land Management administers more than 8 million acres of public lands in Colorado. These lands are often called "the lands no one wanted" because they are composed of public lands that were never disposed of under laws such as the Homestead Act and the Mining Law of 1872, and they were never considered desirable enough to be reserved for National Parks or National Forests.

In Colorado, BLM lands are generally found in the westernmost third of the state, where the Rocky Mountains give way to the arid high mesas and desert canyons of the Colorado Plateau. Other concentrations of BLM land exist in the San Luis Valley and along the Arkansas River between Buena Vista and Pueblo.

Anasazi potsherds, Cross Canyon Wilderness Study Area.

BLM lands might be considered the third province of Colorado, the other provinces being the Rocky Mountains and the High Plains. BLM's province is one of desert river canyons, piñon-juniper woodlands, endangered cactus, multicolored badlands, ponderosa pines, innumerable ancient artifacts of long departed Indian cultures, free-roaming wild horse herds, high lonely mesas, and America's national symbol—the bald eagle. In short, these are the most unpopulated and remote corners of Colorado, and literally the playground of the deer and the antelope.

Colorado's BLM wildlands are "real" wilderness. There are frequently no trails and even fewer trailheads. Signs don't tell you where—and where not—to tread. Route-finding and orienteering skills are at a premium. In exchange, the visitor is rewarded by a sense of true isolation and exploration, by a longing to see what's around the next bend, over the next knoll, behind the next tree. No tracks and no signs indicate anyone has ever ventured beyond the last roadside, and only relics of bygone eras mark the folly of previous dreamers. There is no coddling, and little hand-holding, by the benevolent federal stewards of this land. Of course, with these opportunities for a true wilderness experience comes a great deal of responsibility to leave nothing but footprints—and very light footprints at that.

All the areas described in this guidebook were studied and proposed for designation as wilderness by either BLM (relatively few) or Colorado conservation groups (all the rest). Wilderness designation means the land is left in its natural condition for future generations to enjoy and benefit from. No mining, no logging, no road-building, and no motorized vehicles are allowed to mar areas designated by Congress as wilderness.

BLM lands in Colorado include many ecosystems that are not represented elsewhere in the National Wilderness Preservation System. In particular, significant downstream portions of most of Colorado's major rivers lie in these proposed wildernesses. Ruby Canyon on the Colorado River at the Utah state line, Cross Mountain Gorge of the Yampa, 30 miles of the Dolores River above Bedrock, the Gunnison Gorge below the Black Canyon of the Gunnison, Browns Canyon on the Arkansas, and the Rio Grande at the New Mexico state line are all described as hikes and floats in this guide.

Of the roughly 8 million acres of Colorado BLM lands, I describe hikes here for more than 1 million acres. This million acres represents the land base proposed by Colorado conservationists for wilderness. When combined with adjacent roadless U.S. Forest Service lands, the total is almost 1.3 million acres of de facto wildlands. BLM has proposed wilderness protection for approximately 400,000 acres in a lesser number of these areas, but Congress has designated as wilderness a literal handful to date. Obviously, the areas and hikes described in this guidebook are not a complete list of the recreational opportunities available on Colorado BLM lands. They are, however, the wildest and most natural regions under BLM jurisdiction in Colorado.

Colorado is a state of extraordinary diversity in scenery and ecology. Many of the areas described herein are only a stone's throw off major state and federal highways, yet are hidden from the exploring public by a strategically placed hogback or ridge. As you travel the common and remote byways of Colorado, plan to linger for an afternoon or a weekend at some of these lesser-known hideaways. Many a mesa or slickrock canyon will be revealed with little extra effort.

Because of the generally lower elevation of BLM lands, they are ideal hiking destinations in spring and fall. In springtime, a visitor will often catch the desert at its most glorious wildflower bloom, and in fall many areas glow with brilliant golden cottonwoods and red oakbrush. Other BLM areas form the foothills and transition zones between desert and mountain and are inviting year-round.

Colorado is fortunate to have 39 officially designated wilderness areas, enacted by Congress in 13 separate bills. Only three formally protected wilderness areas are located on BLM lands; nearly all the remainder are managed by the U.S. Forest Service and a couple by the National Park Service. Descriptions and hikes to these National Forest and National Park wilderness areas are detailed in another Westcliffe guidebook, *The Complete Guide to Colorado's Wilderness Areas,* a similar cooperative effort between photographer John Fielder and myself.

—MARK PEARSON, *Durango, Colorado*

Introduction

How to Use This Guide

For ease of identification, the areas in this guide are numbered 1 through 48. Note these reference numbers in the table of contents, on the state map, and in the individual area descriptions.

Only a handful of the areas described contain marked and maintained trails. Where trails exist, I reference them. In many cases, the area descriptions simply provide directions to canyon mouths or rims and suggestions for potential hikes from those jumping-off points. The length and rigor of the hikes is left largely to the individual hiker.

BLM has divided its administration of public lands in Colorado into 11 field offices. These offices roughly conform to geographic regions of the state. For example, the Little Snake Office in Craig covers the Yampa and Little Snake river drainages in northwest Colorado while the Gunnison Field Office covers the Gunnison River basin in western Colorado. For ease of use, areas are organized by geographic region in this book, beginning in the southwest corner of the state and moving clockwise around Colorado through areas defined as the Southwest Region, Midwest Region, Northwest Region, and Central Region. These somewhat arbitrary regions each overlap two or more BLM field offices.

Area descriptions begin with a bulleted list highlighting pertinent attributes: a general sense of location relative to a Colorado town, the area's elevation range, predominant vegetation communities, the amount of roadless country contained in the area, its wilderness status, special features that might be the focus of hikes, and relevant USGS 7.5-minute topographic maps.

The BLM series of 1:100,000 surface management maps is an additional source of information that is often invaluable for determining access. You can obtain these from the local BLM office or from well-stocked sporting goods stores. Addresses and phone numbers for all BLM field offices are listed in Appendix B. Often, local BLM recreation planners can answer questions about routes or give specific advice about road conditions, water availability, and other details for trip planning.

Suggested hikes of varying length and difficulty comprise the bulk of each entry. Hikes fall into one of four categories:

- **Day Hikes** consist of trails and destinations appropriate for a several-hour to all-day excursion.

- **Destination Hikes** include specific locations such as peaks or canyons that may require overnight trips, but might also be reached in one day.

- **Loop Hikes** describe routes that circle through the area and return the hiker to the starting location by a different route.

- **Shuttle Hikes** embrace one-way routes that require two vehicles, with one left at the beginning and one at the ending trailhead.

Opposite: Anasazi tower, Ruin Canyon, Cross Canyon Wilderness Study Area. Photo by John Fielder.

Each hike includes mileage, lowest and highest elevations, and a subjective rating of difficulty. Easy hikes are generally those of short distance or little elevation gain. Moderate hikes may require substantial mileage or elevation gain along well-maintained trails with moderate grades. Strenuous hikes include those routes with greater exposure to weather or topography, faint or nonexistent trails to follow, or steep and sustained grades. The text describing each hike highlights features such as arches, waterfalls, and scenic overlooks encountered along the trail.

Colorado's desert wilderness beckons. Fill your water bottles, grab your pack and boots, and head out for one of the purest wilderness experiences you may ever find!

Desert Etiquette

Desert environments are fragile and show the scars of careless or malicious visitors for generations. Visitors should carefully follow the admonition to take only pictures and leave only footprints. Even this should be strengthened: Minimize the impact of your footprints. Cryptogam, a fragile desert soil, is often found in remote and unfrequented locations. Cryptogamic soil is characterized by a black, knobby surface that looks like the fungus it partially is. Cryptogams hold the soil together and help reduce erosion. Hikers' footprints break this cover and can lead to increased erosion, so pause to consider your route before plunging ahead through undisturbed mats of cryptogamic soil.

Hike on designated trails where they exist. You can expect frequent cross-country travel; however, in these cases, use game trails, water courses, and other features that reduce the creation of new trails.

Water sources in the desert can be few and far between but are vital to the continued health of native wildlife populations. Be careful not to pollute desert springs, streams, and potholes. Camp at least 100 feet from water sources and never bathe or wash dishes in them.

Use a camp stove instead of building fires. Don't build new fire rings. In fact, you might not need rocks if you build a fire on bare ground. Fires sterilize the soil and blacken rocks, leaving unmistakable evidence of your passage; you can reduce damage to soil by removing the topsoil from your fire pit and then replacing it when finished, eliminating evidence of your fire. In this manner, the soil ecology is disturbed less than with traditional fire rings.

Desert ecosystems have low resistance to trampling and other impacts associated with campsites. Try not to camp in the same location for more than two nights in order to reduce the damage to vegetation and to reduce soil compaction.

Bury human feces 6 to 8 inches deep, and burn the toilet paper (if conditions warrant) before filling in the hole.

Be courteous to and considerate of other users of the area. If the area is used for livestock grazing, be sure to close gates behind you and do not harass the livestock.

Pack out whatever you pack in, and try to leave the land without a trace of your visit so the next hikers can imagine they're seeing never-before-explored lands.

Don't let the aridity of desert washes and canyons lull you into forgetting that their shape is due to the explosive force of flash floods. Always consider the possibility of unseen downpours in the surrounding high country as you search for that perfect desert campsite.

One final note: One of the great thrills of hiking Colorado's western deserts is the chance to encounter remnants of thousand-year-old Anasazi and Fremont civilizations. Not only is it illegal to remove or damage cultural artifacts (such actions are punishable by stiff fines and jail time), but such reckless behavior also destroys an irreplaceable resource for future generations. Please be sure to leave all archaeological sites just as you found them and do not disturb pottery sherds, projectile points, corn cobs, structures, petroglyphs, or any other type of artifact. Report any suspicious activity at these sites to an appropriate BLM office.

A Word to Hikers

For the unprepared, the wilderness can be an unforgiving teacher. To ensure the enjoyment of a trip, hikers should possess basic knowledge about wilderness first-aid and about the appropriate equipment for their adventure. What follows is a brief discussion of environmental exposure and the essential equipment every hiker should have when exploring wild and remote BLM lands, many of which are far from the beaten track and located where other visitors or BLM management personnel may be few and far between. Numerous books offer more extensive advice about wilderness emergencies, equipment, camping and orienteering skills, food planning, and weather. The Wilderness Education Association and the National Outdoor Leadership School both publish good books about fundamental wilderness skills. Even the most experienced hiker can use an occasional refresher of outdoor survival skills because the state of knowledge is constantly changing—particularly when it comes to equipment and to wilderness first-aid issues such as hypothermia.

Adverse environmental conditions pose the most potentially dangerous situations for outdoor travelers. You can encounter extremes of both cold and heat in BLM areas in a given season. Wilderness travelers should have a basic understanding of the symptoms of and treatments for the physical reactions to each of these extremes.

Water

Water in the desert is a magical thing. Moisture has a distinctive odor that carries down a canyon, beckoning ever nearer. The fragrance of a moist alcove graced by hanging ferns and a belt of lush greenery is essentially indescribable but certainly unforgettable. Water in many BLM areas is sporadic, transitory, and untrustworthy, but when a cool, clear spring is discovered in the midst of the blazing desert heat, it is a treat difficult to overlook.

Much BLM land, however, is situated in sedimentary formations with significant salt content. Alkali-laden streams and springs flowing in these areas are obvious owing to the white rime of salt that adorns their channels, making them look like a natural margarita glass. Hikers might think twice before imbibing from heavily alkaline waters.

Most BLM land is leased for livestock grazing and/or is home to substantial populations of big game animals. Therefore, hikers should always assume that running water in the desert is home to the parasite *Giardia lamblia* and other microorganisms, and should take appropriate precautions. *Giardia lamblia* is a waterborne organism transferred via fecal mater from infected animals. Minute cysts that survive for weeks or months in even frigid waters enter a new host and can then cause a disease called giardiasis, which has severe flu-like symptoms.

To guard against giardiasis, treat water of uncertain origin by boiling, by filtering, or with chemicals. Experts say giardia cysts are killed by exposure to boiling water at any altitude (it doesn't need to be a hard, rolling boil). Most commonly available water purification filters will also remove the cysts, but be sure to check the manufacturer's instructions. Iodine is the only chemical widely recommended for water purification because the effectiveness of chlorine is influenced by water temperature and siltation. Iodine, however, leaves an aftertaste and may need to be camouflaged by flavored drinks.

You can usually carry sufficient water on day hikes, so only overnight visitors need consider requirements for water purification. Most BLM areas described here have reasonably good sources of water that are easily treated for human use.

Hypothermia

Hypothermia is the lowering of the core body temperature to less than 95° Fahrenheit. Hypothermia can occur in one of two modes: chronic and acute. Chronic hypothermia is the gradual lowering of body temperature over many hours, or even days, and is frequently the result of continued exposure to damp and windy conditions. It can be extremely serious because by the time symptoms appear, the hiker's sources of internal energy have been severely depleted. Two common symptoms characterize chronic hypothermia: exhaustion and lack of coordination. A person experiencing chronic hypothermia will be unable to walk 30 feet in a straight line heel-to-toe. Intense shivering and mild confusion may also occur.

Treat chronic hypothermia by preventing further heat loss, primarily by replacing wet clothing with dry clothing, getting out of the wind, and wrapping the victim with numerous layers of insulating clothing. Chronic hypothermia victims are very dehydrated and should be given fluids—preferably warm—to drink. Warm the victim using hot packs (such as hot water in plastic water bottles) applied to the palms and soles or by using the time-honored treatment of cuddling with one or two other hikers in a sleeping bag. Allow hypothermia victims to rest in order to recover needed energy, but if they appear to be slipping deeper into hypothermia, they need to be evacuated immediately since they can slip into a semicomatose state.

Acute hypothermia results from immersion in cold water and occurs within two hours. A good rule of thumb is that anyone who has been immersed in 50° F water for more than 20 minutes is suffering from severe loss of heat. A serious concern with acute hypothermia victims is a phenomenon known as "afterdrop," whereby the victim's core temperature continues to drop even as he or she is being reheated. Because the acute hypothermia victim's skin temperature is so low, substantial amounts of additional heat can be lost simply as blood circulates from the body core to the skin surface. The ideal treatment for an acute hypothermia victim is immersion in hot water (110° F), but a more practical field treatment may be a blazing bonfire.

Opposite: Canyon scrambling, Bull Canyon Wilderness Study Area. Photo by Dave Cooper.

Cuddling in a sleeping bag with one or two bare-skinned rescuers is another means of adding substantial heat to the victim.

Of course, the best cure is prevention. Proper attire, including layering and protection from wind and rain, is a must. Hikers should be in good physical condition, eat food of high nutritional value at regular intervals, and drink plenty of liquids (as much as 16 ounces per hour). Plan your itinerary in a reasonable fashion to prevent exhaustion.

Heat Stress

Most BLM areas are well-described as deserts, and summertime temperatures routinely exceed 100° F. Heatstroke and heat exhaustion are two environmental stresses for which you should be prepared. Heat exhaustion, the less serious of the two, is characterized by the same symptoms as seen for shock. These include a rapid heart rate, pale color, light-headedness, and frequently profuse sweating. Treatment consists of having the victim lie down, elevating the victim's feet, and providing at least one to two quarts of water.

Heatstroke is an extremely serious condition and definitely poses an emergency. In heatstroke, the body has lost its ability to control heating, and the core temperature of the body can rapidly rise to 105° F and even 115° F. Symptoms include red, hot, and dry skin, since the body is unable to cool by sweating. These conditions are life threatening and the victim's body temperature needs to be immediately reduced. If possible, immerse the victim in cold water, but at a minimum move the victim to a shaded location. Evaporative cooling in the form of wet clothing can help cool the victim, and massaging the victim's extremities can help circulate blood and further reduce the core temperature. The victim should be evacuated from the hot area as soon as possible.

Again, prevention is the best medicine. Some hikers suggest wearing light-colored, long-sleeved shirts and long pants made of cotton; others prefer more exposed skin area and sweating to keep cool through evaporation. In either case, drink plenty of water when hiking in hot weather and stop to rest frequently.

The 10 Essentials

Many wilderness education organizations teach a variation of "the 10 essentials." This is a list of items considered essential for surviving most unexpected events while in the wilderness. One such list consists of the following:

- matches, striker, or lighter, and fire starter
- knife
- emergency shelter such as a poncho or ground cloth
- food and water
- first-aid kit
- signaling devices such as mirrors or whistles
- map and compass
- sunglasses and sunscreen

- extra clothes
- flashlight with extra batteries and bulb

Carry these items in your pack at all times, even on the most innocuous seeming hikes, since you never know when the urge might strike to go just a little farther than planned.

A Word to Boaters

This guidebook includes brief descriptions for floating segments of several Colorado rivers. These are by no means intended to provide explicit information about potential hazards or unique conditions of special concern on any given river; instead, they are intended to offer some ideas for trip planning and opportunities for alternative access to the areas. In all cases, it is best to contact the appropriate BLM office to obtain specific information about launch sites, features of special interest, and river hazards even though permits are not required for any of the river segments described. BLM has prepared river maps indicating access, mileage, campsites, and land ownership for most of these river segments. An excellent source for additional information is *The Floaters Guide to Colorado* by Doug Wheat.

I describe the rivers using a common classification scale ranging from easy (Class I) to unrunnable (Class VI). Several segments described here contain Class II, III, and IV rapids, significant enough to require scouting the rapids before running them.

Most boaters are familiar with the minimum impact camping techniques that are uniformly required on rivers for which permits are issued. It never hurts to review these techniques, however, so accepted practices for reducing or eliminating human impact on the environment are covered here briefly.

Colorado's rivers all receive substantial use that is increasing year-round. As a result, obvious campsites exist along every river; it is best to camp in an already impacted site rather than create new damage at a pristine site.

Most Colorado rivers transport plenty of debris, so fuel for fires in the form of driftwood is in abundant supply. Please bring a fire pan, however, in which to construct your fire, and haul out your ashes with you. Use of a fire pan prevents the blackening of sandy beaches and reduces the negative visual impact of a carpet of charcoal on an otherwise clean beach. A fire pan should have a rim of at least 3 inches. You can soak the ashes thoroughly in a bucket and scoop any that float into a garbage container. Ashes that sink can be dumped into the main current of the river.

Human waste should similarly be hauled out from wilderness rivers. Recent changes in regulations have resulted in a change from the old method of using large rocket boxes lined with plastic garbage bags. Environmental regulations now prohibit disposal of human sewage in landfills; thus the garbage bag method is no longer allowed on regulated rivers. Instead, river managers suggest using new steel or molded plastic toilet boxes with hose fittings that permit them to be flushed clean with water at dump stations designed for recreational vehicles. Look for these toilet boxes in river equipment catalogs or stores.

Basic river safety requires a Type III or Type V life vest for each participant, plus one extra vest per boat. Adequate first-aid kits should be included on each boat, along with an extra oar, repair kit, rescue throw rope, and pump. Certainly, there is no substitute for experience. A situation that might seem innocuous to a novice, such as the approach to a bridge piling, can be fraught with danger. Exercise caution and stop to scout any obstacle with which you are unfamiliar.

That said, floating is an exquisite means of exploring Colorado's canyon country. The riparian corridors that define these rivers offer a refreshing contrast to the often arid and desolate uplands. River travel also provides access to secret canyons and many otherwise inaccessible locations. With proper preparation, floating desert rivers will be an unforgettable journey.

John Fielder

Sunrise, Dolores River Canyon Wilderness Study Area.

Wilderness Explained

What Is Wilderness?

Congress provided a legal description of wilderness in the 1964 Wilderness Act, a law some describe as the nearest example of poetry in legislation. In this landmark law, Congress expressed its desire that "an increasing population, accompanied by expanding settlement and growing mechanization, does not occupy and modify all areas within the United States." As a means of preventing such occupation and modification, Congress created the legal idea of "wilderness." The law created a definition of wilderness this way: "in contrast with those areas where man and his own works dominate the landscape, [wilderness] is hereby recognized as an area where the earth and its community of life are untrammeled by man, where man himself is a visitor who does not remain." (Note that untrammeled means "unmodified" and has no relation to trampling.)

The authors of the Wilderness Act intended that wilderness preserve and perpetuate ecosystems as they functioned when the Europeans first arrived on the North American continent. They envisioned not a static landscape, frozen in time, but a living and dynamic environment full of the fury and calm of nature. Windstorms, fire, avalanches, insect infestations, floods—all these are vital aspects of wilderness every bit as much as the placid lake whose mirrorlike waters reflect crimson clouds at sunset or the bright, sun-dappled forest meadow full of dazzling wildflowers. In short, wilderness represents the epitome of raw, spontaneous nature.

For humans, wilderness represents a place that distills life to its most fundamental concerns of warmth, food, and shelter. It is often difficult for us to shed the pace and trappings of civilization, particularly as we attempt to squeeze that weekend backpacking trip into our busy schedules. For that reason, big wilderness is as beneficial for humans as it is for natural ecosystems. To explore vast wilderness areas, we must abandon worldly timetables and schedules, and instead immerse ourselves in the flows and patterns of wilderness. We rise with the sun, sleep with the darkness, huddle from the storms.

Congress also defined management of areas designated as wilderness. With the goal of precluding expanding settlement and mechanization from dominating the landscape, Congress took pains to prohibit the obvious culprits—logging, mining, and road-building. The Wilderness Act forbids permanent structures and commercial enterprises as well. Congress further abolished the use of motorized vehicles in wilderness as obvious signs of mechanization. More subtly, Congress prohibited all mechanized vehicles, a generous category that includes bicycles and hang gliders, for example. Some might wonder at excluding muscle-powered machines, but remember the wilderness ideal demands that humans abandon their desire to dominate the landscape. The wheel and the gear stand as two of humanity's greatest inventions; together they conquer time and distance. Thus the bicyclist can readily cover 20 or 30 miles or more in a few hours on wilderness trails, where before someone walking might travel at best 12 or 15 miles in a long day. In effect, wheeled machines shrink wilderness and let us further expand our hectic schedules. Hang gliders represent a similar domination of humans over nature, the dream of conquering flight. I fear that those who argue for using mechanized means to explore the wilderness forget that wilderness stands for more than a recreational playground. There is a serious cultural, even spiritual, meaning to wilderness—the idea that in these special places humans willingly forgo their technological dominance over nature and agree to meet nature on her terms.

Political realities dictated that Congress could not preclude all types of human activities, even those which wilderness purists disdain. Since the lion's share of wilderness fell on western public lands in a rural agricultural economy, Congress provided that livestock grazing could continue in wilderness areas, reasoning that cows munching grass couldn't much damage the environment where other large herbivores once grazed. Congress further provided that hunting and fishing would be allowed since for millennia humans had pursued game through the now-recognized wilderness. Congress also left a couple loopholes, acknowledging preexisting rights to water and mineral resources. These loopholes have occasionally created substantial controversy between the wilderness-loving public and private rights holders.

Wilderness and the BLM

The National Park Service and the United States Forest Service (but not the Bureau of Land Management) were directed by the original 1964 Wilderness Act to undertake studies of lands under their jurisdiction and make recommendations to Congress about which lands should be placed in the National Wilderness Preservation System. Congress reserved the final decision as to the designation of wilderness areas for itself.

John Fielder

Black Rocks and sandstone pinnacles, Ruby Canyon, Black Ridge Canyons Wilderness Area.

In Colorado, both the National Park Service and the U.S. Forest Service completed the required wilderness studies and reports throughout the 1970s. Congress acted on many of these recommendations, so that by 2000 approximately 3.4 million acres of federal wilderness had been designated in National Parks and National Forests. The designations covered many of Colorado's most significant wildland resources. Only five areas were designated by the original 1964 Act—Rawah, Mount Zirkel, Maroon Bells, West Elks, and La Garita. The Weminuche and Flat Tops Wildernesses were designated in 1975, Eagles Nest in 1976, and Indian Peaks and Hunter-Fryingpan in 1978. The majority of Colorado's wilderness was set aside by legislation in 1980 and 1993 with the culmination of the Forest Service Roadless Area Review and Evaluation II. The 3.4 million acres of wilderness thus designated, however, amounts to only 6 percent of Colorado's 66 million-acre land base.

During this era, Congress and the public came to recognize the importance of desert wild country under the administration of the BLM. In 1976, Congress passed the Federal Land Policy and Management Act (FLPMA), which for the first time placed BLM on equal footing with the Forest Service. In FLPMA, Congress stated that it was the policy of the United States to retain ownership of the hundreds of millions of acres of BLM public lands throughout the West, and directed BLM to conduct a thorough review of its lands and make recommendations about the wilderness suitability of those lands to Congress by 1993.

In Colorado, BLM initially determined that approximately 1.2 million acres of its 8 million acres were largely roadless. The Wilderness Act defines wilderness as an area with outstanding opportunities for solitude or primitive and unconfined recreation. In applying this definition, BLM decided that while one-third of these roadless lands did have some opportunity for solitude and primitive recreation, those opportunities were not of an outstanding nature. As a result, only 800,000 acres were identified as wilderness study areas by BLM in 1980.

Since 1980, BLM field offices around Colorado have conducted exhaustive reviews of these potential wilderness areas. After considering alternative uses for them such as mining and water projects, BLM has proposed approximately 400,000 acres, or 5 percent of BLM land in Colorado, for designation as wilderness. Colorado BLM officials forwarded their recommendations to the president in October 1991, which were in turn submitted to Congress by President George Bush. Congress acted on the first few of these BLM recommendations in conjunction with 1993 legislation that designated approximately 600,000 acres of National Forest as wilderness areas. The 1993 Colorado Wilderness Act designated two alpine BLM areas as wilderness— Powderhorn and American Flats—and also granted wilderness-type status to the sandstone canyon of Tabeguache Creek. More recently, Congress enacted legislation to designate two of Colorado's premier desert river canyons as wilderness areas—the Gunnison Gorge in 1999 and Black Ridge Canyons in 2000.

Colorado conservation groups conducted field studies separate from BLM. Determining the "outstanding" nature of solitude is obviously a subjective procedure, so in many cases conservation groups proposed areas for wilderness designation that BLM earlier discarded for lack of outstanding solitude or primitive recreation. These areas are included in this guidebook, and you, the reader, will be in the best position

Canoeing through Little Yampa Canyon, Yampa River.

Mark Pearson

to influence the final decision on the fate of these areas. BLM lands proposed for wilderness designation by Colorado conservation groups total more than 1 million acres. Many of these BLM areas are adjacent to roadless Forest Service lands, so when another 300,000 acres of Forest Service wildlands are included, the conservation groups' proposal amounts to more than 1.3 million acres. As Congress weighs the relative merits of the BLM and conservation group proposals for BLM wilderness areas, it will actively solicit input from citizens. If you would like more information about Colorado conservation groups that are active in issues affecting BLM wilderness lands, refer to Appendix C for addresses and phone numbers.

Wilderness Issues

Designation of federal lands as wilderness stirs strong passions among affected interest groups. Conservation groups advocate protection of wilderness areas for many reasons. These include the necessity for unmodified ecological baseline areas to serve as early warning indicators of wholesale environmental changes, a desire to preserve a representative sample of the historic landscape, and the creation of genetic repositories to replenish weakened species and ecosystems in developed regions. Other reasons are to protect scientific warehouses of undiscovered species and flora and fauna with as yet unknown medicinal or utilitarian values, preservation of landscapes with extraordinary aesthetic qualities, and maintaining recreational opportunities that challenge the most-skilled outdoors lovers.

Wilderness designation frequently runs headlong into commercial interests that have traditionally used public lands for a variety of purposes, most prominently logging, livestock forage, mining, and water development. People with other interests, such as motorized recreationists, object to the preservation of selected areas as wilderness because their recreational activity is excluded. There will, however, be few conflicts between wilderness designation of BLM lands and logging simply because most BLM areas are located in semiarid regions and lack commercial timber resources. But the potential for conflicts between other uses and wilderness does exist and deserves some elaboration.

Grazing

The Wilderness Act specifically allows for livestock grazing to continue in the same manner and degree as was occurring at the time the area was designated wilderness. Congress has gone beyond this legislative language in committee reports to explicitly direct federal agencies that there be "no curtailments of grazing in wilderness areas simply because an area is, or has been, designated wilderness, nor should wilderness designations be used as an excuse by administrators to slowly 'phase out' grazing." Ranchers are even allowed exceptions to the general wilderness prohibition against motorized vehicles in wilderness, as long as their use is infrequent and only for required repairs to range developments (such as fences and stock tanks) or for emergencies. In addition, ranchers are permitted to construct new range developments and replace deteriorated facilities as needed to prevent damage to natural resources.

It is apparent from this congressional direction that wilderness designation and continued livestock grazing are compatible. It is the opinion of most conservation organizations that the federal agencies responsible for the administration of grazing in wilderness areas have implemented this directive in a manner that has done little to impair wilderness qualities. Many livestock operators apparently have little quarrel with the existing application of these guidelines. In testimony on several bills concerning Colorado National Forest wilderness additions in 1984, a representative of the Colorado Cattlemen's Association praised this system and noted the lack of problems in wilderness areas between livestock operators and the Forest Service.

Still, individual ranchers and agricultural groups frequently oppose wilderness designations simply because they view wilderness as potentially imposing additional regulation on their commercial use of public lands. These objections are more deeply rooted in ideology than they are in fact.

Mining

The Wilderness Act states that "the minerals in lands designated by this Act as wilderness areas are withdrawn from all forms of appropriation under the mining laws and from disposition under all laws pertaining to mineral leasing." Only valid mineral rights established prior to the designation of a wilderness area, or prior to BLM's identification of an area as a wilderness study area, can be developed.

This outright prohibition of mining in wilderness creates a commonly perceived conflict with wilderness designation. Most of these perceived conflicts on BLM lands arise from energy minerals, such as oil, natural gas, and coal. Hard-rock minerals such as gold and silver pose few conflicts with most BLM wilderness proposals since the majority of these areas are in sedimentary rock formations and are poor source rocks for hard-rock minerals. There are a few exceptions, however, in mountainous regions such as the San Juans where BLM administers several 14,000-plus-foot peaks.

Because few of the proposed BLM wilderness areas lie in either of the two most significant BLM coal-producing regions in Colorado—the North Fork of the Gunnison and the Craig/Hayden area—there are similarly few conflicts with coal mining. One or two areas in the Bookcliffs near Grand Junction contain quantities of low-quality coal, but the Bookcliffs are a minor coal-producing region. BLM's Resource Management Plans report approximately 25 billion tons of recoverable coal reserves on over 1.6 million acres of federal lands in Colorado. In contrast, the proposed wilderness areas cover only 0.7 billion ton of these potential coal reserves on 50,000 acres. The proposed wilderness areas thus include a scant 3 percent of recoverable coal reserves in Colorado, none of which are in the state's prime coal-producing regions.

According to BLM's Resource Management Plans and Umbrella Oil and Gas Leasing Environmental Assessments, almost 8 million acres of BLM-administered mineral lands in Colorado are open to oil and gas leasing. The wilderness acreage proposed by conservation groups is equal to about 13 percent of the BLM acreage open to leasing. Most of the proposed wilderness has been leased at some time or other, but was not extensively explored due to lack of interest by the leaseholders. Despite this record, oil and gas development is likely to be the greatest land-use conflict with potential wilderness designations on BLM lands.

One area, the Roan Plateau, potentially contains significant oil shale resources. Almost a century of tinkering and experimentation has failed to demonstrate any economically viable, not to mention environmentally benign, means of extracting oil from shale. Thus it appears there is little actual conflict between protecting a few thousand acres of one West Slope plateau and exacting this experimental energy source.

Water

As with other federally reserved lands, wilderness areas are entitled to federal water rights sufficient for the purposes of the designation of the wilderness. The purposes of a wilderness designation in most cases include recreation, protection of fish and wildlife habitat, aesthetic values, and maintenance of riparian ecosystems, among others. The concept of reserved water rights dates to a Supreme Court decision in 1908 concerning an Indian reservation in Montana. In that case, the court ruled that it made little sense to reserve land for a specific purpose (in this case for the resettlement of an Indian tribe) if enough water was not also reserved to meet the purposes of the reservation. The court later expanded the reserved rights doctrine to include any federal reservation, including National Parks and National Forests. Conservation groups argue that wilderness, as yet another form of congressional reservation, is similarly entitled to enough water to satisfy its purposes.

Wilderness water rights are adjudicated in state water court pursuant to Colorado water law. The priority date for wilderness water rights is the date of wilderness designation of the area; thus no wilderness area can have a water right more senior than 1964. According to BLM, there are few significant conflicts between wilderness designation and private water rights. In a synopsis of potential water rights conflicts with BLM wilderness prepared by BLM for Congressman George Miller on Aug. 19, 1988, the BLM stated that it expected an in-depth analysis of the issue "will probably demonstrate that the real impacts are small and easily mitigated."

A major reason for the lack of conflicts is that the majority of proposed BLM wilderness areas are headwaters areas; that is, the areas are situated at the heads of watersheds with the result that no water flows into the areas from outside their boundaries. Other areas that might be considered non-headwaters areas (areas into which streams flow) are downstream only from designated wilderness or other protected areas, thus posing no potential conflict with any upstream water user. BLM wilderness areas will carry very junior priority water rights, so most preexisting water uses will not be affected by BLM wilderness water rights because of seniority.

It is also important to note that since the proposed wilderness areas are largely in desert regions, watercourses that flow into non-headwaters areas are generally ephemeral in nature, with limited or nonexistent opportunities for upstream diversion. There are, however, several areas situated on major rivers such as the Dolores, Gunnison, and Yampa.

Many water users in Colorado object to the concept of federal reserved water rights, fearing federal government intervention in what has traditionally been a state arena, despite the fact that all water rights are adjudicated in state water courts. Water users believe that if downstream wilderness areas on major rivers are granted even a very junior water right, the presence of that right could reduce the opportunities for development of new upstream water rights or could prevent some types of changes in use of existing water rights.

Substantial conflicts with water rights may occur where there is or has been proposed a reservoir site that would inundate portions of the proposed wilderness. These instances include major on-stream reservoirs proposed for the Gunnison and Yampa Rivers, but most observers believe the chances are extremely remote that billion-dollar dams will ever be built on these rivers, and therefore the possibility of any real conflict is minimal. This was borne out when Congress designated the Gunnison Gorge as wilderness in 1999 without objections from the one-time dam proponents.

Recreation

As mentioned, wilderness possesses far more values, and perhaps more important values, to civilization than simply as a setting for primitive recreational pursuits such as backpacking and horsepacking. Motorized recreationists often see wilderness designation as a conflict between categories of recreational users, however, and all too often wilderness debates are reduced to trading charges of recreational elitism. The recreational value of wilderness lies in the opportunity to permanently ensure that undisturbed landscapes will always exist for human exploration and challenge. Primitive types of recreation occur largely in wilderness simply because wilderness areas are the only fragments of North America still possessing wild character. Literally millions of acres are available for non-wilderness forms of recreation, on lands that will never be suitable for protection as wilderness. It seems unproductive to argue about the recreational use of shrinking wildlands, when ample alternatives exist for non-wilderness-dependent forms of recreation such as off-road vehicles.

Off-road vehicles come in many shapes and sizes, including four-wheel-drive vehicles, motorcycles, all-terrain vehicles, and snowmobiles. The authors of the Wilderness Act prohibited these machines from designated wilderness under the belief that such obvious signs of civilization and their accompanying noise and potential for environmental damage were incompatible with the objectives of wilderness areas.

Bicycles were similarly prohibited because they represent a mechanical advantage and were deemed inappropriate in wilderness. Machines such as bicycles effectively shrink the wilderness, allowing a visitor to cover distances in a short time that might otherwise require several days of foot travel. The spirit of wilderness is one of shedding the trappings and pace of civilization in favor of the slower rhythms found in nature.

Opposite: Limestone cliffs high above Deep Creek. Photo by John Fielder.

1 American Flats

John Fielder

LOCATION	17 miles west of Lake City
ELEVATION RANGE	11,000–13,000 feet
ECOSYSTEMS	Spruce-fir forest, alpine tundra
SIZE	3,390 acres
WILDERNESS STATUS	Designated as wilderness in 1993
SPECIAL FEATURES	American Lake, tundra, rugged peaks
TOPOGRAPHIC MAPS	Handies Peak, Uncompahgre Peak, Wetterhorn Peak

American Flats is aptly named for the gentle expanse of rolling tundra north of Engineer Pass. Its alpine tundra sits amidst breathtaking 13,000- and 14,000-foot peaks of the San Juan Mountains, and includes 13,266-foot Wildhorse Peak. American Flats was designated as an addition to the Forest Service Uncompahgre Wilderness in 1993 legislation and encompasses the headwaters of Wildhorse Creek and Cow Creek, which flow northward into the wilderness. The flats afford unrestricted views of nearby Wetterhorn

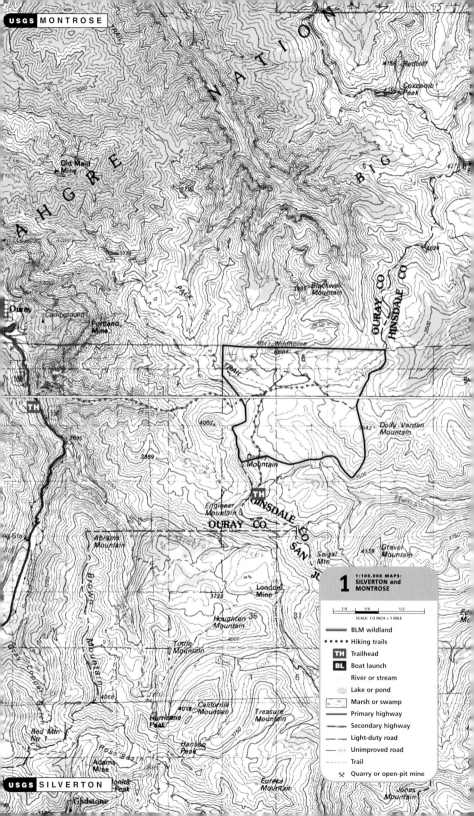

and Uncompahgre Peaks, two Fourteeners (as Colorado's 14,000-plus-foot peaks are called) that rise sharply above the high alpine plain. American Flats also includes American Lake, a small alpine lake perched at the head of Henson Creek.

CONTACT INFORMATION: Gunnison Field Office, Bureau of Land Management, 216 N. Colorado St., Gunnison, CO 81230, 970-641-0471, http://www.co.blm.gov/gra/gra-hmepge.htm.

DESTINATION HIKE AMERICAN LAKE

ONE-WAY LENGTH: 2 miles
LOW AND HIGH ELEVATIONS: 12,400 and 12,600 feet
DIFFICULTY: Easy

American Flats is easily accessible from the popular Engineer Pass Road. An abandoned vehicle track that is now only two fading ruts across the tundra leads directly across the flats and circles east to American Lake. This track leaves the Engineer Pass Road approximately 2.5 miles beyond its fork with Schafer Gulch, immediately east of the rugged ridge that forms the Hinsdale-Ouray County line, and is marked by a BLM sign prohibiting vehicles. Some of the easiest alpine hiking in all of Colorado is found along this route; the gentle to nonexistent grade is particularly suited for elderly or infirm hikers who wish to venture amidst the blinding summer displays of alpine wildflowers. There is interest here for the historically minded as well. In 1874 members of the Hayden Survey crossed the undulating plateau of American Flats to its western edge, from which they studied the possibilities of climbing Mount Sneffels.

SHUTTLE HIKE BEAR CREEK TRAIL

ONE-WAY LENGTH: 6 miles
LOW AND HIGH ELEVATIONS: 8,500 and 12,500 feet
DIFFICULTY: Strenuous

You can also reach American Flats from the west via the Bear Creek or Horse Thief Trails from Ouray and the Red Mountain Pass highway. The thrilling Bear Creek Trail begins along Highway 550 south of Ouray, just south of the highway tunnel. This old supply route clings to cliff faces as it passes along narrow ledges with spine-tingling drop-offs, eventually working up to American Flats and the gentle trail out to the Engineer Pass Road. Of course, it's much easier to begin at American Flats and hike downhill to the highway.

Cross Canyon

2

John Fielder

25 miles northwest of Cortez	**LOCATION**
5,000–6,600 feet	**ELEVATION RANGE**
Cottonwoods, sagebrush, piñon-juniper woodlands	**ECOSYSTEMS**
25,248 acres	**SIZE**
Not proposed for wilderness by BLM	**WILDERNESS STATUS**
Numerous archaeological sites, desert riparian zone, Canyons of the Ancients National Monument	**SPECIAL FEATURES**
Cahone, Champagne Spring, Negro Canyon, Pleasant View, Papoose Canyon, Ruin Canyon, Ruin Point	**TOPOGRAPHIC MAPS**

Cross Canyon, and its tributaries Cahone Canyon, Cow Canyon, and Ruin Canyon, drop abruptly from surrounding mesas into 300- to 900-foot-deep canyons. The canyons comprise the northwestern corner of Colorado's newest National Monument, the Canyons of the Ancients National Monument proclaimed by President Bill Clinton in June 2000. There is no better example of undisturbed landscapes and intertwined natural and cultural resources for which the Monument was proclaimed.

Cross Canyon includes more than 20 twisting miles of canyon itself and more than 25 miles of tributaries. The canyon bottoms are lined with cottonwood trees framing a cool stream that in some areas features inviting pools and waterfalls. The water is largely spring fed, but cattle grazing in the canyons suggests filtering water for consumption. The long riparian canyons not only provide a haven for myriad species of wildlife, but also were a source of sustenance for the large number of Anasazi Indians who lived there between A.D. 450 and 1300. The ruins and artifacts left in this area are literally everywhere, in concentrations of 40 to 60 (and even 100) sites per square mile, making it a denser collection of cultural resources than anywhere else in the United States. Kivas, room blocks, and small storage structures are hidden among the rocks and cliffs, and an intact square tower similar to those found at Hovenweep National Monument may be found in Ruin Canyon. Finding rock art on the canyon walls and frequent pieces of pottery in the dirt makes exploring these isolated canyons exciting and mysterious, but please don't deface or remove any traces of ancient cultures.

The native piñon-juniper woodlands that dominate the upland mesas surrounding Cross Canyon have seen extensive development by agriculture, and by exploration for oil, gas, and carbon dioxide. However, the canyon slopes are covered with numerous shrubs, such as mountain mahogany, serviceberry, and rabbitbrush, in addition to the prevalent piñon-juniper woodlands. Mule deer, mountain lions, and even black bears live in the canyon as well as raptors such as golden and bald eagles and peregrine falcons.

Spring and fall are inviting months to visit Cross Canyon—spring for the lime-green buds of early cottonwood leaves, fall for the brilliant golden glimmering of those very same trees. Visitors in the late spring months of May and June may encounter fierce hordes of cedar gnats with insatiable appetites and apparent imperviousness to bug dope.

CONTACT INFORMATION: San Juan Field Office, Bureau of Land Management, 15 Burnett Court, Durango, CO 81301, 970-247-4874, http://www.co.blm.gov/sjra/sjra.html.

DAY HIKE ▸ CROSS CANYON MOUTH

ONE-WAY LENGTH: Several miles to many
LOW AND HIGH ELEVATIONS: 5,100 and 5,500 feet
DIFFICULTY: Easy

The most popular hike in Cross Canyon wanders up the canyon's wide and inviting lower end. A trickling stream under a thick canopy of cottonwoods makes this particularly appealing on hot spring and summer days. To reach the mouth of Cross Canyon, take the McElmo Canyon road west from Cortez to the Hovenweep National Monument headquarters just over the state line into Utah (north of the Ismay trading post). Head north about 3 miles from the visitor center, and turn west for a short 1-mile jog over to Cross Canyon. Follow a spur to its terminus in the mouth of Cross Canyon. Several fading petroglyphs are located on the boulders just east of the parking area. Numerous archeological sites occur within the first few miles of Cross Canyon, including one large community draped around and atop a prominent outcrop in the middle of the canyon.

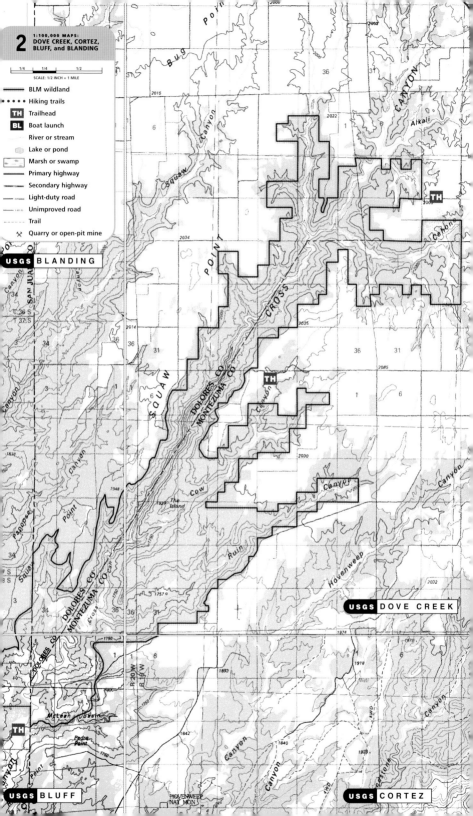

2 1:100,000 MAPS:
DOVE CREEK, CORTEZ,
BLUFF, and BLANDING

SCALE: 1/2 INCH = 1 MILE

	BLM wildland
•••••	Hiking trails
TH	Trailhead
BL	Boat launch
	River or stream
	Lake or pond
	Marsh or swamp
	Primary highway
	Secondary highway
	Light-duty road
	Unimproved road
	Trail
✕	Quarry or open-pit mine

USGS **BLANDING**

USGS **DOVE CREEK**

USGS **BLUFF**

USGS **CORTEZ**

DAY HIKE McCLEAN BASIN

ONE-WAY LENGTH: 6 miles
LOW AND HIGH ELEVATIONS: 5,100 and 6,000 feet
DIFFICULTY: Moderate

A slight modification of the previous Cross Canyon hike is to head east from the Cross Canyon parking area (rather than north) and walk along the jeep trail to the canyon rim above McClean Basin. A primary feature of this hike is the dramatic McClean Basin towers, a pair of solitary towers with unique glazed brick bands that stand as silent sentinels over the vast empty basins of the Four Corners. The towers are nestled just below the canyon rim. After a well-deserved breather admiring the towers, you can continue up the road, across a narrow neck on the mesa, and drop down an old oil exploration road back into a tributary of Cross Canyon. A pleasant stroll along Cross Canyon returns you to your vehicle.

LOOP HIKE LOWRY RUIN LOOP

ONE-WAY LENGTH: 15 miles
LOW AND HIGH ELEVATIONS: 5,500 and 6,600 feet
DIFFICULTY: Moderate

One easy access into Cross Canyon is from BLM's Lowry Ruin National Historic Site. From Highway 666 near Pleasant View, follow the signs to the ruins (approximately 9 miles west along County Road CC). Lowry Ruin sits at the head of Cow Canyon on the boundary of the roadless area. From the parking lot at the ruins, head south down the drainage into Cow Canyon. This canyon intersects with Cross Canyon in about 8 miles. For an overnight trip, you can hike up Cross Canyon 5 or 6 miles, and then strike out cross-country south and east back to Cow Canyon near Lowry Ruins.

SHUTTLE HIKE CROSS CANYON ENTIRETY

ONE-WAY LENGTH: 22 miles
LOW AND HIGH ELEVATIONS: 5,100 and 6,600 feet
DIFFICULTY: Moderate

Hiking the entire length of Cross Canyon offers perhaps the longest wilderness canyon walk in southwest Colorado. For much of its length, Cross Canyon is a lush, water-filled riparian corridor with abundant cottonwoods and cattails. To start the hike from the north, turn west from Highway 666 onto County Road R in the hamlet of Cahone and follow it through a couple of right-angle corners to its end as County Road S. BLM land beckons just over the fence, from which one can rapidly scramble into a large tributary of Cross Canyon. To find the canyon itself involves a long 1.5 miles of route-finding through piñon-juniper woodlands. From this point, the route is a relatively easy stroll along cattle and game trails that parallel the watercourse. Inviting grassy campsites under arching cottonwoods occur with increasing frequency down canyon. You'll see more and larger archeological sites toward the lower reaches of the canyon as well. The hike's terminus is at the jump-off point for the Cross Canyon day hike described on page 36.

Dolores River Canyon

3

John Fielder

17 miles west of Naturita	**LOCATION**
5,000–6,600 feet	**ELEVATION RANGE**
Box elder, tamarisk, sagebrush, piñon-juniper woodlands	**ECOSYSTEM**
38,465 acres	**SIZE**
29,415 acres proposed for wilderness by BLM	**WILDERNESS STATUS**
Dolores River, slickrock canyons, scenic vistas, petroglyphs	**SPECIAL FEATURES**
Anderson Mesa, Bull Canyon, Davis Mesa, Lisbon Gap, Paradox, Wray Mesa	**TOPOGRAPHIC MAPS**

Dolores River Canyon is a pristine desert canyon land containing some of the most outstanding canyon scenery in Colorado. The area includes a segment of the Dolores River recommended as a wild river under the Wild and Scenic Rivers Act, surrounding benchlands and mesa uplands, and portions of five major tributary canyons. Twelve geological formations are exposed by the river in the gorge—the predominant formation being the spectacular cliff—forming red Wingate sandstone. The cliffs rise to benches 500 to 700 feet above the river, with the canyon rim 1,100 feet above the river. The tributary canyons include La Sal Creek—a deep and twisting canyon cut by a perennial stream—Coyote Wash, Spring Canyon, Bull Canyon, and Wild Steer Canyon, all delightful canyons with sculpted slickrock and plunge pools.

Dolores River Canyon is home to a variety of wildlife, including the endangered peregrine falcon known to be nesting in Paradox Valley and believed to be hunting in the Dolores River Canyon area. Mule deer, mountain lions, and bobcats are common inhabitants of the area; golden eagles and bald eagles are known to nest and hunt here. Dolores River Canyon is also home to reintroduced populations of desert bighorn sheep and river otters.

Vegetation varies from piñon-juniper woodlands, oakbrush, and sagebrush on the mesa uplands to riparian species of plants along the river, including tamarisk, willows, box elder, rushes, sedges, and occasional cottonwoods. A number of rare plants grow within the area, including the Eastwood monkeyflower (said to grow in shallow caverns in cliffs on the lower portion of Coyote Wash), Kachina daisy, and *Mertensia arizonica*.

CONTACT INFORMATION: San Juan Field Office, Bureau of Land Management, 15 Burnett Court, Durango, CO 81301, 970-247-4874, http://www.co.blm.gov/sjra/sjra.html.

DAY HIKE NYSWANGER MESA

ONE-WAY LENGTH: 3 miles
LOW AND HIGH ELEVATIONS: 5,100 and 6,600 feet
DIFFICULTY: Moderate

A hike across Nyswanger Mesa offers absolutely stunning views of the surrounding snowcapped peaks of the La Sals and San Juans. An abandoned jeep trail, now impassable to vehicles, heads up the cliffs less than a mile west of Bedrock. Park along Highway 90, and follow this trail across the mesa. A network of bladed ways, relics from wantonly destructive uranium exploration, crisscross the piñon-juniper woodlands and sagebrush meadows of the mesa, but creates a relatively small impact on its overall naturalness. In about 3 miles, you will reach the southern point of the mesa, and look straight down into the Dolores River Canyon and La Sal Creek. From this vantage point, La Sal Creek and its tributaries carve a wild labyrinth through glaring white sandstone cliffs, set off by a green mat of piñon-juniper woodlands and highlighted by the snowcapped La Sal Mountains.

DESTINATION HIKE COYOTE WASH

ONE-WAY LENGTH: 1.5 miles
LOW AND HIGH ELEVATIONS: 5,100 and 5,500 feet
DIFFICULTY: Easy

Silveys Pocket offers an easy route into Coyote Wash for those without means of floating the river. Proceed through Gypsum Valley past the river boat launch, across the river bridge, and another 10 miles or more over a watershed divide to a basin called Silveys Pocket. You can drive on the old uranium exploration roads as far as you dare, but ultimately no closer than about 1.5 miles to Coyote Wash. An easy walk delivers you to the heart of Coyote Wash, about 1.5 miles from the wash's confluence with the Dolores River. Hikers can spend one day or several exploring up and down the wash.

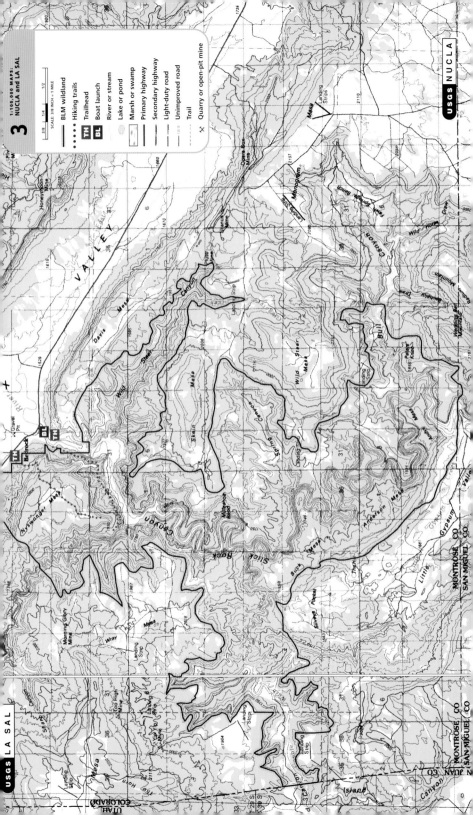

3

1:100,000 MAPS:
NUCLA and LA SAL

SCALE: 3/8 INCH = 1 MILE

3/8   1/4   1/2   1 MILE

▬▬▬	BLM wildland
• • • •	Hiking trails
TH	Trailhead
BL	Boat launch
	River or stream
	Lake or pond
	Marsh or swamp
	Primary highway
	Secondary highway
	Light-duty road
	Unimproved road
	Trail
✕	Quarry or open-pit mine

DESTINATION HIKE — LA SAL CREEK

ONE-WAY LENGTH: 4 miles
LOW AND HIGH ELEVATIONS: 5,000 and 5,100 feet
DIFFICULTY: Easy

La Sal Creek is accessible either by boat or overland from Bedrock. To hike into La Sal Creek, park at the Bedrock boat ramp, and follow the now-faded jeep trail along the west bank of the river 4 miles to the mouth of La Sal Creek. La Sal Creek is perhaps the largest creek draining the La Sal Mountains, but water quality may be suspect due to agricultural practices upstream and a metals mine just outside the roadless area boundary (approximately 3 miles upstream from the Dolores). La Sal Creek offers a deep, narrow canyon for exploration. Ambitious hikers can proceed farther up the Dolores beyond La Sal Creek, particularly in summer and fall when the river's level is frequently only 20 cubic feet per second (cfs).

RIVER TRIP — GYPSUM VALLEY/BEDROCK

ONE-WAY LENGTH: 36 miles
LOW AND HIGH ELEVATIONS: 5,000 and 5,300 feet
DIFFICULTY: Class II and III

This stretch of the Dolores River is very popular for rafting, kayaking, and canoeing. As is often the case, floating the river provides the greatest access to numerous outstanding hiking locations. The rafting season usually occurs during May and early June and there are several Class II and III rapids in the canyon, though since McPhee Dam was completed upstream there has frequently been insufficient spring runoff to support a boating season. To float just the wilderness section, boaters launch at Little Gypsum Valley, about 14 miles west of Highway 141, and take out at Bedrock in the Paradox Valley on Highway 90. Launching at Slickrock where Highway 141 crosses the Dolores River adds another 14 miles to the float trip, but includes some river stretches with agricultural and oil development activities. Rafters generally figure a minimum flow of at least 800 cfs is needed to negotiate the canyon, with canoeists and kayakers able to get by with considerably less. The BLM routinely updates scheduled releases throughout the spring on its website.

Among the half-dozen tributary canyons, Coyote Wash is a favorite stopping place for rafters to walk barefoot in the sandy streambed. Bull Canyon includes a cold plunge pool, and Spring Creek has several low alcoves. Petroglyphs and pictographs are found in the tributary canyons and under large alcoves in the main gorge.

Handies Peak 4

15 miles southwest of Lake City	**LOCATION**
9,500–14,048 feet	**ELEVATION RANGE**
Aspen groves, spruce-fir forest, alpine tundra	**ECOSYSTEM**
67,683 acres	**SIZE**
7,120 acres proposed for wilderness by BLM	**WILDERNESS STATUS**
14,048-foot Handies Peak, 15 miles of Continental Divide, glacial valleys, alpine lakes, Colorado Trail	**SPECIAL FEATURES**
Finger Mesa, Handies Peak, Howardsville, Lake San Cristobal, Pole Creek Mountain, Redcloud Peak	**TOPOGRAPHIC MAPS**

Handies Peak, when combined with Carson Peak on adjacent National Forest lands, is one of the largest unprotected roadless areas remaining in Colorado. The area contains 15 miles of the Continental Divide in the midst of the exceptionally scenic San Juan Mountains, sitting at the headwaters of both the Rio Grande and Lake Fork of the Gunnison River. Handies Peak (14,048 feet) is the most prominent feature in the northern end of the area, while two Thirteeners, Carson Peak (13,657 feet) and Pole Creek Mountain (13, 716 feet), dominate the expansive alpine tundra to the south. Handies Peak is the fortieth highest peak in Colorado, and the highest peak under BLM jurisdiction outside of Alaska.

The landforms of this area present intriguing contrasts. The Lake Fork side is precipitous and rugged, characterized by massive volcanic peaks and huge glaciated valleys, dotted with numerous waterfalls and moss-covered grottoes. These valleys provide access to the high rolling tundra and volcanic peaks of the central part of the area. Deep valleys drain south into the Rio Grande River. A particularly unique feature of these southerly drainages is the presence of volcanic "beehives," cones of ash and lava, some of which sit astride Pole Creek in the form of arches.

The almost 70,000-acre chunk of wild mountains surrounding Handies Peak comprises one of the last puzzle pieces to completing a continuous string of wilderness areas along the spine of the San Juan Mountains from New Mexico to central Colorado. The Rio Grande and Lake Fork of the Gunnison both rise in the high peaks of the Continental Divide here. The Lake Fork's tributaries crash thousands of feet to the valley floor in a series of spectacular cascades and waterfalls, while the Rio Grande's tributaries pursue a

John Fielder

Handies Peak from Grizzly Gulch, Handies Peak Wilderness Study Area.

more leisurely course through soft volcanic sediments. The vast, sweeping expanses of upper Pole Creek remind one of nothing so much as the immensity of Alaskan wilderness. Three distinctive landscapes define the Handies Peak area. Vertical cliffs rise out of the Lake Fork of the Gunnison valley on the north, broken by numerous waterfalls and fern and moss grottoes. Rolling tundra interspersed with rugged volcanic peaks characterizes the central portion, while the southern end contains several deep, glaciated valleys.

The Handies Peak roadless area suffers from administrative gerrymandering and proximity to the Weminuche Wilderness. The roadless area falls into three separate federal jurisdictions: the Bureau of Land Management manages the northern quarter as the Handies Peak Wilderness Study Area, Gunnison National Forest manages another quarter that consists of the sliver of land between BLM land and the Continental Divide, and Rio Grande National Forest administers the half that lies south of the divide. When conducting wilderness studies, each agency claimed its portion too small or unmanageable for protection as wilderness, or stated that the nearby half-million-acre Weminuche Wilderness suffices for wilderness protection in the San Juans. BLM has in fact proposed for wilderness a tiny area surrounding 14,048-foot Handies Peak, but none of the agencies recognize the realities of ecosystem management in providing ecological corridors that connect large protected reserves. Looking at a map of the San Juans, Handies Peak clearly fills the gap between the Weminuche Wilderness to the south and the La Garita and Uncompahgre Wilderness Areas to the north. If our wilderness reserves are to serve as reservoirs of biological diversity far into the future, then provision must be made for movement between these reserves by recognizing and protecting connections such as Handies Peak.

CONTACT INFORMATION: Creede Ranger District, Rio Grande National Forest, 3rd and Creede Ave., Creede, CO 81130, 719-658-2556; or Cebolla Ranger District, Gunnison National Forest, 216 N. Colorado St., Gunnison, CO 81230, 970-641-0471; or Gunnison Field Office, Bureau of Land Management, 216 N. Colorado St., Gunnison, CO 81230, 970-641-0471, http://www.co.blm.gov/gra/gra-hmepge.htm.

DAY HIKE POLE CREEK

ONE-WAY LENGTH: 3–5 miles
LOW AND HIGH ELEVATIONS: 10,500 and 12,000 feet
DIFFICULTY: Easy to moderate

A stroll of varying length proceeds up Pole Creek's valley, which cuts through volcanic ash and tuff. Keep your eyes open the first few miles for volcanic beehives, including one such formation that the stream has tunneled through to create a natural volcanic bridge. The valley widens at its confluence with the West and Middle Forks, before climbing again into the open, alpine expanses of the upper drainage.

DESTINATION HIKE · HANDIES PEAK

ONE-WAY LENGTH: 3–4 miles
LOW AND HIGH ELEVATIONS: 10,500 and 14,048 feet
DIFFICULTY: Moderate

One popular destination in this area is 14,048-foot Handies Peak. Two common approaches depart from the Cinnamon Pass Road. The longer route heads up the Grizzly Gulch Trail from Burrows Park, climbing steeply and continuously into the high cirque below the peak. The route heads to the saddle between Handies Peak and 13,542-foot Whitecross Mountain, another worthy destination, from which the ridge easily leads to the summit. The other route ascends Handies Peak from American Basin and begins 1,000 feet higher. Taking off from a trailhead at the end of the road into American Basin, on the peak's west side, hike almost to Sloan Lake and then proceed east to the saddle and onto the summit.

DESTINATION HIKE · CATARACT LAKE

ONE-WAY LENGTH: 5 miles
LOW AND HIGH ELEVATIONS: 9,600 and 12,100 feet
DIFFICULTY: Moderate

A well-maintained trail ascends steeply from the Lake Fork of the Gunnison River near the ghost town of Sherman to Cataract Lake. The trail follows Cataract Creek and climbs past plunging cascades in seemingly endless switchbacks over the valley's lip into the mild terrain of upper Cataract Gulch. Several small lakes dot the alpine valley; Cataract Lake, a fairly large body of water, lies just below the treeless Continental Divide. Backpackers planning on extended stays may want to climb 13,657-foot Carson Peak, 2 miles east via the Colorado Trail, or impressive 13,841-foot Half Peak whose 1,000-foot sheer north face belies an easy approach from the south.

LOOP HIKE · LOST TRAIL CREEK

ONE-WAY LENGTH: 20 miles
LOW AND HIGH ELEVATIONS: 9,800 and 12,900 feet
DIFFICULTY: Moderate

Two forks of Lost Creek create an appealing loop through the area's eastern half. The route passes through wide alpine valleys and includes a 5-mile segment of the Colorado Trail. Hikers can easily bag 13,657-foot Carson Peak along the way or dally at Cataract Lake. From the trailhead near Lost Trail Campground on Forest Road 520 along the Rio Grande, follow Lost Creek as it circles north and joins the Colorado Trail. Near Cataract Lake, a trail forks south into West Lost Trail Creek for the leisurely return to the trailhead. From the West Lost Trail Creek valley, 13,716-foot Pole Creek Mountain offers a strenuous challenge for those so inclined. In 1991, a massive landslide buried West Lost Creek in mud and sediment, making travel and route-finding difficult for a short distance.

3/8   1/4   1/2

SCALE: 3/8 INCH = 1 MILE

—————— BLM wildland
• • • • • Hiking trails
TH Trailhead
BL Boat launch
—————— River or stream
⬭ Lake or pond
⬚ Marsh or swamp
—————— Primary highway
- - - - - Secondary highway
—·—·— Light-duty road
——— Unimproved road
- - - - - Trail
⤫ Quarry or open-pit mine

SHUTTLE HIKE | CUBA GULCH/CATARACT GULCH

ONE-WAY LENGTH: 18 miles
LOW AND HIGH ELEVATIONS: 9,600 and 12,900 feet
DIFFICULTY: Moderate

This circuit connects two plunging glacial gorges with the rolling alpine tundra of upper Pole Creek and Cataract Lake. The vehicle shuttle required is only 3 miles, but it is along the rough four-wheel-drive road to American Basin, so hikers might want to make this a loop trip by walking the short distance along the road. Beginning at Cuba Gulch, the trail switchbacks past a series of foaming cascades and waterfalls, over the valley's lip, and into a wide, willow-choked alpine valley. After gaining the Continental Divide at almost 13,000 feet, the route drops into the Middle Fork of Pole Creek, and connects with the main Pole Creek Trail (the Colorado Trail). Upper Pole Creek is another impressive, limitless alpine valley. The route returns to the Gunnison Basin at a shallow pass above Cataract Lake, and then descends steeply down Cataract Creek to the terminus at the Lake Fork.

John Fielder

25 miles south of Naturita	**LOCATION**
6,300–8,800 feet	**ELEVATION RANGE**
Piñon-juniper woodlands, Douglas fir, ponderosa pine	**ECOSYSTEM**
21,080 acres	**SIZE**
Not proposed for wilderness by BLM	**WILDERNESS STATUS**
Shale badlands, sandstone buttes, fossils, wild horses	**SPECIAL FEATURES**
Glade Mountain, McKenna Peak, North Mountain, South Mountain	**TOPOGRAPHIC MAPS**

M cKenna Peak possesses diverse values including a rich fossil resource of clams and brachiopods from the Cretaceous era (100 million years ago), a diverse range of vegetative communities running from grassland to coniferous forests, an established herd of wild horses, and scenic, eroded adobe badlands presided over by imposing sandstone cliffs rising 2,000 feet above the plain.

The McKenna Peak roadless area ranges in elevation from 6,300 to 8,800 feet. The lower-elevation western and southern portions of the area comprise gentle, barren shale flats broken by occasional mesas and buttes of eroded shale highlands. McKenna Peak itself is a highly symmetrical, barren, gray-colored cone with radiating ridge spines and gullies. Vegetation here is sparse, composed of scattered grasses, colorful wildflowers, and widely separated piñons and junipers lining the ridges.

An impressive ridge of sandstone cliffs forms a towering backdrop rising 2,000 feet above the shale badlands. Lush forests of ponderosa pine and Douglas fir exist atop these cliffs, providing refreshingly cool refuges in summer from the furnacelike heat of the lower badlands. These forests include an extremely important winter wildlife habitat for large numbers of deer and elk in the area bordering North Mountain, now considered to have one of the largest deer and elk herds in all of Colorado. The wild horse herd of about 100 roams the western reaches of the area in the Spring Creek Basin. A very rocky jeep trail heads into the basin from the Disappointment Valley road. Bald eagles winter in the lower reaches of the area, and peregrine falcons have been sighted here as well. Mountain lions, bobcats, and black bears are also known to inhabit McKenna Peak.

CONTACT INFORMATION: San Juan Field Office, Bureau of Land Management, 15 Burnett Court, Durango, CO 81301, 970-247-4874, http://www.co.blm.gov/sjra/sjra.html.

DAY HIKE ❯ McKENNA PEAK

ONE-WAY LENGTH: 3 miles
LOW AND HIGH ELEVATIONS: 6,600 and 8,400 feet
DIFFICULTY: Moderate

To hike to the top of 8,400-foot McKenna Peak, start from the Disappointment Valley road that heads east from Highway 141 between Slickrock and Gypsum Gap. Remember, McKenna Peak is the shale cone in front of and below the high sandstone cliffs. Simply follow a winding badland gully that heads directly north 3 miles to the base of McKenna Peak, and scramble up any of its steep symmetrical slopes. In wet weather, the shale turns to heavy, slippery clay that makes walking almost impossible.

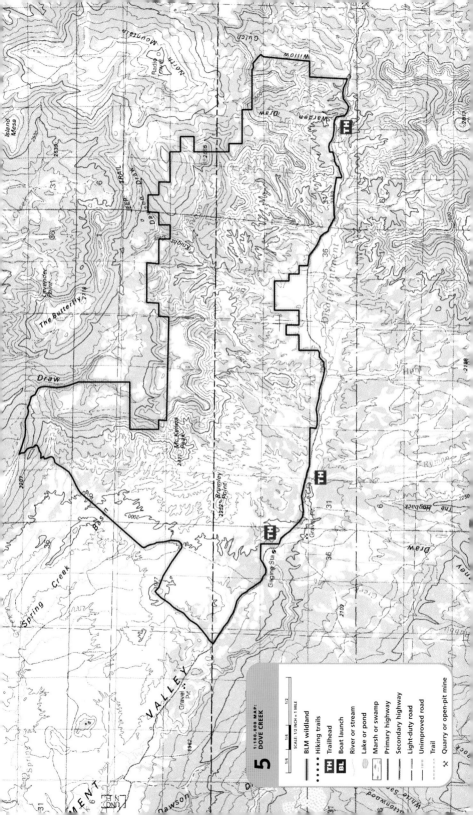

DAY HIKE BRUMLEY POINT

ONE-WAY LENGTH: 2 miles
LOW AND HIGH ELEVATIONS: 6,600 and 7,400 feet
DIFFICULTY: Easy

Brumley Point consists of a sandstone-capped butte rising above the plain of Disappointment Valley. A fringe of piñon pine and juniper woodland graces the summit, and determined hikers will discover a small arch amidst sandstone outcrops atop the butte. Because of its vantage point hundreds of feet above the valley floor, the summit opens up sweeping vistas from the San Juan Mountains to the La Sals in Utah. The hike to Brumley Point is a relatively short walk across a broad plain and an arroyo or two. Park along the Disappointment Valley Road at any appropriate location and strike out cross-country for the prominent butte.

DAY HIKE WARDEN DRAW

ONE-WAY LENGTH: 2 miles
LOW AND HIGH ELEVATIONS: 7,300 and 8,800 feet
DIFFICULTY: Moderate

Scaling one of the huge sandstone cliffs results in a particularly outstanding sense of isolation as you peer into the yawning spaciousness of the unfolding badlands below. The butte west of Warden Draw offers one such opportunity. At the east end of the roadless area, park along a jeep trail in the mouth of Warden Draw, and hike north a short distance until a route up the steep, soft slopes of the butte becomes apparent through the forest. A slot in the rim sandstone provides the final route to the top. Once through the bright yellow sandstone rim, hikers are rewarded by the cool shade of the Douglas fir trees that populate the protected north and west slopes of the butte. There are few contrasts so substantial as surveying shimmering heat waves radiating off of shale badlands from a cool retreat such as that provided by a Douglas fir forest high above the desert.

Powderhorn 6

John Fielder

5 miles northeast of Lake City	**LOCATION**
8,600–12,600 feet	**ELEVATION RANGE**
Ponderosa pine, aspen groves, spruce-fir forest, timberline-alpine tundra	**ECOSYSTEMS**
60,100 acres	**SIZE**
Designated wilderness in 1993	**WILDERNESS STATUS**
Alpine tundra, cirque basins, lakes, scenic vistas	**SPECIAL FEATURES**
Cannibal Plateau, Mineral Mountain, Powderhorn Lakes, Rudolph Hill	**TOPOGRAPHIC MAPS**

On the northern fringe of the San Juan Mountains, the Cannibal and Calf Creek Plateaus create a seemingly endless, undulating plain of tundra, broken only by several steep escarpments bejeweled by Powderhorn and other lakes. Local researchers at Western State College in Gunnison call these plateaus the largest continuous extent of tundra in the lower 48 states, a claim easy to believe as one strides across their limitless expanse. Few other areas in Colorado give rise to an equivalent sense of vastness, as the

12,000-foot plateau affords panoramic views of the San Juan, Elk, and Sawatch Ranges and their numerous Fourteeners.

Lava and ash thousands of feet thick underlie these high plateaus. Glaciation chiseled abrupt cirques and scoured depressions now filled with water, proven attractions for generations of anglers. Though located on the northern flank of the usually wet San Juan Mountains, the lower elevations of the Gunnison Basin receive modest precipitation, and as a result, sagebrush meadows characterize the wilderness here. Widely separated ponderosa pines intermingle with the sagebrush, and wetter pockets support groves of aspen. Moving higher onto the plateaus, precipitation increases markedly and fills the abundant lakes and beaver ponds of the long, shallow, willow-packed valleys. Elk and mule deer find this habitat to their liking and several hundred of both roam the area.

Cannibal Plateau gained its distinctive name from the exploits of Colorado's most notorious man-eater, Alferd Packer. In the winter of 1874, Packer and five friends set out from Montrose for the trading post at Saguache. In a classic example of mistaken direction, the group followed the Gunnison's Lake Fork south instead of taking the main fork east, and they wound up trapped at the foot of a broad alpine plateau. Only one of the group, Alferd Packer, was ever again seen alive, and his tale granted him both notoriety and jail time. After killing some or all of his companions, Packer proceeded to consume them for sustenance.

Powderhorn is the Bureau of Land Management's first designated wilderness area in Colorado. The 1964 Wilderness Act did not originally apply to the BLM, and only after the enactment of the Federal Land Policy and Management Act in 1976 could BLM review and propose areas for wilderness designation. Powderhorn was one of the first areas so reviewed. The northern three-quarters of the wilderness falls on BLM-administered lands; the southern quarter consists of the roadless Calf Creek watershed of the Gunnison National Forest. Since Congress was considering the National Forest segment in deliberations leading to the 1993 Colorado Wilderness Act, it logically followed to designate the adjacent BLM roadless lands as part of the same wilderness area. This multi-agency wilderness designation offers an excellent example of ecosystem management, whereby arbitrary boundary lines are ignored in favor of real watersheds on the ground.

CONTACT INFORMATION: Gunnison Field Office, Bureau of Land Management, 216 N. Colorado St., Gunnison, CO 81230, 970-641-0471, http://www.co.blm.gov/gra/gra-hmepge.htm.

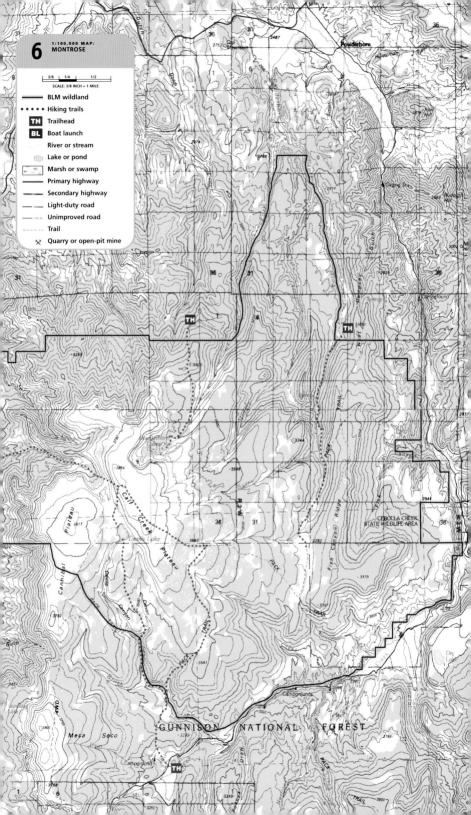

SCALE: 3/8 INCH = 1 MILE

—————— BLM wildland
• • • • • Hiking trails
TH Trailhead
BL Boat launch
River or stream
Lake or pond
Marsh or swamp
—————— Primary highway
—————— Secondary highway
— — — Light-duty road
— — — Unimproved road
— — — Trail
✕ Quarry or open-pit mine

GUNNISON   NATIONAL   FOREST

CEBOLLA CREEK
STATE WILDLIFE AREA

DAY HIKE POWDERHORN LAKES

ONE-WAY LENGTH: 4 miles
LOW AND HIGH ELEVATIONS: 11,200 and 11,900 feet
DIFFICULTY: Easy

The shortest trail to a wilderness lake, and consequently the most heavily used, takes off from the Powderhorn Lakes Trailhead 10 miles down the Indian Creek Road (County Road 58) from Highway 149. Starting off in Engelmann spruce and subalpine fir, the trail winds across the plateau through grassy meadows and beaver-filled creeks to its destination at Powderhorn Lakes. A broken wall of volcanic rock forms the dark background to these timberline lakes. Both lakes offer good fishing for cutthroat trout.

DESTINATION HIKE DEVILS LAKE

ONE-WAY LENGTH: 6.8 miles
LOW AND HIGH ELEVATIONS: 8,500 and 12,000 feet
DIFFICULTY: Moderate

BLM's acquisition of the Devils Creek property along the Gunnison's Lake Fork and new trail construction opened up a new and engaging route to Devils Lake from Highway 149, 7 miles north of Lake City. Cannibal Plateau's high escarpment towers over the deep valley carved by the Lake Fork. Few rivers can match the Lake Fork's stunning beauty at the height of fall color, its glittering crystal waters reflecting sunshine as brilliant as the golden foliage of surrounding aspen forests. From this scenic trailhead, the route climbs along Devils Creek onto the plateau, gaining 1,500 feet of elevation in the first 2 miles. Hikers reach the lake, set in a treeless alpine meadow, in another 4.5 miles after 1,800 feet in additional elevation gain. BLM's wilderness managers hope development of this new trail will relieve some of the crowding on the Powderhorn Lakes Trail.

DESTINATION HIKE EAST FORK POWDERHORN CREEK

ONE-WAY LENGTH: 5.6 miles
LOW AND HIGH ELEVATIONS: 9,300 and 10,600 feet
DIFFICULTY: Easy

Hikers seeking greater solitude might try the lesser visited eastern reaches of the wilderness, where a lack of large lakes draws fewer anglers. One such route leads through Powderhorn Park from the northeastern boundary, and anglers will still find plenty of fishing opportunities for brook trout in the abundant beaver ponds. From the East Fork Trailhead at the end of the Ten Mile Springs Road (Road 3034), this hike follows the East Fork of Powderhorn Creek, past abundant beaver ponds, up to the old cabin called Robbers Roost, then continues on to Powderhorn Park, a long and wide meadow at 10,600 feet. There is no reliable water in Powderhorn Park, so you are better off camping near Robbers Roost or along the East Fork.

LOOP HIKE) CALF CREEK PLATEAU

ONE-WAY LENGTH: 18 miles
LOW AND HIGH ELEVATIONS: 10,400 and 12,600 feet
DIFFICULTY: Moderate

Powderhorn's diversity of landforms—forests, meadows, lakes, and sweeping panoramas from the alpine plateaus—unroll before hikers looping around this route. Starting at the Deer Lakes Campground along Forest Road 788 on the wilderness area's southern boundary, hike north to Brush Creek and follow it 1 mile to its junction with Devils Canyon. From here, the Cañon Infierno Trail climbs through spruce, fir, and alpine meadows onto the Cannibal Plateau before dropping to the shallow saddle between the Cannibal and Calf Creek Plateaus. Devils Lake rests in this saddle, 8 miles from the trailhead. One return route feints north first, to the high point of the Calf Creek Plateau, before looping in a winding meander across the plateau back to Brush Creek via the Calf Creek Plateau Trail. A worthwhile side trip adds 4 miles round-trip to the loop by wandering down to Powderhorn Lakes from the Calf Creek Plateau. A much longer circuit can be created by looping north into the heart of the Powderhorn country via the Middle Fork and East Fork Trails.

7 Redcloud Peak

John Fielder

LOCATION	5 miles southwest of Lake City
ELEVATION RANGE	9,000–14,034 feet
ECOSYSTEM	Spruce-fir forest, aspen, willows, alpine tundra
SIZE	37,000 acres
WILDERNESS STATUS	27,884 acres proposed for wilderness by BLM
SPECIAL FEATURES	Two 14,000-plus-foot peaks, Cooper Lake, glacial valleys
TOPOGRAPHIC MAPS	Lake City, Lake San Cristobal, Redcloud Peak, Uncompahgre Peak

Redcloud Peak contains some of the most spectacular alpine country in Colorado—indeed, in the United States. Within it are two of Colorado's Fourteeners: 14,034-foot Redcloud Peak and 14,001-foot Sunshine Peak. The mountains plunge from more than 14,000 feet to the depths of the Lake Fork valley 5,000 feet below in a horizontal distance of less than a mile. The steep lower slopes were carved by glaciers, and are blanketed by spruce-fir forests and stands of aspen.

Three main drainages dissect the area. Of these, Alpine Gulch is the largest, its tributaries collecting runoff from the northeastern slopes of the area. Silver Creek and Cooper Creek drain the western flanks of the high peaks, and Cooper Lake is nestled high at the head of Cooper Creek. Trails traverse each of these drainages, providing recreational access to the high peaks and alpine tundra. The prospect of bagging the Fourteeners draws many hikers to the area.

A deposit of alunite underlies Red Mountain, which forms the scenic backdrop to Lake City. Alunite is an alternate ore to bauxite for producing aluminum, with by-products of sulfuric acid and potash. A mining company approached the BLM in 1983 to lease and mine this deposit. BLM prepared an environmental assessment of a proposed open-pit mine, which indicated that 2,000 feet would be removed from the top of Red Mountain, and the upper end of Alpine Gulch would be turned into a huge tailings pile of stockpiled ore. Congress later banned the issuance of mineral leases within wilderness study areas, so no final decision was ever reached by BLM on the lease application, though all indications were that it ultimately would have been denied.

CONTACT INFORMATION: Gunnison Field Office, Bureau of Land Management, 216 N. Colorado St., Gunnison, CO 81230, 970-641-0471, http://www.co.blm.gov/gra/gra-hmepge.htm.

DAY HIKE   REDCLOUD AND SUNSHINE PEAKS

ONE-WAY LENGTH: 5.7 miles
LOW AND HIGH ELEVATIONS: 10,400 and 14,034 feet
DIFFICULTY: Moderate

Silver Creek is the area's most popular trail because it's the most direct route to the two Fourteeners. From Lake City, head south out of town, past Lake San Cristobal, the BLM's Mill Creek Campground, and continue right on the Cinnamon Pass Road at the abandoned townsite of Sherman. The Silver Creek Trailhead is about 3 miles farther along the road. The trail climbs gradually above timberline through a broad alpine valley to the saddle northeast of Redcloud Peak. From there, it is a short climb up the ridge to the summit. Total distance from the trailhead is about 4.5 miles. Sunshine Peak is another mile south along the summit ridge from Redcloud. Either backtrack to return to the trailhead, or descend steeply into the gulch on the west side of the saddle between the peaks and join up with Silver Creek midway along its length.

DAY HIKE   COOPER CREEK

ONE-WAY LENGTH: 4 miles
LOW AND HIGH ELEVATIONS: 10,600 and 12,800 feet
DIFFICULTY: Moderate

The Cooper Creek Trail begins 1 mile west of the Silver Creek Trailhead on the Cinnamon Pass Road. The valley of Cooper Creek is similar to that of Silver Creek, but a small alpine lake graces the head of this valley. The Cooper Creek Trail provides access to several unnamed Thirteeners. Because it does not lead to the Fourteeners, Cooper Creek receives much less hiking use than does Silver Creek.

DESTINATION HIKE ▶ ALPINE GULCH

ONE-WAY LENGTH: 6 miles
LOW AND HIGH ELEVATIONS: 9,100 and 12,500 feet
DIFFICULTY: Moderate to strenuous

Alpine Gulch is the longest valley in the area, and offers scenic views of steep cliffs and flower-covered meadows. The gulch branches into several major tributaries that provide more opportunities to avoid the sights and sounds of other hikers. One can also climb out of the cirque basins of either western branch to reach high ridges in the heart of the roadless area. To reach Alpine Gulch, take the Henson Creek Road west from Lake City. Alpine Gulch intersects Henson Creek a little more than 2 miles up the road. The Alpine Gulch Trail crosses Henson Creek via a bridge, but beyond that the trail makes many creek crossings as it wends its way up the valley. The trail leads to several old mines and prospects and ends atop Grassy Mountain. From here, you can also gain access to the backside of Red Mountain.

SHUTTLE HIKE ▶ WILLIAMS CREEK/ALPINE GULCH

ONE-WAY LENGTH: 13 miles
LOW AND HIGH ELEVATIONS: 9,100 and 12,500 feet
DIFFICULTY: Moderate to strenuous

The Williams Creek Trail begins along the Lake Fork just before the Williams Creek Campground, approximately 6.5 miles west of the highway. An attraction of this trail is that about half its length is above treeline, with sweeping panoramic vistas. Follow the trail up through the forest, briefly joining an old jeep road where you take a middle path at a three-way fork. The last several miles to Grassy Mountain are marked by rock cairns across the tundra. Join the Alpine Gulch Trail atop Grassy Mountain and descend north to the trailhead along Henson Creek. This route makes for a relatively quick and easy vehicle shuttle of only a dozen miles or so between the two trailheads.

8 Snaggletooth

John Fielder

LOCATION	25 miles northwest of Cortez
ELEVATION RANGE	5,800–6,600 feet
ECOSYSTEMS	Ponderosa pine forest, box elder, cottonwoods, sagebrush, piñon-juniper woodlands
SIZE	31,684 acres
WILDERNESS STATUS	Not proposed for wilderness by BLM
SPECIAL FEATURES	Ponderosa Gorge of the Dolores River, Snaggletooth Rapid
TOPOGRAPHIC MAPS	Doe Canyon, The Glade, Joe Davis Hill, Secret Canyon

Snaggletooth contains the renowned Ponderosa Gorge of the Dolores River. The gorge provides one of the West's most exquisite wilderness adventures—a quick-paced float on an icy-cold mountain river past cathedral stands of ancient, yellow-barked ponderosa pines. Spectacular campsites present themselves mile after mile in this segment—grassy parks amidst towering ponderosa giants. Soaring cliffs of brilliant red Wingate sandstone provide a fitting background to this incredible wilderness setting.

Snaggletooth covers 30 river miles from the popular Bradfield Bridge raft launch downstream past fearsome Snaggletooth Rapid. This segment is at once among the most cherished and rarest wilderness river floats in the Southwest: cherished because of the serene beauty of the Ponderosa Gorge, and rare because of the short boating season, complicated by McPhee Reservoir and vast irrigation diversions. The boating season typically runs for a few weeks in May, usually bracketing Memorial Day weekend. Depending on snowpack and runoff, some years the boating season begins as early as mid-April or extends as late as mid-June.

While the Ponderosa Gorge is breathtaking in its beauty, the river below the great U-turn at Mountain Sheep Point offers charms of a different sort. The river corridor here begins its transformation from mountain stream to desert river. The corridor vegetation grows progressively sparser and drier, with box elders and the omnipresent non-native tamarisk taking hold instead. Piñon-juniper woodlands, rather than ponderosa pine and Douglas fir, dominate the higher canyon slopes. The ponderosa forest, dense below Bradfield Bridge raft launch on the wilderness area's upper boundary, thins dramatically below the Dove Creek Pump Station boat launch and is replaced by overhanging clumps of box elder that offer refreshingly cool and secluded campsites for river runners.

Due to the river's great recreational appeal, BLM manages the area to preserve and enhance its extraordinary recreation opportunities. BLM estimates more than 12,500 visitor days annually during the typically brief snowmelt period of May and June. The river is generally considered boatable by 14- to16-foot rafts at flows above 800 cfs. Canoes and kayaks can get through with flows as low as 250 cfs. Contact the BLM for predicted flow releases from McPhee Reservoir before confirming your river trip as releases can change unexpectedly depending on weather and snowpack.

The entire segment of the Dolores River flowing through the proposed wilderness was studied and recommended for designation under the Wild and Scenic Rivers Act in a study completed in 1976. The recommendation was forwarded to Congress, but no congressional action was ever taken. A temporary mineral withdrawal associated with the Wild and Scenic study expired in 1981, leaving the river corridor susceptible to road construction, mining, and other activities incompatible with the river's extraordinary scenic and recreational values.

Boaters enjoy the area's significant cultural resources, including an intact cliff dwelling located just upstream of the Dove Creek pump station. This dwelling, and numerous other Anasazi features, make the area important for future research to understanding prehistoric cultures. Just upstream, McPhee Reservoir inundated vast areas of prehistoric dwellings.

River otters, reintroduced to the Dolores River by the Colorado Division of Wildlife, now thrive. Other wildlife in the corridor includes mule deer, black bears, mountain lions, and numerous raptors as well as species that depend upon mature ponderosa pine forests, such as Abert squirrels and flammulated owls. The river also supports a healthy trout population that attracts anglers year-round.

CONTACT INFORMATION: San Juan Field Office, Bureau of Land Management, 15 Burnett Court, Durango, CO 81301, 970-247-4874, http://www.co.blm.gov/sjra/sjra.html.

RIVER TRIP — BRADFIELD BRIDGE/DOVE CREEK PUMP STATION

ONE-WAY LENGTH: 19 miles
LOW AND HIGH ELEVATIONS: 6,000 and 6,400 feet
DIFFICULTY: Class II and III

Float trips offer the ideal mode for explorations of the Snaggletooth area. Trips of various lengths are possible, including multi-day combinations with the downstream Dolores River Canyon unit. A popular day trip, or short overnight trip, runs the 19 miles from Bradfield Bridge launch to the Dove Creek Pump Station. This is the heart of the Ponderosa Gorge, with abundant memorable campsites between miles 5 and 16. The river flows swiftly through many riffles, but no significant rapids occur in this section, making it ideal for canoes and inflatable kayaks as well as rafts and hardshell kayaks. A short car shuttle from Bradfield to the Pump Station takes a little more than an hour round-trip.

RIVER TRIP — BRADFIELD BRIDGE/SLICKROCK

ONE-WAY LENGTH: 47 miles
LOW AND HIGH ELEVATIONS: 5,400 and 6,400 feet
DIFFICULTY: Class III and IV

A classic three-day float trip carries boaters through a dramatic ecological transition from the ponderosa forests of the upper gorge to the barren desert of the Disappointment Valley. This trip includes the imposing Class IV whitewater rapid at Snaggletooth—a long, rock-strewn rapid named for a jagged, toothlike obstacle at its lower end. Some rafters portage the rapid rather than tempt its rocky clutches, particularly at very low water levels (800 cfs or less). Snaggletooth Rapid is at river mile 27, a few miles below the Dove Creek Pump Station. This lower segment offers the most thrilling whitewater, with Class III Little Snag and Three-Mile Rapids providing more excitement. Many boaters extend the trip another three days by floating an additional 50 miles downstream through the Dolores River Canyon unit to Bedrock. Some float as far as the Colorado River confluence at river mile 171, one of the longest wild river floats outside the Grand Canyon!

SCALE: 3/8 INCH = 1 MILE

BLM wildland
Hiking trails
TH Trailhead
BL Boat launch
River or stream
Lake or pond
Marsh or swamp
Primary highway
Secondary highway
Light-duty road
Unimproved road
Trail
✕ Quarry or open-pit mine

DAY HIKE — MOUNTAIN SHEEP POINT

ONE-WAY LENGTH: 3 miles
LOW AND HIGH ELEVATIONS: 7,100 and 8,300 feet
DIFFICULTY: Easy to moderate

The Snaggletooth area is most easily explored via the river, but one scenic hike presents unparalleled views of the Dolores River Canyon. From the glade on the adjacent San Juan National Forest, you can hike onto the prominent peninsula called Mountain Sheep Point and simultaneously obtain long views up and down the canyon. From the Bradfield Bridge boat launch, drive 21 miles north on Forest Development Road 504 to Big Water Spring. At the spring, head west about 0.75 mile on Forest Road 219 to the corral. The terrain is flat here, so direction finding can be a bit challenging. One option is to park at the corral and walk south-west on a fading logging track through scrub aspen about 1 mile before starting the downtrend to the point. Or, for more avid four-wheelers, you can take the left-hand vehicle fork just beyond the corral, drive on a very rough, boulder-strewn road another mile, at which point you can park and hike south across a shallow draw several hundred yards to old logging tracks. These eventually lead out toward the point, finally disappearing into ponderosa pine and oakbrush along the ridgeline. You can stop and enjoy the view at this point (3 miles from the corral) or bushwhack all the way to the very end of Mountain Sheep Point.

DESTINATION HIKE — DOLORES RIVER OVERLOOK

ONE-WAY LENGTH: 0.25 mile
LOW AND HIGH ELEVATIONS: 8,000 feet
DIFFICULTY: Easy

No more spectacular picnic area exists in all of Colorado than the Dolores River Overlook. On a point 2,000 feet above the whispering rapids below, the overlook provides a soaring overview of the Dolores River's eons of geologic scouring. To the south, dark pine forests line the gorge far into the distance, while to the north the canyon broadens out to thousand-foot red sandstone cliffs. Simply follow the signs to the Dolores River Overlook, 8 miles east of Highway 666 near Dove Creek. The actual overlook is an easy quarter-mile stroll from the picnic area.

Squaw and Papoose Canyons 9

John Fielder

Sunrise on sandstone walls and Utah's Abajo Mountains, Squaw/Papoose Canyon Wilderness Study Area.

40 miles northwest of Cortez	**LOCATION**
5,900–8,300 feet	**ELEVATION RANGE**
Cottonwoods, sagebrush, piñon-juniper woodlands	**ECOSYSTEMS**
14,180 acres	**SIZE**
Not proposed for wilderness by BLM	**WILDERNESS STATUS**
Archaeological resources, rare and diverse reptiles and amphibians, Canyons of the Ancients National Monument	**SPECIAL FEATURES**
Champagne Spring, Hatch Trading Post, Papoose Canyon, Ruin Canyon, Ruin Point	**TOPOGRAPHIC MAPS**

quaw and Papoose Canyons generally parallel each other, trending northeast to southwest as they cross the Colorado–Utah border. The canyons begin as rocky arroyos but rapidly cut into the Dakota Sandstone and Morrison Formation to form rugged, steep canyon walls of exposed rock outcrops, boulders, and talus slopes.

Both canyons are rich in archaeological resources. This region of Colorado and Utah contains one of the greatest concentrations of Anasazi Indian sites, as many as 40 to 60 sites per square mile, and includes round towers, Hovenweep towers, pit houses, pueblos, cliff dwellings, lithic scatter, pottery sherds, agricultural sites, and a wide variety of pictographs and petroglyphs. Please don't deface or remove these traces of ancient cultures; leave them for others to observe and enjoy.

Squaw and Papoose Canyons support numerous species of wildlife, many of which have been displaced from the surrounding uplands due to agricultural and other development activities. Larger mammal species include mule deer, mountain lions, and black bears. The diverse topography allows for a similar abundance of bird species including resident golden eagles and migratory bald eagles. Peregrine falcons may occasionally visit the area. Squaw and Papoose Canyons are considered to have the most abundant and diverse reptile and amphibian population in Colorado, including many rare and localized species and subspecies.

A wide variety of vegetation occurs in the area, beginning with the piñon-juniper woodlands and sagebrush that dominate the canyon rims. The slopes contain trees and shrubs including rabbitbrush, Mormon tea, mountain mahogany, Gambel oak, serviceberry, and cliffrose. Vegetation is thicker along the canyon floors with numerous grasses; cactus and yucca; wildflowers such as Indian paintbrush, penstemon, yarrow, phlox, and lupine; and riparian flora including rushes, sedges, cattails, willows, tamarisk, box elder, and cottonwoods. The canyons also contain many perennial springs that offer dependable sources of water.

CONTACT INFORMATION: San Juan Field Office, Bureau of Land Management, 15 Burnett Court, Durango, CO 81301, 970-247-4874, http://www.co.blm.gov/sjra/sjra.html.

LOOP HIKE MARES TAIL CANYON

ONE-WAY LENGTH: 6 miles
LOW AND HIGH ELEVATIONS: 5,600 and 6,400 feet
DIFFICULTY: Moderate

To reach the west side of Squaw Canyon, head west from Dove Creek on H Road, and then zigzag on 6 Road and L Road, following signs to Bug Point southwest toward the state line. Follow a road south along the state line that dead-ends on the rim of the canyon in about 4 miles (you will know you are at the state line when the road makes two consecutive right-angle corners). From this point, you can scramble east several hundred feet down into Squaw Canyon and either explore the canyon 4 miles upstream to private land, or head downstream about 2 miles to the confluence of Mares Tail Canyon. Meander up Mares Tail 2 or 3 miles to any convenient point at which you can scramble out of the canyon east back to your vehicle. An old seismic exploration line provides one obvious route out of the canyon.

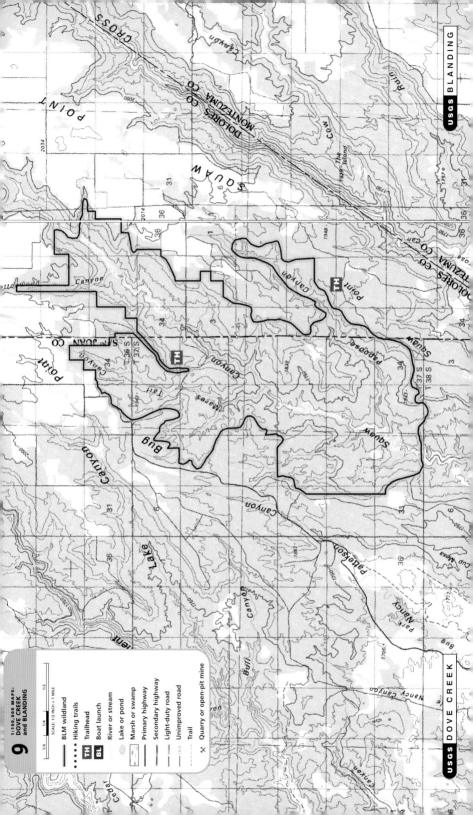

9 1:100,000 MAPS:
DOVE CREEK
and BLANDING

SCALE 1/2 INCH = 1 MILE

1/4   1/4   1/2   1/2 MILE

BLM wildland
Hiking trails
TH Trailhead
BL Boat launch
River or stream
Lake or pond
Marsh or swamp
Primary highway
Secondary highway
Light-duty road
Unimproved road
Trail
✕ Quarry or open-pit mine

DOLORES CO
MONTEZUMA CO

DOLORES CO
TEZUMA CO

SAN JUAN CO

SQUAW POINT

CROSS

POINT

Point

Squaw

Point

Lake

Bug Canyon

Canyon

Canyon

Canyon

Mares Canyon

Tail Canyon

Bug Canyon

Nancy Canyon

Bull Canyon

Park Nancy

Patelson

Cow Ruin

The Island

SHUTTLE HIKE SQUAW CANYON/PAPOOSE CANYON

ONE-WAY LENGTH: 13 miles
LOW AND HIGH ELEVATIONS: 5,400 and 6,400 feet
DIFFICULTY: Moderate

The branching nature of the Squaw and Papoose Canyons creates the opportunity for extended, multi-day explorations of the canyons and their many fascinating cultural treasures. This shuttle begins at the Squaw Canyon jump-off point for the hike described on page 68, but instead of heading back north at Mares Tail Canyon, proceed down the length of Squaw Canyon another 5 miles to Papoose Canyon. Papoose Canyon is around 9 miles in length in its entirety, but you can hike out of the canyon at any point to reach your shuttle vehicle. To reach the east side of Papoose Canyon for the end point of your shuttle, take H Road west from Dove Creek, but rather than heading southwest on L Road, stay on 6 Road south to the east side of Squaw Canyon, following the signs to Squaw Point. Take the road southwest along the mesa between Papoose Canyon and Cross Canyon. Park at any convenient location on public land along this road at the end of your hike. This road deteriorates significantly the farther you go, and ultimately may be impassable beyond the state line to the bottom of Squaw Canyon, particularly in wet weather. The rim here offers sweeping views of the canyon system.

Tabeguache 10

6 miles north of Nucla	**LOCATION**
5,600–7,400 feet	**ELEVATION RANGE**
Cottonwood riparian, piñon-juniper woodlands, ponderosa pine, oakbrush	**ECOSYSTEM**
17,240 acres	**SIZE**
Designated as a protected "area" in 1993 legislation	**WILDERNESS STATUS**
Perennial stream, slickrock canyon, ponderosa forest	**SPECIAL FEATURES**
Nucla, Windy Point	**TOPOGRAPHIC MAPS**

Tabeguache Creek and its North Fork begin in fertile subalpine bowls atop the Uncompahgre Plateau. The main fork plunges quickly into a steep-walled canyon of brilliant red Wingate sandstone, while the North Fork takes a more leisurely route, winding 5 miles through an unbroken expanse of vibrant aspen before it too drops abruptly into a deep canyon lined by red sandstone cliffs. The red cliffs, normally associated with desert terrain, seem somehow out of place surrounded by the lush greenery in this unique melding of canyon and mountain country.

The area is named for the Tabeguache band of Utes who roamed the Uncompahgre Plateau until 1880, when they were exiled to the Uintah Reservation in Utah. The word *tabeguache* loosely translates as "place where the snow melts first" or "sunny side." True to its name, Tabeguache Creek drains the southwestern escarpment of the Uncompahgre Plateau, a broad shield that rises gradually from the east to a deceptive elevation more than a mile above its surrounding plains. Carved by the San Miguel and Dolores Rivers, the western edge of the uplift drops more precipitously. One of the two ranges of the ancestral Rockies was called Uncompahgria, and geologists surmise the existing plateau to be the underlying bedrock of that now-erased mountain range.

In the turbulent heart of Tabeguache Canyon, hikers quickly forget the serenity of the aspen forests high on the benchlands above. Here, along unruly Tabeguache Creek, stately ponderosa pines line the stream bank 1,000 feet below forests of piñon pine and juniper. This is an unusual reversal of the normal succession of life zones, for normally piñon-juniper woodlands precede ponderosa pines in elevation. Cool mountain air flowing down the canyon carries the biological characteristics of the uplands with it and causes this upside-down reversal of life zones. Consequently, hikers descending from Pinto Mesa find themselves passing downward from the Upper Sonoran life zone, dominated by piñon-juniper woodlands, into the ponderosa pine and Douglas fir of the Transition life zone.

Tabeguache occupies an odd niche among Colorado's system of protected areas, a niche shared with two other areas—Roubideau and Piedra. In Colorado's 1993 wilderness legislation, Congress granted it most of the protections normally accorded a wilderness area, although it is not officially designated so. Congress called Tabeguache and the other two "areas." The reason stems from the fact that, unlike the rest of the areas designated wilderness in 1993, Tabeguache is not truly a headwaters area; instead, some streams flow into the area from non-wilderness Forest Service lands upstream. Because private water rights existed upstream, Congress deemed it necessary to leave Tabeguache undesignated for the present in order to preserve a fragile compromise about protecting instream flows in the other official wilderness areas. For Tabeguache, this means its glorious aspen forests have been spared the chainsaw, its minerals have been withdrawn from potential development, and its quiet forests retain their peaceful solitude, free from motorized vehicles. But water development projects could still proceed, even if they dewatered the area's streams.

Tabeguache's 1993 protection denoted a milestone in the appreciation of wild places. Though it was proposed for wilderness protection by the Forest Service in 1979, Congress left Tabeguache out of Colorado's 1980 wilderness legislation in favor of more spectacular areas, such as Mount Sneffels and the Wilson Mountains in the nearby San Juan Mountains. At the time, the lonely, forested low-elevation canyon of Tabeguache Creek seemed less worthy than the photogenic high peaks. From the point of view of biological richness, however, Tabeguache easily rates as important as any rocky, alpine wilderness. Tabeguache deserves notice for another reason as well. Its protection marks the first time Congress has ignored arbitrary administrative boundaries (lines on the map) in Colorado to encompass a larger watershed that spans two federal agencies. The Forest Service controls the upper half of the area, but the BLM oversees the lower arid reaches of the canyon.

CONTACT INFORMATION: Uncompahgre Field Office, Bureau of Land Management, 2505 S. Townsend Ave., Montrose, CO 81401, 970-240-5300, http://www.co.blm.gov/ubra/ubra.html and Norwood Ranger District, Uncompahgre National Forest, 1760 E. Grand Ave., Norwood, CO 81423, 970-327-4261, http://www.fs.fed.us/r2/gmug.

Eric Finstick

Tabeguache Creek.

BLM wildland
Hiking trails
TH Trailhead
BL Boat launch
River or stream
Lake or pond
Marsh or swamp
Primary highway
Secondary highway
Light-duty road
Unimproved road
Trail
Quarry or open-pit mine

SCALE 1/2 INCH = 1 MILE

UNCOMPAHGRE

Columbine Pass

Campground

Tabeguache Trail

JEEP TRAIL

Cañón Point

Spruce Mountain

Pack Trail

Round Mountain

Piñon Mountain

Windy Point

Landing Strip

Pinto Mesa

Doby Canyon

Pack Trail

Box Canyon

Third Canyon

Park Canyon

Wild Cow Mesa

DAY HIKE   INDIAN TRAIL

ONE-WAY LENGTH: 2 miles
LOW AND HIGH ELEVATIONS: 6,000 and 7,200 feet
DIFFICULTY: Moderate

Tabeguache's small size and narrow configuration results in short but steep hikes. From Pinto Mesa, the poorly maintained Indian Trail leads directly into the canyon's bottom, descending from piñon-juniper woodlands down decrepit sandstone cliffs to the ponderosa pines along the creek bottom. To reach the trail, travel 8 miles north of Nucla on the Columbine Pass Road (Forest Road 503), turn north onto Forest Road 660, and climb onto Pinto Mesa. Skirt an agricultural field, turn north, and park a mile farther where the road becomes severely eroded. This road leads to a sign denoting the Indian Trail and a series of steep switchbacks into the canyon bottom. As you descend, notice that the opposite walls are composed of Wingate sandstone overlaid by Entrada sandstone, with the usually intervening layer of Kayenta sandstone largely absent. The trail ultimately disappears in dense shrubs along the creek's banks. Tabeguache Creek is all but impossible to cross in the spring, unless you are lucky enough to find a fallen ponderosa forming a natural bridge over the water. In summer, you can hopscotch over the creek via boulders. On the far side of the creek, a faint trail picks up heading downstream.

DAY HIKE   NORTH FORK TABEGUACHE CREEK

ONE-WAY LENGTH: 3 miles
LOW AND HIGH ELEVATIONS: 8,600 and 8,900 feet
DIFFICULTY: Easy

An unmarked trailhead along the Divide Road provides the jumping-off point for the Fortyseven Trail and a pleasant stroll through succulent aspen groves of the North Fork drainage. Using your topographic map, pay close attention to map mileage or corners along the Divide Road and pull off at an open area along the road's south side where the trail intersects. Walk south from this open area; the trail quickly becomes apparent where it descends a short hill to the creek. From there, the trail winds past marshy areas and small stock ponds before meandering through level benches populated by a dense forest of aspen en route to the Fortyseven Cow Camp.

DAY HIKE LOWER TABEGUACHE CREEK

ONE-WAY LENGTH: 3 miles
LOW AND HIGH ELEVATIONS: 5,700 and 6,300 feet
DIFFICULTY: Easy

Several abandoned roads lead into the arid lower section of the canyon on BLM land. Using your topographic map, drive northwest out of Nucla on the high standard road past old coal mines, and turn right onto an old track just north of Coal Canyon. Park where convenient, then hike northeast along this track to Gypsy Park and Ross Fort Park where colorful adobe soils inhibit growth of the piñon-juniper. The path forks, and one route drops into Tabeguache Creek. In late summer and fall, you can easily negotiate the creek by way of boulder hopping or numerous stream crossings. An occasional trail proceeds upstream along the creek 4 miles to the National Forest boundary. The canyon here is shallow with rounded cliffs of Entrada sandstone and several overhanging alcoves hidden among the dense riparian vegetation.

SHUTTLE HIKE INDIAN TRAIL/LOWER TABEGUACHE CREEK

ONE-WAY LENGTH: 8 miles
LOW AND HIGH ELEVATIONS: 5,700 and 7,200 feet
DIFFICULTY: Moderate to strenuous

The routes described on page 75 and above for the Indian Trail and Lower Tabeguache Creek can be combined to create a shuttle hike that extends the lower half of the canyon (the upper half is trailless and choked with dense brush). Leaving one vehicle on Pinto Mesa on Forest Road 660, hike into the canyon and cross the creek. In spring, Tabeguache Creek is a raging, hazardous torrent and can be safely crossed only via a log. Once on the north side, proceed downstream 4 or 5 miles with a lot of bushwhacking, passing Fortyseven Creek and Stinking Springs along the way. Using your topographic map, keep a sharp eye out for the trail out of the canyon to Gypsy Park and your other vehicle.

Weber Mountain and Menefee Mountain

11

John Fielder

20 miles east of Cortez	**LOCATION**
6,500–8,300 feet	**ELEVATION RANGE**
Piñon-juniper woodlands, oakbrush, mountain mahogany, ponderosa pine, Douglas fir	**ECOSYSTEM**
14,572 acres	**SIZE**
Not proposed for wilderness by BLM	**WILDERNESS STATUS**
Scenic buttes, bighorn sheep, Mexican spotted owl	**SPECIAL FEATURES**
Mancos, Thompson Park, Trail Canyon	**TOPOGRAPHIC MAPS**

Weber and Menefee Mountains are wilderness islands amidst the developed agricultural lands of the Mancos River Valley. As such, they provide extremely important undisturbed wildlife habitat. Both mountains are prominent buttes, rising from 6,500 to 8,300 feet, capped with resistant Point Lookout sandstone that creates a girdling barrier of cliffs. These sheer cliffs, combined with dense vegetation, create the almost impenetrable solitude many species of wildlife find so necessary. Around the mountains, farming and ranching have stripped the land, leaving only the mountains with good vegetative cover.

Mule deer herds migrate along the bottom slopes of the mountains for winter range. Weber Mountain and adjacent Menefee Mountain provide a valuable refuge, offering ridgetops that blow free of snow and protective valleys in between. Deer can migrate through the area without any manmade obstructions to the lower, warmer lands of the Ute Indian Reservation to the south. A small herd of bighorn sheep, originally introduced into adjacent Mesa Verde National Park in 1946, frequents Weber Mountain. Perhaps 20 black bears, up to 10 mountain lions, and a number of bobcats inhabit the area as well. Golden eagle nests have been identified on Menefee Mountain. The endangered Mexican spotted owl has been sighted on the Ute Reservation immediately south and in adjacent Mesa Verde National Park.

Vegetation consists of piñon-juniper woodlands, oakbrush, and mountain mahogany with scattered stands of Douglas fir and ponderosa pine above 7,000 feet. The ruggedness creates prime opportunities for hiking, backpacking, and climbing, and the cliff tops offer dramatic vantage points for sightseeing and photography.

Weber and Menefee Mountains offer wonderful opportunities for solitude, fine scenery, and backcountry recreation in close proximity to Mesa Verde National Park. The existing Mesa Verde Wilderness is closed to recreational use, as is all the backcountry in Mesa Verde, for the purpose of protecting the archaeological sites in the National Park.

Weber Mountain is the western of the two mountains and forms the viewshed from the main entrance road into the park. The spires and pinnacles of an intrusive volcanic plug, midway down the west side of the mountain, look appealing for hikes, but Weber Mountain consists almost entirely of private land. Two large canyons drain the south end of the mountain and offer rugged routes to the mountain crest, but require permission from the local landowner for access. In addition, if you cross over to the Ute Mountain Tribal Park south of Weber Mountain, you will need a permit from the Ute Mountain Tribe headquartered in Towaoc.

CONTACT INFORMATION: San Juan Field Office, Bureau of Land Management, 15 Burnett Court, Durango, CO 81301, 970-247-4874, http://www.co.blm.gov/sjra/sjra.html.

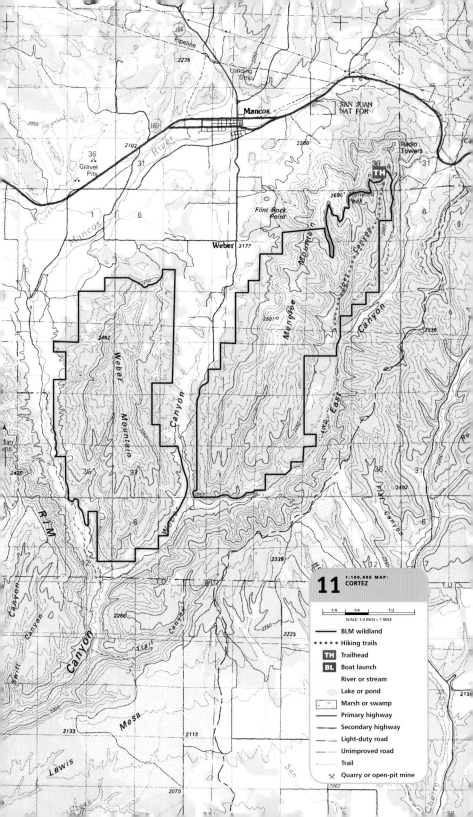

SAN JUAN NAT FOR

Mancos

Radio Towers

Gravel Pits

Flint Rock Point

Weber 2177

Menefee Mountain

Bridges Canyon

Weber Canyon

Mancos River

East Canyon

Flat Canyon

Swift Canyon

Lewis

Mesa

Canyon

R/M

11 1:100,000 MAP:
CORTEZ

SCALE: 1/2 INCH = 1 MILE

| 1/4 | 1/4 | 1/2 |

BLM wildland
•••• Hiking trails
TH Trailhead
BL Boat launch
River or stream
Lake or pond
Marsh or swamp
Primary highway
Secondary highway
Light-duty road
Unimproved road
Trail
Quarry or open-pit mine

DAY HIKE JOES CANYON

ONE-WAY LENGTH: 4 miles
LOW AND HIGH ELEVATIONS: 7,200 and 8,300 feet
DIFFICULTY: Moderate

Joes Canyon provides an interesting transition from Menefee Mountain's summit ridge to the open meadows that surround its lower slopes. At the crest of the large horseshoe curve atop Mancos Hill on Highway 160, turn south on the farthest west dirt road, and then immediately turn hard right on the branch leading to the many prominent radio towers at Menefee's north end. Park at the head of Joes Canyon near a stock pond and immediately descend through a surprising aspen grove down the obvious stock and game trail. Ancient Douglas fir and ponderosa pine trees are scattered throughout the canyon's length. The trail ultimately joins an old jeep trail in the open lower end of Joes Canyon and meets private property at an old cabin. Rather than precisely retrace your steps back to your car, you can follow several westerly branching tributary canyons can lead you up steep slopes through dense, old timber to the radio tower road and an easy walk back to the car.

DAY HIKE MENEFEE MOUNTAIN

ONE-WAY LENGTH: 2 miles
LOW AND HIGH ELEVATIONS: 6,100 and 8,100 feet
DIFFICULTY: Moderate

The west side of Menefee Mountain is generally barricaded by private land from the Weber Canyon Road, but there is one public land access point on the extreme southwest corner of the mountain. Follow South Main Street out of Mancos to the Weber Canyon Road. At Menefee's southern end, a faint road marked by a BLM/Public Land sign climbs steeply up a slope strewn with large sandstone boulders scattered amidst ancient junipers. Following deer paths and ridgelines, bushwhack your way to the mountain's summit ridge.

Cave along the Dolores River.

John Fielder

12 Adobe Badlands

Mark Pearson

LOCATION	3 miles north of Delta
ELEVATION RANGE	5,200–8,300 feet
ECOSYSTEM	Sagebrush, piñon-juniper woodlands
SIZE	10,525 acres
WILDERNESS STATUS	Not proposed for wilderness by BLM
SPECIAL FEATURES	Scenic vistas, badlands topography
TOPOGRAPHIC MAPS	North Delta, Point Creek

Adobe Badlands is notable for its mazelike adobe formations of gray and yellow Mancos shale interspersed with intriguing canyons, mesas, and arroyos on the southern slopes of the Grand Mesa. The badlands offer scenic vistas of Grand Mesa, the Uncompahgre Plateau, and the San Juan Mountains. Two endangered cactus species, the spineless hedgehog cactus and *Sclerocactus glaucidus,* are thought to inhabit the area.

At first glimpse, the Adobe Badlands appear unforgiving and void of life, but with closer inspection, you'll see wildlife

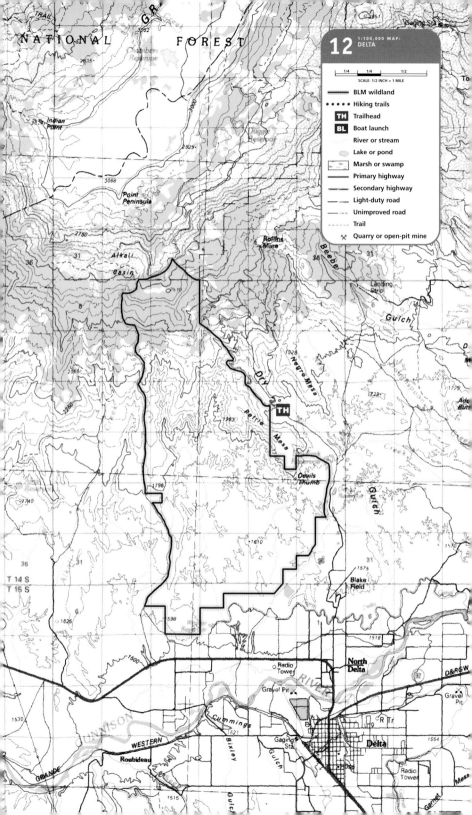

SCALE: 1/2 INCH = 1 MILE

─────	BLM wildland
• • • • •	Hiking trails
TH	Trailhead
BL	Boat launch
─────	River or stream
⬡	Lake or pond
▨	Marsh or swamp
═════	Primary highway
─────	Secondary highway
─────	Light-duty road
─────	Unimproved road
- - - -	Trail
✕	Quarry or open-pit mine

NATIONAL FOREST

Indian Point

Point Peninsula

Alkali Basin

Rollins Mine

Beebe

Landing Strip

Gulch

Dry

Negro Mesa

Petrie Mesa

TH

Devils Thumb

Gulch

Creek

Blake Field

T 14 S
T 15 S

Radio Tower

North Delta

Gravel Pit

D&RGW

Gravel Pit

RIVER

GUNNISON

Cummings

Bixley Gulch

WESTERN

Roubideau

GRANDE

Gaging Sta

Delta

Radio Tower

Garnet Mesa

flourishing everywhere. Birds, such as the house finch, Gambel's quail, and piñon jay are common in the area, and you'll occasionally see golden eagles, turkey vultures, and red-tailed hawks. Desert striped whipsnakes and northern sagebrush lizards are some of the common reptiles found in the Adobes. Pronghorn also roam the slopes of the area.

The Mancos shale that comprises the badlands was deposited between 135 million to 65 million years ago by an ancient sea, and you can find marine fossils in the shale. Volcanic eruptions later deposited a basaltic caprock that now forms the top of Grand Mesa. Erosion has since created the spectacular badlands that now occupy much of the area.

CONTACT INFORMATION: Uncompahgre Field Office, Bureau of Land Management, 2505 S. Townsend Ave., Montrose, CO 81401, 970-240-5300, http://www.co.blm.gov/ubra/ubra.html.

DAY HIKE | DEVILS THUMB

ONE-WAY LENGTH: 1.5 miles
LOW AND HIGH ELEVATIONS: 5,700 and 6,300 feet
DIFFICULTY: Easy

The roadless area lies immediately north of Highway 50 outside Delta. Take the airport road (County Road 1575) north at the highway curve in north Delta, and veer west just below the hilltop runway. This road skirts past an abandoned reservoir and angles toward the Grand Mesa along the eastern side of Adobe Badlands. Devils Thumb, a prominent eroded pinnacle, juts from the end of Petrie Mesa and is a short hike from the road. Park near the abandoned reservoir, approximately 2.5 miles north of the airport, and head cross-country to the thumb. Or, continue on the road to the north side of Petrie Mesa, and hike the obvious abandoned jeep trail up the mesa and out its length to Devils Thumb. You'll find many vantage points for stunning views of the San Juan Mountains, particularly when the peaks are snow covered in spring or fall.

Bangs Canyon 13

Mark Pearson

5 miles south of Grand Junction	**LOCATION**
4,900–8,400 feet	**ELEVATION RANGE**
Piñon-juniper woodlands, sagebrush, Douglas fir, aspen	**ECOSYSTEM**
21,130 acres	**SIZE**
Not proposed for wilderness by BLM	**WILDERNESS STATUS**
Ecological transition, perennial streams	**SPECIAL FEATURES**
Island Mesa, Whitewater	**TOPOGRAPHIC MAPS**

Bangs Canyon provides remarkable backcountry recreation opportunities just minutes from downtown Grand Junction. Located east of the Colorado National Monument, the area includes several wild canyons, including Bangs Canyon and North East Creek. Water cut through the Morrison and Entrada sediments to form these brilliantly colored hideaways on the flanks of the Uncompahgre Uplift. Vegetation ranges from Douglas fir and aspen on the Uncompahgre Plateau to saltbush desert on the south bank of the Gunnison River.

Though near Grand Junction, Bangs Canyon possesses a great sense of remoteness and solitude. The boundaries of the area are largely defined by rough four-wheel-drive roads and by the Gunnison River. Access to the western edge of the area from Grand Junction is relatively quick, but it may take a couple hours to get to the upper reaches of North East Creek on the south end of the area. East Creek carves a scenic canyon, lined with cottonwoods and pools, along State Highway 141 on the unit's eastern side.

CONTACT INFORMATION: Grand Junction Field Office, Bureau of Land Management, 2815 H Rd., Grand Junction, CO 81506, 970-244-3000, http://www.co.blm.gov/gjra/gjra.html.

DAY HIKE BANGS CANYON VIA TABEGUACHE TRAIL

ONE-WAY LENGTH: 4 miles
LOW AND HIGH ELEVATIONS: 4,700 and 5,600 feet
DIFFICULTY: Moderate

The Tabeguache Trail intersects Highway 141 at an indistinct trailhead 1.25 miles southwest of Whitewater where the highway bridges East Creek. Heading north, in a few minutes you climb out of the canyon and away from the highway noise onto the mesas that slope gently up to the Uncompahgre Plateau. Hike up the trail to a point just past a couple metal stock ponds on the right where a two-track trail goes right (north). Keep bearing left at any other tracks until you ultimately reach the high ridge over Bangs Canyon. A cattle dugway allows access to Bangs Canyon, from here to the junction of Bangs and West Bangs Canyons. If you have good eyes, you can find the dugway at this point.

DAY HIKE ROUGH CANYON

ONE-WAY LENGTH: 2 miles
LOW AND HIGH ELEVATIONS: 5,400 and 6,200 feet
DIFFICULTY: Easy-moderate

You can also access Bangs Canyon via Little Park Road south of Grand Junction. From downtown Grand Junction, follow the signs toward the Colorado National Monument and take Broadway across the Colorado River. Once over the river, turn left onto Monument Road, and turn left again almost immediately onto Rosevale Road. Rosevale Road curves around a corner and in several blocks intersects Little Park Road. Take Little Park Road south approximately 6 miles (1.5 miles beyond the end of the pavement) to a dirt road that branches south. This road goes directly to Bangs Canyon, and forms the western boundary of the roadless area. The first drainage crossed is Rough Canyon. Though not part of the Bangs Canyon roadless area, Rough Canyon is a pleasant hike that includes pools, waterfalls, and petroglyphs. A short 2-mile hike upstream returns you close to the Little Park Road.

SCALE: 1/2 INCH = 1 MILE

1/4   1/4   1/2

BLM wildland
•••• Hiking trails
TH Trailhead
BL Boat launch
River or stream
Lake or pond
Marsh or swamp
Primary highway
Secondary highway
Light-duty road
Unimproved road
Trail
Quarry or open-pit mine

USGS GRAND JUNCTION

USGS DELTA

Grand Junction

Pear Park

Rosevale

Orchard Mesa

COLORADO

Whitewater

Horse Point

Gaging Stations

Gravel Pit

Gravel Pits

Rough

Hells Hole

Horse Mesa

Canyon

Bangs

Island Mesa

West

Notch Spring

Bangs

Cordura Spring

Bench

Bangs Canyon

Nancy Hanks Gulch

JEEP

TRAIL

Ninemile Hill

Milburn Bench

Cactus

LOOP HIKE WEST BANGS CANYON/BANGS CANYON

ONE-WAY LENGTH: 12 miles
LOW AND HIGH ELEVATIONS: 4,700 and 6,400 feet
DIFFICULTY: Moderate

West Bangs Canyon is a 3-mile drive beyond Rough Canyon along a four-wheel-drive road that doubles as the Tabeguache Trail. Park near the crossing of West Bangs Canyon, and follow the canyon about 5 miles downstream to the confluence with Bangs Canyon. Return about 5 miles back up Bangs Canyon until you intersect the Tabeguache Trail (a rough jeep road at this point) and follow the Tabeguache Trail back 2 miles to the starting point. These canyons are cut largely through the Morrison Formation, which creates soft canyon walls of green and gray shale. The canyons are relatively broad and shallow.

Black Ridge Canyons

John Fielder

10 miles west of Grand Junction	**LOCATION**
4,700–6,800 feet	**ELEVATION RANGE**
Piñon-juniper woodlands, sagebrush, cottonwoods	**ECOSYSTEM**
75,000 acres	**SIZE**
73,937 acres designated as wilderness in 2000	**WILDERNESS STATUS**
Colorado River, sandstone arches, slickrock canyons, eagles and peregrine falcons, desert bighorns	**SPECIAL FEATURES**
Battleship Rock, Bitter Creek Well, Colorado National Monument, Mack, Ruby Canyon, Sieber Canyon, Westwater 4 SE	**TOPOGRAPHIC MAPS**

Black Ridge is an outstanding example of deep, sheer-walled slickrock canyons. The scenery is somewhat similar to that of Colorado National Monument, but is much more varied. The Monument features only relatively short, dry canyons and a few rock pinnacles. Black Ridge Canyons contains three major canyon systems (much longer than anything in the Monument), innumerable spires and pinnacles, the second greatest concentration of natural arches in the Southwest, perennial streams with rich riparian vegetation, a huge 300-foot cavern cut by a stream meandering in Mee Canyon, and about 20 miles of frontage along the Colorado River in Ruby and Horsethief Canyons. This stretch of the Colorado River has been recommended for Scenic designation under the Wild and Scenic Rivers Act. BLM estimates that the river alone receives 7,000 visitor days of use per year.

Black Ridge Canyons contains critical wildlife habitat for many species. Desert bighorn sheep have been reintroduced into the area; the herd presently consists of 30 to 40 animals. Deer, mountain lion, and many raptors, including the peregrine falcon, also inhabit Black Ridge Canyons. The river corridor provides wintering grounds for bald eagles, and active golden eagle nesting sites exist within the area.

Black Ridge Canyons is also home to several rare and endangered species. These include four species of endangered fish in the Colorado River—humpback chub, pikeminnow (formerly named Colorado River squawfish), bonytail chub, and razorback sucker—as well as a rare butterfly, *Papilio indra minori,* the short-tailed black swallowtail. The area also harbors a variety of uncommon desert plant communities. In fact, Black Ridge Canyons contains a greater number of rare and imperiled plant, animal, and invertebrate species than any other desert wilderness in Colorado.

In the late 1980s, the National Park Service cast a covetous eye on Black Ridge Canyons, with a desire to expand the boundaries of the Colorado National Monument westward to encompass the wild canyons under BLM's administration. BLM launched a counteroffensive with a proposed National Conservation Area that included Black Ridge Canyons as its wilderness core, but also including Ruby Canyon along the Colorado River as well as extensive tracts of BLM land north of the river in the area around Rabbit Valley. These additional lands proposed for the National Conservation Area included the Kokepelli Trail, a popular route for mountain biking west of Grand Junction.

Congress finally moved to act on the pending Black Ridge Canyons wilderness proposal and the associated National Conservation Area in 2000, in response to a threat by Interior Secretary Bruce Babbitt to push proclamation of a new National Monument. At the end of 2000, Congress enacted the Black Ridge Canyons Wilderness Area and the Colorado Canyons National Monument, both under BLM's management.

Black Ridge Canyons is a large area with many and varied access opportunities. The area is easily explored by raft or canoe, short day hikes, or long multi-day backpack trips.

CONTACT INFORMATION: Grand Junction Field Office, Bureau of Land Management, 2815 H Rd., Grand Junction, CO 81506, 970-244-3000, http://www.co.blm.gov/gjra/blackridgewsa.htm.

RIVER TRIP — LOMA/WESTWATER

ONE-WAY LENGTH: 26 miles
LOW AND HIGH ELEVATIONS: 4,600 and 4,700 feet
DIFFICULTY: Class I and II

The Colorado River is one of the most popular avenues for visiting Black Ridge Canyons. The segment from Loma to the Westwater Ranger Station is flat water suitable for most types of watercraft. To find the Loma boat launch, take the Loma exit on Interstate 70 (I-70) west of Grand Junction, drive south across the overpass, and follow the signs left to the boat ramp. Once you are on the river, one of the first attractions is the hidden mouth of Rattlesnake Canyon, 3.3 miles downstream on river left. A steep climb up Rattlesnake Canyon will take you to the arches in the Entrada sandstone along the canyon rim. Mee Canyon, 14 miles downstream from Loma, is a popular campsite and river hike. Pinnacles, windows, and turrets line the canyon mouth and occur in groups throughout the lower several miles of the canyon. Other popular campsites along the river include those at Black Rocks, 2 miles beyond Mee Canyon, and at the mouth of Knowles Canyon, several miles farther downstream. Knowles Canyon offers many miles of hiking and tributaries. The Westwater Ranger Station, and the takeout for this segment of the river, is 26 river miles from Loma. Floating beyond the ranger station and through Westwater Canyon requires a permit from BLM. The Westwater Ranger Station is at the end of an 8-mile access road that leaves from the Westwater Exit on I-70 just over the Utah state line.

DESTINATION HIKES — DEVILS CANYON

ONE-WAY LENGTH: 3 miles
LOW AND HIGH ELEVATIONS: 4,600 and 5,400 feet
DIFFICULTY: Easy to moderate

Devils Canyon offers the closest wilderness trailhead to Grand Junction and Fruita. To reach the trailhead, take Highway 340 south from the Fruita Exit on I-70. Turn right at the Kingswood Estates subdivision just south of the river, and follow the road a mile or so west to the Devils Canyon Trailhead. Devils Canyon is the first canyon west of the Colorado National Monument, and is a similarly short but dramatic slickrock canyon cut into the northern edge of the Uncompahgre Plateau. The trail initially follows an old road constructed for a proposed residential subdivision in the mouth of Devils Canyon. When the developer declared bankruptcy in the mid-1980s, quick action by BLM personnel resulted in public purchase of the defaulted property from the lender. Hikers can explore several miles into Devils Canyon.

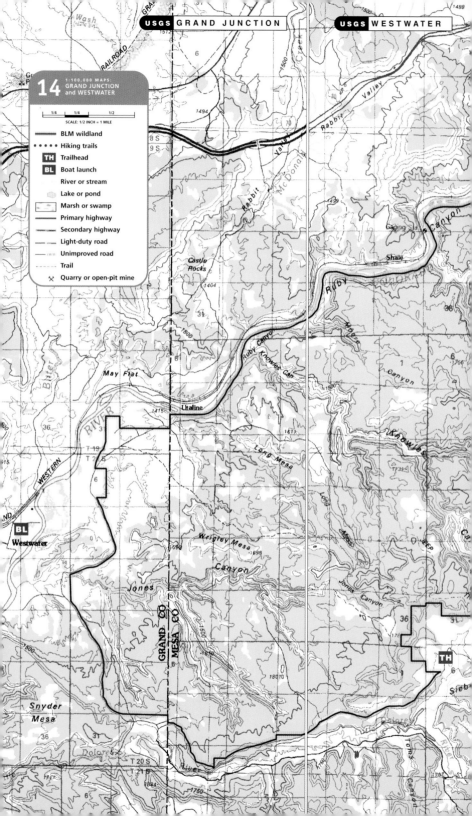

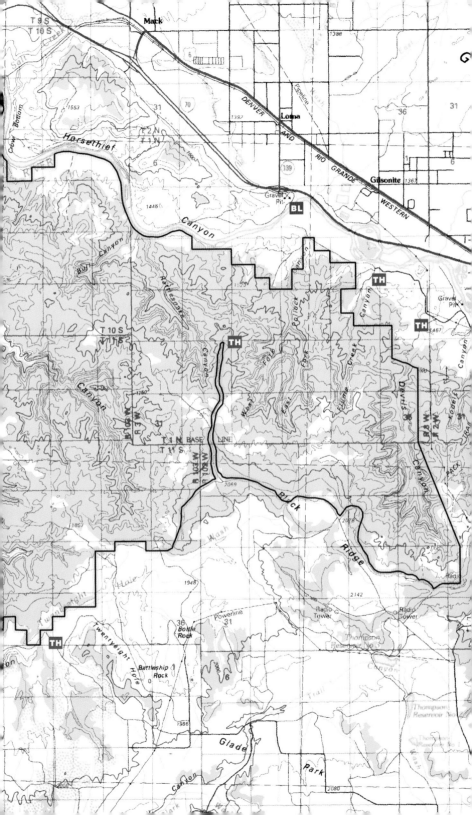

DESTINATION HIKE RATTLESNAKE ARCHES FROM FLUME CANYON

ONE-WAY LENGTH: 7 miles
LOW AND HIGH ELEVATIONS: 4,600 and 5,600 feet
DIFFICULTY: Moderate to strenuous

The Rattlesnake Canyon arches have gained increasing attention in recent years. In recognition of this, BLM constructed a trail to the arches from the river near Fruita. This hiking trail, surprisingly steep in places, begins at a trailhead west of Fruita in the mouth of Flume Canyon, and traverses approximately 7 miles across East and West Pollock Canyons to Rattlesnake Canyon. The trailhead is located on the same road just another mile west of the Devils Canyon Trailhead described on page 91. The trail offers immediate seclusion from the bustle of the Grand Valley, with increasingly sweeping panoramas as you gain altitude. About a dozen arches are carved through the Entrada sandstone rimrock above Rattlesnake Canyon.

DESTINATION HIKE RATTLESNAKE ARCHES FROM HUNTER ACCESS ROAD

ONE-WAY LENGTH: 0.5 mile
LOW AND HIGH ELEVATIONS: 5,600 and 5,900 feet
DIFFICULTY: Easy

You can also reach the arches via one of two rough, 13-mile jeep roads that begin just outside the Colorado National Monument. Near the midpoint along the rim drive in the Monument, turn south onto the dirt road to Glade Park; after a 0.25 mile, turn west onto the Black Ridge Hunter Access Road. From this point, two roads follow the north slope of Black Ridge leading to the Rattlesnake Canyon Trailhead, each open a different season. The Upper Road is open from April 15 to Aug. 15; the Lower Road is open from Aug. 15 to Feb. 15. Both roads are closed to motorized travel from Feb. 15 to April 15 to prevent severe rutting when the soil is most thoroughly saturated. BLM has constructed a parking area at the end of the roads, and a short trail takes you to the arches, of which a dozen are scattered along a mile of the canyon rim. Be warned that these roads are entirely impassable when wet, owing to the Morrison shale on which they are built.

DESTINATION HIKE KNOWLES CANYON

ONE-WAY LENGTH: 2–15 miles
LOW AND HIGH ELEVATIONS: 4,400 and 6,200 feet
DIFFICULTY: Easy to strenuous

BLM constructed two trailheads in the Twentyeight Hole country for access to the more remote, western reaches of Black Ridge Canyons. You can reach these trailheads by traveling through the Monument to the Glade Park store, then heading 1 mile north to the first major road west, BS Road. Follow BS Road 12 miles west to the Knowles Canyon Trailhead, just after you cross Twentyeight Hole wash (or Sieber Canyon). A 1.5-mile trail leads to a jeep trail that skirts the head of Knowles Canyon. You can follow this trail into the canyon, or you can pioneer your own route into the bottom. Knowles Canyon is the longest canyon system in the area, and traveling its entire length to the river makes it a multi-day trip.

DESTINATION HIKE JONES CANYON

ONE-WAY LENGTH: 3–12 miles
LOW AND HIGH ELEVATIONS: 4,600 and 6,300 feet
DIFFICULTY: Easy to strenuous

The second trailhead along Sieber Canyon is several miles farther west of the Knowles Canyon Trailhead. A locked gate denotes the end of the public road, and also marks the trailhead to Jones Canyon. This trailhead is one of your best bets for seeing few other people. The trail follows one of several old jeep trails across the expansive mesas and buttes of Black Ridge Canyons' western extent. The branching nature of Jones Canyon offers an opportunity for a looping hike down one fork and out a different tributary.

Sandstone arch, Rattlesnake Canyon, Black Ridge Canyons Wilderness Area.

15 Demaree Canyon

Mark Pearson

LOCATION	25 miles northwest of Grand Junction
ELEVATION RANGE	5,000–7,500 feet
ECOSYSTEM	Douglas fir, piñon-juniper woodlands, oakbrush-mountain mahogany, greasewood, sagebrush
SIZE	24,500 acres
WILDERNESS STATUS	Not proposed for wilderness by BLM
SPECIAL FEATURES	Desert scenery, views of the La Sal Mountains
TOPOGRAPHIC MAPS	Carbonera, Howard Canyon

Demaree Canyon is a chunk of the wild canyons of the Bookcliffs in extreme western Colorado. The roadless area consists of the Bookcliffs escarpment, rising more than 2,500 feet out of the featureless desert plains of the Grand Valley and culminating in rugged ridges. Four large canyons dissect this desolate terrain, spanning the cliff front between East and West Salt Creeks.

The canyons of Demaree are cut through the tan and brown sandstone of the Mesa Verde Group, underlaid by gray

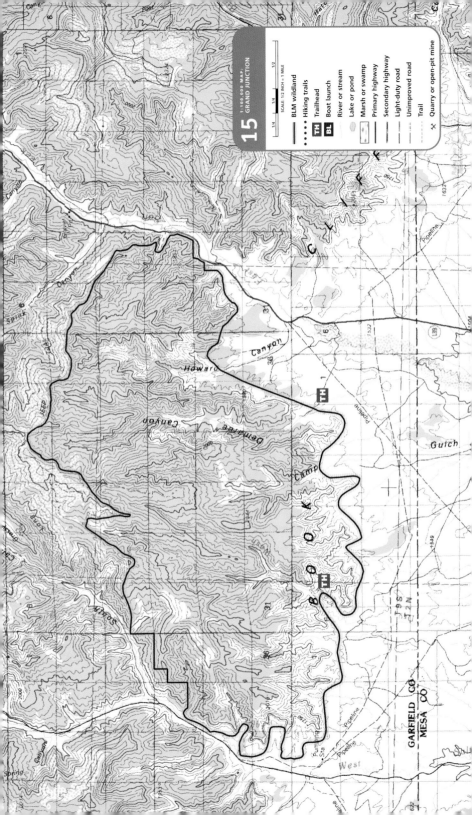

Mancos shale. Forests of piñon and juniper blanket the steep slopes of uplifted cliffs, interspersed with dense thickets of mountain mahogany and oakbrush. Intermittent streams occasionally carve bowls and channels through the soft sandstone.

Hikers gain an immediate sense of intimacy upon entering the canyon from the open plain of the Grand Valley. Splashes of cactus wildflowers enliven the otherwise gray and forest green backdrop. The canyons gradually close in and lead to steep head-walls. An oil and gas road bladed across the tops of these imposing slopes forms the northern boundary of the roadless area. From these ridges you gain stirring views of the snowcapped La Sal Mountains, rising from behind the red rock canyons of the Uncompahgre Plateau.

CONTACT INFORMATION: Grand Junction Field Office, Bureau of Land Management, 2815 H Rd., Grand Junction, CO 81506, 970-244-3000, http://www.co.blm.gov/gjra/demareewsa.htm.

DAY HIKE DEMAREE CANYON

ONE-WAY LENGTH: 5 miles
LOW AND HIGH ELEVATIONS: 5,300 and 6,600 feet
DIFFICULTY: Easy to moderate

Demaree Canyon is readily accessible from either the east or west. The eastern boundary of the unit is the Douglas Pass Road, Highway 139. Take the highway north from I-70 at the Loma exit to a point about 1.5 miles north of the Mesa-Garfield county line. A road takes off to the west, skirts a stock pond, and imme-diately crosses East Salt Creek, which is a shallow ford during all but the height of spring runoff. The road will take you to the mouth of Demaree Canyon a mile farther on, at which point you can abandon your vehicle for hiking boots. The streambed of Demaree Canyon makes a pleasant hiking path and leads past out-crops of sandstone and several narrow channels to the source of the canyon.

DAY HIKE DRY CANYON WASH

ONE-WAY LENGTH: 6 miles
LOW AND HIGH ELEVATIONS: 5,300 and 6,600 feet
DIFFICULTY: Easy to moderate

Access to Demaree Canyon from the west is via Baxter Pass Road. From Loma, head west on old Highway 50 to Mack and follow the signs to Baxter Pass and Bonanza, Utah. The Mitchell Road turns east from this road 1 mile north of the Mesa-Garfield county line. The Mitchell Road generally forms the southern boundary of the Demaree Canyon roadless area and takes you directly to the mouth of Dry Canyon Wash. An oil and gas road is punched a couple miles up this canyon, but the canyon is pristine beyond the end of the road.

Dominguez Canyons 16

John Fielder

20 miles southeast of Grand Junction	**LOCATION**
4,800–9,000 feet	**ELEVATION RANGE**
Cottonwood riparian zone, piñon-juniper woodlands, ponderosa pine, Douglas fir, aspen, and spruce	**ECOSYSTEM**
87,483 acres	**SIZE**
74,488 acres proposed for wilderness by BLM	**WILDERNESS STATUS**
Waterfalls, pools, petroglyphs, desert bighorn sheep	**SPECIAL FEATURES**
Dominguez, Escalante Forks, Good Point, Jacks Canyon, Keith Creek, Triangle Mesa	**TOPOGRAPHIC MAPS**

Big and Little Dominguez Canyons comprise a spectacular slickrock canyon wilderness. The canyons are endowed with all the components of a desert paradise—perennial streams and plunge pools carved out of glistening black schist, brilliant red sandstone walls, gracious cottonwoods, desert bighorn sheep, an endangered cactus (the spineless hedgehog), numerous petroglyph panels, and many soaring raptors.

The canyons drain the northeastern corner of the Uncompahgre Plateau and front the Gunnison River for almost 15 miles. Little Dominguez is the longer of the two, approximately 20 miles from top to bottom. It joins larger Big Dominguez Canyon just before their confluence with the Gunnison River. The area is the largest BLM roadless area in the state and spans an extraordinary array of ecosystems ranging from upper Sonoran desert characterized by piñon-juniper woodlands along the Gunnison to Douglas fir and ponderosa pine forest on canyon slopes, culminating in aspen and spruce-fir forests in the highest elevations.

Dominguez Canyons hosts one of the greatest concentrations of rare and imperiled plants, fish, and amphibians in Colorado. Among these rare species, two amphibians, the canyon treefrog and northern leopard frog, make their homes here. Uncommon hanging gardens grace hidden alcoves, the canyon-bog orchid pops up here and there, and the Uinta Basin hookless cactus dots the hot, dry canyon slopes and mesas.

For many years, dam builders targeted this stretch of the Gunnison River for yet another dam, this one called Dominguez Dam in "honor" of the magnificent tributary canyons that would be flooded. Poor economics, the significance of the Gunnison River as spawning grounds for endangered native fish such as the pikeminnow, and changing attitudes spelled the death knell for the dam.

CONTACT INFORMATION: Grand Junction Field Office, Bureau of Land Management, 2815 H Rd., Grand Junction, CO 81506, 970-244-3000, http://www.co.blm.gov/gjra/dominguezwsa.htm.

DESTINATION HIKE ▶ CACTUS PARK

ONE-WAY LENGTH: 5 miles
LOW AND HIGH ELEVATIONS: 5,400 and 6,600 feet
DIFFICULTY: Moderate

Big Dominguez Canyon is the most accessible of the two major canyons, and the Cactus Park Trail drops straight into the heart of it. To reach the Cactus Park Trailhead, drive 9 miles southwest of Whitewater on Highway 141, turn east at the signed Cactus Park intersection, and drive another 7 miles on a dirt road to the canyon's rim. The last few miles require a high-clearance vehicle. BLM constructed a short, steep primitive trail from the rim into the middle of Big Dominguez Canyon. Several miles downstream from this point is the confluence with Little Dominguez. A mile or so above the confluence you'll see a slot waterfall and several large boulders covered with petroglyphs. From the point the trail reaches the canyon bottom, the Gunnison River is about 3.5 miles downstream and the Big Dominguez Campground is 10 miles upstream to the west.

DESTINATION HIKE BIG DOMINGUEZ CANYON

ONE-WAY LENGTH: 13 miles
LOW AND HIGH ELEVATIONS: 4,800 and 7,300 feet
DIFFICULTY: Moderate

BLM's Big Dominguez Campground provides the jumping-off point for hikes from the head of the canyon. You reach the campground via Highway 141, but the turnoff is the Divide Road, 5 miles beyond the Cactus Park Road. The Divide Road is a well-maintained Forest Service road that accesses the Uncompahgre Plateau. After you've climbed onto the plateau, in about 5 miles a sign identifies the turnoff to Dominguez Campground. The campground is another 5 miles down its own road, which becomes quite hazardous when wet. The campground is a pleasant, shaded spot nestled among ponderosa pine, cottonwood trees, and willows along Big Dominguez Creek at the head of the roadless area. From here, it is perhaps 13 miles down the canyon to the confluence with Little Dominguez, and about 10 miles to the Cactus Park Trail.

LOOP HIKE BIG DOMINGUEZ/LITTLE DOMINGUEZ

ONE-WAY LENGTH: 34 miles
LOW AND HIGH ELEVATIONS: 4,800 and 8,400 feet
DIFFICULTY: Strenuous

Dominguez is a large and varied area that can easily absorb several days or a week of exploration. The twin forks of Big and Little Dominguez Canyons invite an obvious multi-day loop exploration of the area. Such a circuit requires cross-country travel between the canyons and particularly entails substantial bush-whacking in the upper reaches of Little Dominguez. Beginning at the Big Dominguez Campground, you will need to travel about 5 miles due south toward Black Point and the upper end of Little Dominguez. You can follow roads accessing the old chainings on the mesa between the canyon and follow various easy spurs to the rim of Little Dominguez, at which point it becomes a more difficult, brushy bushwhack. Once you're in Little Dominguez, spend several days exploring its length down to the confluence and back along Big Dominguez to the campground. An elderly recluse lives in a small cabin in Little Dominguez, so please respect his privacy. He sold his land to BLM for inclusion in the wilderness after his death, and BLM permits him to live out the remainder of his years in the canyon.

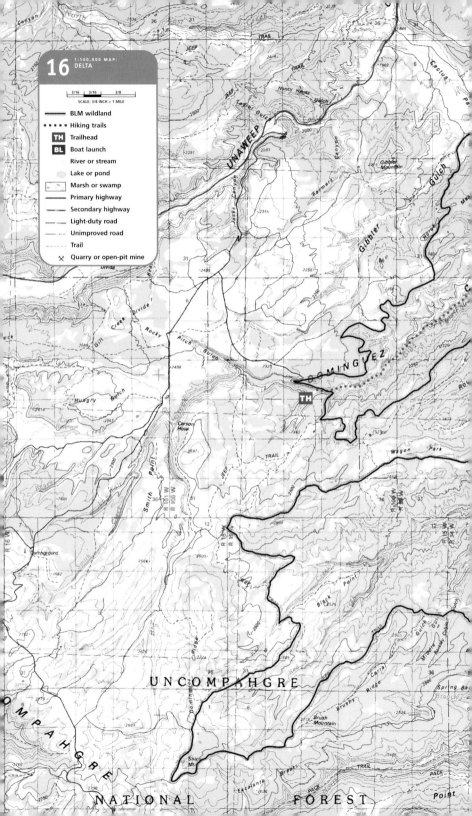

1:100,000 MAP:
DELTA

SCALE: 3/8 INCH = 1 MILE

——— BLM wildland

• • • • Hiking trails

TH Trailhead

BL Boat launch

——— River or stream

Lake or pond

Marsh or swamp

——— Primary highway

– – – Secondary highway

– · – · Light-duty road

· · · · · Unimproved road

· · · · · Trail

✕ Quarry or open-pit mine

UNAWEEP

DOMINGUEZ

Gibbler
Gulch

TH

UNCOMPAHGRE

NATIONAL   FOREST

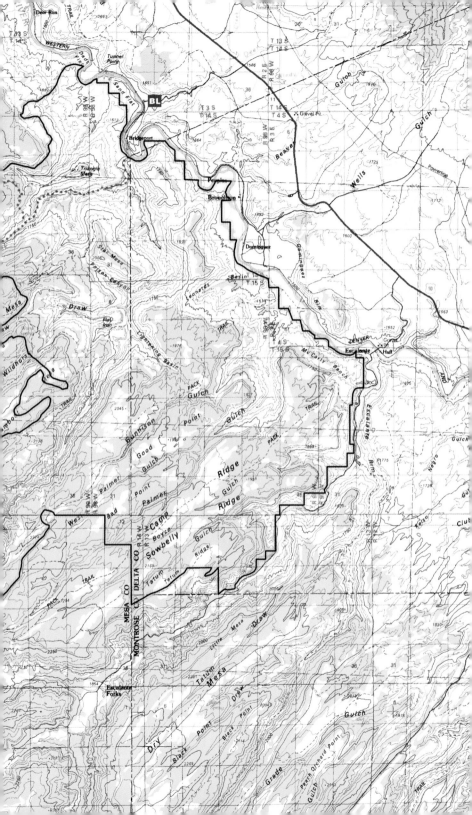

RIVER TRIP ESCALANTE/WHITEWATER

ONE-WAY LENGTH: 29 miles
LOW AND HIGH ELEVATIONS: 4,700 and 4,800 feet
DIFFICULTY: Class I and II

Another popular access to Dominguez is the mouth of the canyon via the Gunnison River. The Gunnison River through the Dominguez Canyon section is an easy Class I and II raft or canoe trip, and the canyon mouth is a favored campsite. Waterfalls and pools mark the entrance of the canyon, and the confluence of Big and Little Dominguez is only a mile up the canyon. Because of the increasing popularity of the campsite at the mouth of Dominguez Canyon, BLM has created additional river camps upstream of Dominguez that also provide hiking access into the canyon's mouth.

Boaters generally launch at the Escalante Canyon bridge several miles downstream from Delta (accessed from Highway 50), and can take out either at Bridgeport (mile 13) or the highway bridge at Whitewater (mile 29). The Escalante launch is at the Escalante Canyon bridge over the Gunnison River, west of Highway 50 between Grand Junction and Delta. The boat launch is on the bridge's north side. The Whitewater take-out is just off Highway 141 west of Whitewater. From the highway, turn south onto Desert Road and travel three-quarters of a mile before turning right at the gate going through the old Department of Energy compound. From here, drive about another half mile and park. The take-out is under the railroad bridge. Boaters should bring a portable toilet and fire pan, as is always good river etiquette.

In previous years, the public was able to reach Dominguez across a decrepit wooden bridge at Bridgeport, just a few hundred yards downstream of the canyon mouth. The bridge, which is private, has been condemned by BLM and is now off-limits to public use. It is still possible to cross the river at this point in a canoe or other watercraft, but please respect the closure of the bridge. You can reach Bridgeport via Bridgeport Road, a dirt road that leaves Highway 50 about a mile east of the Mesa-Delta county line. Bridgeport is also a possible take-out for river trips starting at Escalante.

John Fielder

Waterfall in Big Dominguez Canyon, Dominguez Canyon Wilderness Study Area.

17 Granite Creek

Mark Pearson

LOCATION	30 miles southwest of Grand Junction
ELEVATION RANGE	4,600–7,600 feet
ECOSYSTEM	Piñon-juniper woodlands, cottonwood and box elder riparian zone
SIZE	9,520 acres
WILDERNESS STATUS	Not proposed for wilderness by BLM
SPECIAL FEATURES	Perennial stream, slickrock canyon
TOPOGRAPHIC MAPS	Steamboat Mesa, Two V Basin

Granite Creek is a lush, red sandstone canyon tributary of the Dolores River. The canyon, with a depth as great as 800 feet and cut through classic Wingate sandstone cliffs, is dotted with picturesque fins, columns, windows, and buttes. The higher-elevation, eastern end of Granite Creek Canyon is relatively open and straight, while the western end of the canyon where it joins the Dolores River is so serpentine that the stream runs 7 miles to cover 3 horizontal miles.

Granite Creek begins amidst piñon-juniper and oakbrush benches on the extreme northwest edge of the Uncompahgre Plateau

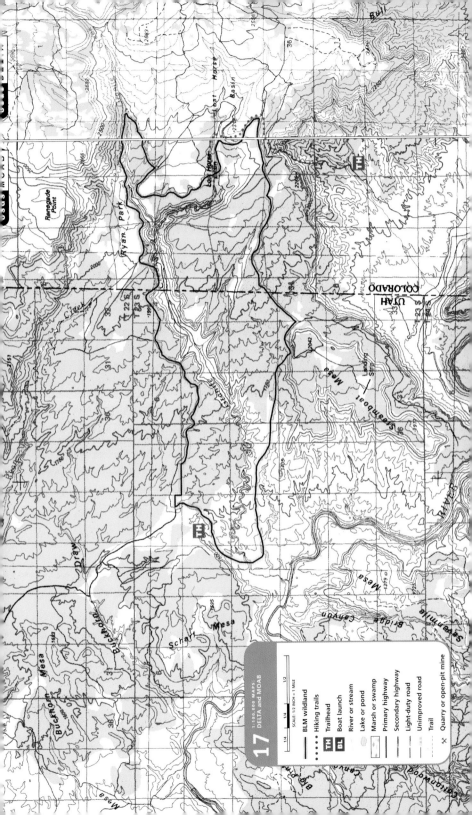

in an area called the Dolores Triangle. The Dolores Triangle is one of the most remote and unvisited corners of Colorado, and consists of the triangle of land between the Colorado and Dolores Rivers along the Colorado–Utah state line. The canyon rims offer spectacular views of the river canyons and the snow-capped La Sal Mountains, while down below, perennial Granite Creek creates a lush riparian habitat that includes cottonwoods and box elders.

CONTACT INFORMATION: Grand Junction Field Office, Bureau of Land Management, 2815 H Rd., Grand Junction, CO 81506, 970-244-3000, http://www.co.blm.gov/gjra/gjra.html.

DAY HIKE UPPER GRANITE CREEK VIA GATEWAY

ONE-WAY LENGTH: 5 miles
LOW AND HIGH ELEVATIONS: 5,200 and 7,400 feet
DIFFICULTY: Moderate

An intriguing and extremely scenic access to Granite Creek is from the Dolores River Canyon downstream of Gateway. From Gateway, follow County Road 4.2 for 6 miles on the north side of the river to a rough track that parallels a fence-line running north. Drive along the track as long as you please, but a reasonable parking place is at the creek crossing about 3 miles distant. This track ultimately climbs 2,000 feet in perilous fashion until it reaches a fault that provides a break in the Wingate sandstone cliffs. The cliff-hugging track is often impassable to vehicles (even when it is in premium condition!), but makes for a splendid hike. Upon reaching the top of the cliffs, take the left branch of the road, pass through an old burn, and branch right to a road that forms the perimeter of the Granite Creek roadless area. From this road, there are several routes into the westward trending canyon. A primitive road provides an easy hiking route through the canyon bottom.

DAY HIKE LOWER GRANITE CREEK

ONE-WAY LENGTH: 10 miles
LOW AND HIGH ELEVATIONS: 4,400 and 5,900 feet
DIFFICULTY: Moderate

You can also reach Granite Creek from Grand Junction via Glade Park. From Grand Junction, drive through the Colorado National Monument to Glade Park; follow DS Road approximately 20 miles west across the state line into Utah by turning right at the T intersection. In less than a mile, the road branches to the left and heads toward the Dolores River ford above Dewey Bridge, Utah. Follow the road about 7.5 miles to the west, and then fork left along the road that heads south and crosses Buckhorn Draw in another 7.5 miles. Drive approximately 2.7 miles beyond Buckhorn Draw to the rim of Granite Creek, and park where a right fork drops down toward Granite Creek. From here it's about 2 miles into the bottom of Granite Creek. A miner has bulldozed this road down the cliffs to the canyon bottom; this road defines the downstream boundary of the roadless area. Once in the canyon, it is an arduous 9- to 10-mile hike up the canyon to the state line.

RIVER TRIP   GRANITE CREEK VIA DOLORES RIVER

ONE-WAY LENGTH: 32 miles
LOW AND HIGH ELEVATIONS: 4,100 and 4,500 feet
DIFFICULTY: Class III and IV

As a tributary of the Dolores River, Granite Creek is easily accessible by raft (when the Dolores has water). The 32-mile stretch of the Dolores River between Gateway and Dewey Bridge receives less recreational use, and includes at least one challenging Class IV rapid (Stateline) as well as several beautiful desert canyons. Granite Creek is a major canyon on the north bank of the river, approximately 18 river miles below Gateway. The roadless section of the canyon begins only a mile upstream from the Dolores River, and is well worth a side trip for boaters.

18 Gunnison Gorge

John Fielder

LOCATION	10 miles northeast of Montrose
ELEVATION RANGE	5,400–8,200 feet
ECOSYSTEM	Piñon-juniper woodlands, sagebrush, cottonwood, box elder
SIZE	17,700 acres
WILDERNESS STATUS	17,700 acres designated wilderness in 1999
SPECIAL FEATURES	Gunnison River, gold medal trout fishery, granite canyon
TOPOGRAPHIC MAPS	Black Ridge, Red Rock Canyon

Gunnison Gorge consists of the 13 miles of the Gunnison River downstream of the newly redesignated Black Canyon of the Gunnison National Park. Three basic geographic features define the Gunnison Gorge—a sheer inner river gorge, a slightly broader outer gorge, and rolling uplands.

The inner gorge consists of Precambrian schist and gneiss, dissected by intrusive pegmatite dikes. Riparian vegetation, including box elder, cottonwood, and stands of nonnative tamarisk, exist along the river. Through this section the Gunnison River gained great popularity during the 1980s among both commercial and private rafting and kayaking enthusiasts. High water flows, generally during spring runoff, draw whitewater boaters, but the more dominant appeal is the gold medal trout fishery that reestablished itself since the upstream construction of Blue Mesa Reservoir. Of national renown, this fishery draws thousands of anglers annually down one of several access trails, and supplies commercial fishing guides with business well into the fall.

A broad multicolored canyon flares outward from the inner canyon rim, creating a double canyon in effect. The rock strata is a colorful blend of red, buff, lavender, green, and gray sedimentary rock layers. Red Canyon cuts the outer gorge laterally at its mid-point, leaving a hanging canyon gaping above the river. Its magnificently colored walls contort and fold repeatedly. The Colorado Division of Wildlife recently reestablished bighorn sheep populations in the upper gorge.

Although dam proposals that would inundate much of the gorge have been considered for decades, two water rights holders (Colorado-Ute Electric Association and the City of Delta) negotiated to exchange their conditional water rights for decreed rights in Blue Mesa Reservoir upstream from the area or to transfer their rights to other locations downstream from the wilderness area. A third water rights holder (Pittsburg & Midway) donated a portion of its water rights for instream flow purposes. Meanwhile, the river through the Gunnison Gorge is a congressionally designated study river, which has been recommended by the National Park Service and BLM for designation as a wild river under the federal Wild and Scenic Rivers Act.

Beginning in 1984, local boosters in Montrose and Delta pushed for redesignation of the Black Canyon of the Gunnison from National Monument status to a National Park. Though the management changes little if at all under the two designations, park advocates hoped both for increased tourism from a National Park designation and for increased management budgets in the Black Canyon. Seeing a golden opportunity, conservationists and fishing interests combined forces to get the downstream Gunnison Gorge added into the legislation, and consequently the Gunnison Gorge was finally designated wilderness in 1999—almost 15 years after the first bill was introduced in Congress. The bill also redesignated the Black Canyon of the Gunnison as a National Park, and transferred 4,400 acres at the upper end of the Gunnison Gorge into the new National Park.

The BLM charges fees for overnight and day use of the Gunnison Gorge, and claims that 100 percent of the fees remain in the local office to help offset management costs for the gorge. Fees help pay for public information, control of tamarisk and other weeds, campsite rehabilitation, and facility maintenance. A single day permit is $3, while overnight use is $5 per day, with a minimum of $10 per visit.

Due to the Gunnison Gorge's popularity, BLM permits camping only in designated sites along the river and allows a maximum stay of two nights (three days). You can reserve campsites at trailhead register boxes. Wood fires are not allowed, and groups are restricted to no more than 12 people.

CONTACT INFORMATION: Uncompahgre Field Office, Bureau of Land Management, 2505 S. Townsend Ave., Montrose, CO 81401, 970-240-5300, http://www.co.blm.gov/ubra/gorgenca.htm.

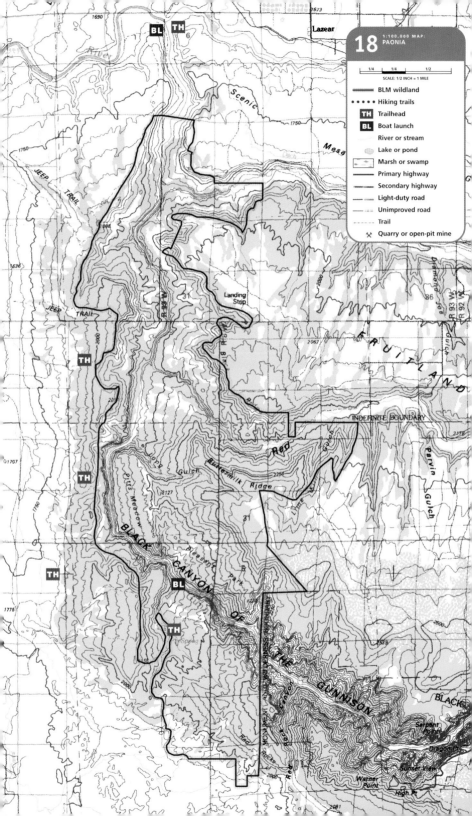

SCALE: 1/2 INCH = 1 MILE

1/4	1/4	1/2

BLM wildland
Hiking trails
TH Trailhead
BL Boat launch
River or stream
Lake or pond
Marsh or swamp
Primary highway
Secondary highway
Light-duty road
Unimproved road
Trail
✕ Quarry or open-pit mine

Lazear

Scenic

Mesa

JEEP TRAIL

JEEP TRAIL

Landing Strip

FRUITLAND

INDEFINITE BOUNDARY

Pervin Gulch

Red

Gulch

Buttermilk Ridge

Long Gulch

Pitts Meadow

BLACK CANYON OF THE GUNNISON

Blossom Park

Little

BLACK

Serpent Point

Dragon Point

Sunset View

Warner Point

High Pt

DESTINATION HIKE   CHUKAR TRAIL

ONE-WAY LENGTH: 1.1 miles
LOW AND HIGH ELEVATIONS: 5,400 and 5,900 feet
DIFFICULTY: Easy

The Chukar Trail, the most heavily used trail, is the boat launch access; it requires boaters to carry their crafts 1.1 miles to the river's edge from the trailhead. Lack of road access helps control river use naturally, although horsepackers are available for hire to portage gear. The Chukar Trail actually approaches the gorge from the south, after a circuitous route out of Peach Valley. The closest highway access to the Chukar Trail is from Olathe, where you turn east on Falcon Road from Highway 50, 1 mile south of town. Falcon Road turns into Peach Valley Road in 3.7 miles, and it's another 1.4 miles to the Chukar Trail turnoff. From the turnoff, drive 7 miles to the Chukar Trailhead (the last few miles are over rough clay roads that become impassable when wet). Two hiker camps are located along the river.

DESTINATION HIKE   BOBCAT TRAIL

ONE-WAY LENGTH: 1.5 miles
LOW AND HIGH ELEVATIONS: 5,300 and 6,100 feet
DIFFICULTY: Strenuous

The most primitive of the four trails leading into the gorge from its western ridge is the Bobcat Trail. The trail is undeveloped and hard to follow, with a difficult descent over a steep rock face in the last half mile. The Bobcat Trail accesses two hiker camps along the river. To reach the trailhead, take the Falcon Road east from Highway 50, 1 mile south of Olathe, and follow along the Peach Valley Road to reach the Bobcat Trail access road about 2 miles north past the Chukar Trail turnoff. From this junction, the trailhead is another 1.5 miles of rough jeep road.

DESTINATION HIKE   DUNCAN TRAIL

ONE-WAY LENGTH: 1.5 miles
LOW AND HIGH ELEVATIONS: 5,300 and 6,200 feet
DIFFICULTY: Strenuous

The Duncan Trail, a well-established route into the middle of the gorge, receives lots of use. The last half mile again provides a challenge due to steepness and loose scree. Stay on the north side of the scree, cross below an old mine, and climb a final ridge before dropping the last couple hundred yards to the river. This trail accesses four hiker camps along the river. The Duncan Trail is located off the Peach Valley Road 1.4 miles north of the Bobcat Trail access. A rough, 2.5-mile jeep road leads to the trailhead from the Peach Valley Road.

DESTINATION HIKE UTE TRAIL

ONE-WAY LENGTH: 4.5 miles
LOW AND HIGH ELEVATIONS: 5,300 and 6,500 feet
DIFFICULTY: Moderate

As the longest trail into the gorge, the Ute Trail offers the best perspective of the varied geology and ecosystems. The trail access is located along the north end of the Peach Valley Road about 2.3 miles north of the Duncan Trail access road. A jeep road climbs steeply 2.5 miles to the Gunnison Gorge rim and the trailhead. The Ute Trail, which begins at the picnic area on the rim, drops 4.5 miles into Gunnison Gorge at Ute Park. Hikers wishing to spend the night will find several choice campsites in the grassy meadows and piñon-juniper trees along the river. You can also access the Peach Valley Road and the various trailheads from the north via Highway 92. At Austin, turn south onto County Road 2200 and follow signs to the Gunnison Gorge National Conservation Area.

John Fielder

Gunnison Gorge, Gunnison Gorge Wilderness Area.

DESTINATION HIKE   NORTH FORK/SMITH FORK

ONE-WAY LENGTH: 4 miles
LOW AND HIGH ELEVATIONS: 5,100 and 5,300 feet
DIFFICULTY: Easy

A river's edge trail offers easy access for anglers wanting to fish the gorge's lower end. The trail takes off from the BLM Gunnison Forks Day Use Area, and follows the river's east bank for 4 miles to the Smith Fork. There are four hiker campsites along the route. The Gunnison Forks Day Use Area is located about 13 miles east of Delta on Highway 92 and is marked by an obvious sign.

RIVER TRIP   CHUKAR/GUNNISON FORKS

ONE-WAY LENGTH: 13.5 miles
LOW AND HIGH ELEVATIONS: 5,100 and 5,400 feet
DIFFICULTY: Class III and IV

The Gunnison Gorge offers one of Colorado's most spectacular wilderness river floats. Although a number of commercial outfitters run the river, the lack of road access to the river launch site, coupled with the river's technical nature, greatly reduces public boating pressure. The gorge is easily floated in a single day, which reduces the need for large amounts of gear. The river launch site is at the Chukar Trail, a 1-mile hike down to the river. You can contract a BLM-permitted horse-packer to carry in your gear. The BLM publishes a convenient river map that notes rapids and their difficulty along with suggested runs. The take-out is at the Gunnison Forks Day Use Area. Spring flows can range between 2,000 and 6,000 cfs, while late summer flows in dry years can drop as low as 300 cfs. Rafts over 12 feet are not recommended at flows under 800 cfs.

19 Hunter Canyon

Mark Pearson

LOCATION	10 miles northwest of Grand Junction
ELEVATION RANGE	5,400–8,100 feet
VEGETATION/ECOSYSTEM	Piñon-juniper woodlands, mountain mahogany, Douglas fir
SIZE	14,300 acres
WILDERNESS STATUS	Not proposed for wilderness by BLM
SPECIAL FEATURES	Slot canyons, Douglas fir, and ponderosa pine
TOPOGRAPHIC MAPS	Corcoran Peak

Hunter Canyon is an area of striking contrasts, ranging from narrow, serpentine canyons snaking onto the plains of the Grand Valley to chalk-colored cliffs that form a lofty escarpment at the headwaters of the area. Hunter Canyon spans a continuous range of ecosystems from the arid desert of the Grand Valley to relatively lush Douglas fir forests in adjacent upland mesas.

Hunter Canyon itself carves a deep, winding canyon of a type uncommon in the Bookcliffs of western Colorado. In an abrupt fashion, the canyon breaks through the sheer, cliff-forming Mesa Verde Formation and out onto the Grand Valley. The stream

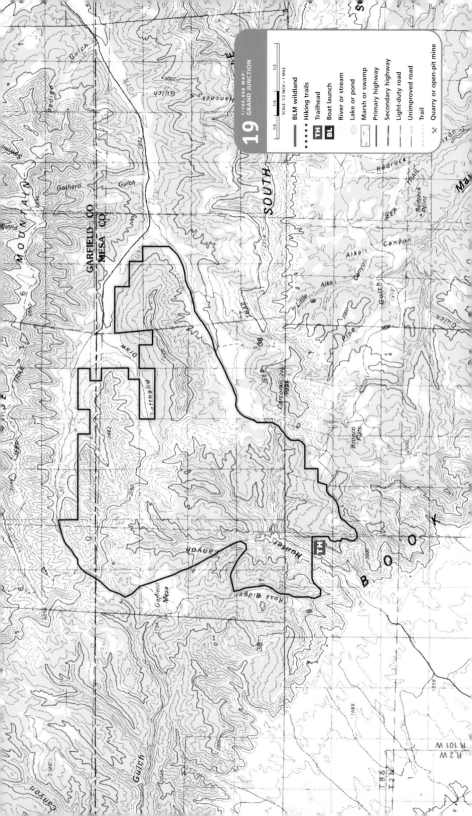

SCALE: 1/2 INCH = 1 MILE

1/4   1/4   1/2

BLM wildland

Hiking trails

TH Trailhead

BL Boat launch

River or stream

Lake or pond

Marsh or swamp

Primary highway

Secondary highway

Light-duty road

Unimproved road

Trail

✕ Quarry or open-pit mine

undercuts the rock walls, creating narrow defiles in the canyon's upper reaches, one of which can be waded to a point beneath a towering waterfall. Large, isolated ponderosa pines line the canyon bottom, providing welcome shade in the noon-day summer sun.

The deep, silent canyon gives way to high mesas covered by sagebrush, mountain mahogany, and piñon-juniper woodlands. Moving higher, nearing the 8,400-foot mark, the area evolves into rolling forests and gentle canyons, ultimately culminating in an escarpment of chalk-white cliffs of the Green River Formation, which creates a dramatic backdrop to Hunter Canyon. These wetter, higher elevations provide for increased vegetative vigor in the form of Douglas fir, aspen, and flowering shrubs.

CONTACT INFORMATION: Grand Junction Field Office, Bureau of Land Management, 2815 H Rd., Grand Junction, CO 81506, 970-244-3000, http://www.co.blm.gov/gjra/gjra.html.

DESTINATION HIKE ▶ HUNTER CANYON

ONE-WAY LENGTH: 3 miles
LOW AND HIGH ELEVATIONS: 5,600 and 6,600 feet
DIFFICULTY: Easy

To reach Hunter Canyon, drive west from Grand Junction on Highways 6 and 50, past the I-70 interchange, to 21 Road. Follow 21 Road north through the irrigated farm country, cross the Highline Canal, and drive another 7 miles across the desert to the face of the Bookcliffs. An oil and gas access road has been bladed in the bottom of Hunter Canyon in recent years, so leave your vehicle where convenient and continue up the canyon on foot. The Middle Fork branches east a couple miles into the canyon. This fork twists and turns as it ascends past undercut banks and small pour-overs. Both the main stem and the Middle Fork are populated by Douglas fir and scattered ponderosa pine. There is running water in both streams during the spring.

John Fielder

5 miles northeast of Grand Junction	**LOCATION**
5,000–7,300 feet	**ELEVATION RANGE**
Piñon-juniper woodlands, greasewood, sagebrush	**ECOSYSTEM**
26,525 acres	**SIZE**
Not proposed for wilderness by BLM	**WILDERNESS STATUS**
1,000-foot-deep Main Canyon, Bookcliffs escarpment, hoodoos, perennial streams, wild horses	**SPECIAL FEATURES**
Cameo, Round Mountain, Winter Flats	**TOPOGRAPHIC MAPS**

Little Bookcliffs encompasses the stunning cliffs and canyons of the east end of the Bookcliffs. Thousand-foot canyon walls rise from the entrance to Main Canyon at its confluence with the Colorado River, and portions of the 2,000-foot vertical face of the Bookcliffs that frame the Grand Valley are incorporated into the area. The sheer enormity of these unscalable walls, combined with the unparalleled views from the mesas above them, create an incomparable wilderness experience.

The roadless area includes two-thirds of the Little Bookcliffs Wild Horse Range, one of only three such designated Wild Horse Ranges in the United States, and the only one in the Colorado Plateau Province. The 80 to 120 wild horses that roam the area are most frequently seen in Coal Canyon and Main Canyon, and offer unique opportunities for observation and photography while you're hiking, backpacking, or horseback riding. It is not uncommon to encounter a stud and his harem band of mares. Portions of Little Bookcliffs are also critical winter range for mule deer.

Little Bookcliffs is one of very few remaining roadless areas in the Bookcliffs region of west central Colorado. The area is atypical of wilderness in Colorado, owing to its deep canyons and rolling forested piñon-juniper mesas. Four major canyons cut through the area: Main, Cottonwood, Spring, and Coal. These twisting canyons contain trickling desert streams graced by cool cottonwoods and Douglas fir in their upper reaches. Plunge pools and waterfalls frequent the canyons. Several natural bridges and numerous pinnacles (hoodoos) dot the tan and gray canyon walls.

CONTACT INFORMATION: Grand Junction Field Office, Bureau of Land Management, 2815 H Rd., Grand Junction, CO 81506, 970-244-3000, http://www.co.blm.gov/gjra/lbcwsa.htm.

DAY HIKE   MAIN CANYON

ONE-WAY LENGTH: 5 miles
LOW AND HIGH ELEVATIONS: 5,000 and 5,300 feet
DIFFICULTY: Easy

Main Canyon forms the heart of the Little Bookcliffs roadless area. I-70 provides easy access to both Main Canyon and Coal Canyon. Take the Cameo exit on I-70 east of Palisade, cross the Colorado River, and drive directly past the Public Service power plant. Follow the only legal road beyond the power plant (the others are indicated by "No Trespassing" signs) up the mouth of Coal Canyon. The canyon veers westward in approximately 1.5 miles, and at this point there is a cattle guard across the road. Park in the cleared parking area just before the cattle guard and below a roadcut in the low ridge that separates Coal Canyon from Main Canyon. From the parking area, either follow the roadcut over the ridge to Main Canyon, or find one of the horse trails just west of the road that also takes you into Main Canyon. A old jeep trail traverses the lower reaches of Main Canyon and makes for an easy hiking route. Farther along Main Canyon, beyond Spring Creek, several lonely cottonwoods have taken root and the beginnings of giant alcoves appear high on the canyon walls. Spring Creek enters from the west a couple miles up the canyon and its hoodoos are worthy of exploration. About 3 miles beyond Spring Creek, Main Canyon splits with the right branch continuing another 6 or 7 miles to source tributaries such as Alkali Canyon; the left branch heads west as Cottonwood Canyon.

LOOP HIKE   COAL CANYON/SPRING CANYON

ONE-WAY LENGTH: 14 miles
LOW AND HIGH ELEVATIONS: 5,000 and 6,900 feet
DIFFICULTY: Moderate

The Coal Canyon Road is closed to motorized vehicles between Dec. 1 and May 30 to protect the wild horse herd. This closure makes spring an ideal time for hikers to explore Coal Canyon via this scenic loop day hike or overnight trip. From the Coal Canyon parking area at the locked gate, simply hike up the Coal Canyon Road 3 miles to a gas pad, then follow the Hoodoo Trail that hugs the right side of the canyon and veers north. It's 4 miles to the top of Hoodoo Trail, at which point you cross over into Spring Canyon and descend through U-shaped slickrock bowls and a braided gravel stream for 5 miles to Main Canyon. Spring Creek is graced by a staggering selection of hoodoos and gradually opens up as you descend it. A tributary on the north quickly dead-ends in an alkaline alcove. Back in Main Canyon, it's a short 2-mile hop back over the saddle to the starting point.

LOOP HIKE   ROUND MOUNTAIN

ONE-WAY LENGTH: 21 miles
LOW AND HIGH ELEVATIONS: 5,000 and 6,800 feet
DIFFICULTY: Moderate

The coral pattern of the canyons in Little Bookcliffs allows for a series of multi-day backpacks. It is relatively easy to scramble out of any of the canyons, and the piñon-juniper woodlands on the intervening plateaus do not pose a significant obstacle to cross-country travel. A hiker could easily spend several days hiking the length of Main Canyon, crossing over Round Mountain south into Cottonwood Canyon, and then returning down Cottonwood back to Main Canyon. There is running water most of the year in these canyons, though it may be high in alkali content and is likely polluted by wild horses.

SHUTTLE HIKE — MONUMENT ROCKS/MAIN CANYON

ONE-WAY LENGTH: 9 miles
LOW AND HIGH ELEVATIONS: 5,000 and 6,700 feet
DIFFICULTY: Moderate

You can reach Monument Rocks, a primitive BLM picnic area and campground, over dirt roads via the town of DeBeque and the Winter Flats Road. Take the I-70 exit at DeBeque, cross the Colorado River, and turn left in the middle of town on Fourth Street. Take a left at the gas station and follow the street to its end, where you turn right onto the Winter Flats Road. The Winter Flats Road is built across clay and shale, and wet weather makes it impassable. Drive the Winter Flats Road 20 miles west, take a left fork, and drive another 12 miles to Monument Rocks. A horse trail drops from Monument Rocks into Cottonwood Canyon, and from there it's an easy walk to Main Canyon and out to the Coal Canyon parking area.

Tamarisk in October, Main Canyon, Little Bookcliffs Wilderness Study Area.

21 The Palisade

John Fielder

LOCATION	50 miles southwest of Grand Junction
ELEVATION RANGE	4,500–9,400 feet
VEGETATION/ECOSYSTEM	Blackbrush, piñon-juniper woodlands, cottonwood, ponderosa pine, oakbrush, aspen
SIZE	26,150 acres
WILDERNESS STATUS	Not proposed for wilderness by BLM
SPECIAL FEATURES	Dolores River Canyon, shale hoodoos, The Palisade, Unaweep Seep, Unaweep Canyon rim
TOPOGRAPHIC MAPS	Dolores Point North, Fish Creek, Gateway, Steamboat Mesa, Two V Basin

The Palisade sits astride the edge of the Uncompahgre Uplift, forming an ecological bridge between the red slickrock tributaries of the Dolores River and the lush aspen and ponderosa forests of Unaweep Canyon. Unaweep Canyon is a broad U-shaped canyon carved deep into the Uncompahgre Plateau by the ancient Gunnison and Colorado Rivers. The walls of Unaweep Canyon, composed of stark black and gray schists, gneiss, and granite, tower to heights of 4,000 feet above the canyon floor. This great relief is the cause of The Palisade's most outstanding feature—its wide diversity of ecological character. Rainfall ranges from much less than 10 inches per year to more than 30 inches. As expected, plant and animal life vary in accordance with this diversity; few places offer such a wide range of natural characteristics over so small an area.

The roadless area encompasses many miles of the rim of Unaweep Canyon. Out of sight and hearing of the ranches on the plateau above, and towering some 3,000 feet above the canyon floor below, the rim (and especially the ledge topping the pre-Cambrian granitic cliffs) appears to be related to neither. Stands of aspen adorn the rim. Owing to the rugged cliffs along either side of the canyon, this is one of the most photogenic places in Colorado. At the far eastern end of the rim, Fish Creek tumbles down a spectacular series of waterfalls, dropping 1,700 feet in 1.5 miles.

The western portion of The Palisade is a barren basin of low relief cut through the Chinle and Wingate Formations along the Dolores River. At the edges of the basin, on all sides, are numerous hoodoos—standing columns of soft shale capped by rocks of a more resistant nature. The shale is a literal rainbow of color, predominantly a milky blue in color, but also tinted in places with green or purple and capped with red or brown stains. Springs feed two permanent streams in this area, giving rise to delightful strings of pools and waterfalls graced by stately cottonwoods. The benchlands are dominated by blackbrush, a low desert shrub with sparse gray-green leaves, scattered piñon pines, and juniper.

CONTACT INFORMATION: Grand Junction Field Office, Bureau of Land Management, 2815 H Rd., Grand Junction, CO 81506, 970-244-3000, http://www.co.blm.gov/gjra/palisadewsa.htm.

| **DAY HIKE** | UNAWEEP SEEP/NORTH WEST CREEK |

ONE-WAY LENGTH: 2 miles
LOW AND HIGH ELEVATIONS: 5,700 and 7,400 feet
DIFFICULTY: Moderate

The eastern boundary of The Palisade runs along West Creek at the lower end of Unaweep Canyon and exists in stark contrast to the Dolores River desert to the west. Lush stands of cottonwoods grace the creek below towering black cliffs. Forests of ponderosa pine lead upward, giving way to piñon-juniper, oakbrush, and ultimately aspen. Unaweep Seep sits perched on the northwest bank of West Creek. The seep—the collective name for a number of springs—creates an outstanding natural botanical display, which is listed on the register of Colorado State Natural Areas. The combination of cool summer air, a long growing season due to its relatively low elevation, and abundant moisture creates an astounding abundance and variety of plants. Relatively uncommon species such as ground cherry and blackberry occur here, and more prosaic species, notably box elder, alder, and smooth sumac, reach unusual sizes. The seep is an obvious feature that appears at the highway bridge approximately 10 miles east of Gateway. From the seep, walk downstream along West Creek and up the imposing valley of North West Creek. This is a rugged and brushy hike; it may require fortitude.

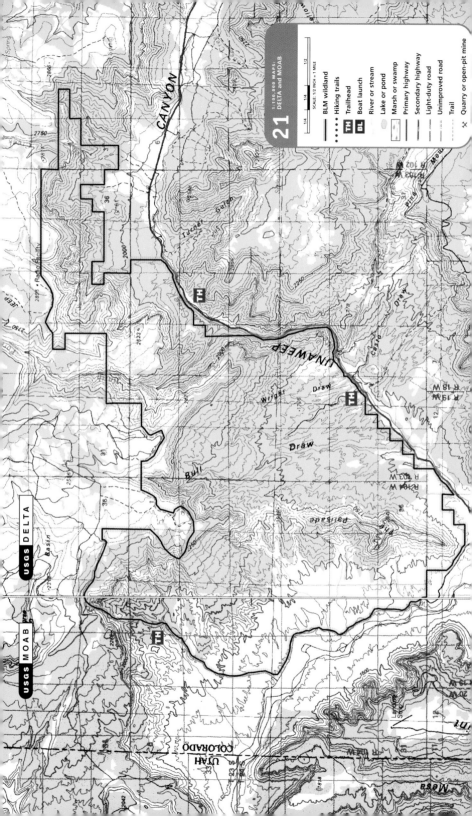

1:100,000 MAPS
DELTA and MOAB

SCALE 1/2 INCH = 1 MILE

| 1/4 | 1/4 | 1/2 |

BLM wildland
Hiking trails
TH Trailhead
BL Boat launch
River or stream
Lake or pond
Marsh or swamp
Primary highway
Secondary highway
Light-duty road
Unimproved road
Trail
× Quarry or open-pit mine

USGS DELTA

USGS MOAB

CANYON

UNAWEEP

Tucker Gulch

Wright Draw

Draw

Bull Draw

Basin

Palisade

Casto Draw

Big

UTAH
COLORADO

Mesa

DAY HIKE LOWER DOLORES RIVER

ONE-WAY LENGTH: 1–2 miles
LOW AND HIGH ELEVATIONS: 5,300 and 6,600 feet
DIFFICULTY: Moderate

The broad, open valley of the Dolores River downstream of Gateway offers appealing explorations. From Gateway, follow County Road 4.2 for 6 miles on the east side of the river to a rough track that parallels a fenceline running north. Drive along the track as long as you please, but no farther than its creek crossing about 3 miles distant. The wash offers a short but dramatic hike below Wingate sandstone cliffs and past scenic hoodoos eroded out of the colorful Moenkopi Formation. Any of the several branches lead steeply to hidden pools, trickling water slides, and solitary cottonwoods.

DAY HIKE BULL DRAW

ONE-WAY LENGTH: 3 miles
LOW AND HIGH ELEVATIONS: 5,000 and 6,100 feet
DIFFICULTY: Easy

Bull Draw drains the center of the roadless area. Bull Draw is a wide-open basin of gravelly hills covered with piñon-juniper woodlands. The basin provides immediate views of The Palisade and the multi-fingered butte to its north. To access Bull Draw, hike up the two-track trail just west and across from the Casto Draw Road (County Road 6.3). The basin's open terrain allows one to pick and choose ridges or draws to explore for numerous looping hike opportunities. Bull Draw can be hot and dry, so it's particularly suited for a cool fall or winter day.

DESTINATION HIKE THE PALISADE

ONE-WAY LENGTH: 2 miles
LOW AND HIGH ELEVATIONS: 4,900 and 7,000 feet
DIFFICULTY: Strenuous

The Palisade itself is a narrow fin of sandstone surrounded on all sides by vertical walls of Wingate sandstone and capped with the carved slickrock of the Entrada. Stands of Douglas fir dot the shaded north slopes of this fin, and hoodoos line its western slopes. Imposing as it appears, The Palisade can be climbed. The Grand Junction group of the Colorado Mountain Club describes a route that begins on the west side from a dirt road 3.7 miles along County Road 4.2. Head for the most logical rib to the base of cliffs that are broken down, climb a series of ledges, and traverse northerly following cairns, flagging, ropes, and wires. Avoid the last cliff band by traversing south and scrambling over the sandstone dome. Head north across The Palisade to a chimney, which leads to more scrambling before reaching the summit. A rope is likely required for belay and confidence.

22 Roan Plateau

East Fork Parachute Creek.

LOCATION	10 miles northwest of Rifle
ELEVATION RANGE	5,700–9,300 feet
ECOSYSTEMS	Riparian forest, piñon-juniper woodlands, Douglas fir, aspen, spruce-fir forest
SIZE	38,900 acres
WILDERNESS STATUS	Not proposed for wilderness by BLM
SPECIAL FEATURES	Waterfall, fossils, rare plants, native cutthroat trout
TOPOGRAPHIC MAPS	Anvil Points, Forked Gulch, McCarthy Gulch, Rio Blanco

The Roan Plateau is immediately familiar, by form if not by name, to anyone who travels I-70 between Rifle and Grand Junction. The Roan Plateau towers more than 3,000 feet above the highway; the massive cliffs at its rim are formed from the Green River Formation's sandstone and shale. A dark brown line is apparent in the cliffs, even from Interstate 70, and denotes the presence of an oil-bearing strata called the Mahogany Ledge.

For decades, the U.S. Department of Energy managed the Roan Plateau as a Naval Oil Shale Reserve. Various experimental recovery techniques were explored at Anvil Points, but the technological and environmental hurdles proved too great to consider oil shale as a realistic source of petroleum products. The oil-bearing layers of the Green River Formation thicken as one moves north into the Piceance Basin. Consequently, most commercial oil shale development efforts took place farther north, leaving the Roan Plateau relatively unscathed.

In 1997, management of the Roan Plateau transferred from the Department of Energy to the BLM. Prior to its transfer, the plateau was managed primarily for livestock grazing, although it was also open to public recreation. Since BLM's formal assumption of management of the plateau, more attention will be paid to primitive recreation and wilderness values. There is an abundance of livestock grazing developments such as stock ponds, fences, and roads on many of the plateau's ridgelines, but once you drop down into the valleys themselves, the evidence of human activity rapidly disappears. Given the widespread livestock grazing, it may be best to plan hiking trips before early summer when the sheep and cattle are released on the range.

Several parallel drainages flow west off Roan Plateau into Parachute Creek. The plateau presents a mosaic of vegetation, with broad stands of aspen intermixed with sagebrush meadows. On the wetter north-facing slopes, Engelmann spruce and subalpine fir invade aspen stands. Douglas fir, blue spruce, and cottonwoods dominate the streamside vegetation.

The Roan Plateau's gentle valleys and rolling hills end abruptly in the 1,500-foot-deep canyons carved by the East Fork and East Middle Fork of Parachute Creek on the plateau's western edge. A 200-foot waterfall denotes the East Fork's drop off the plateau. A similar size waterfall pours off the East Middle Fork, but is located on private land farther west. This unique geology, with high waterfalls plunging off the edge of the plateau, creates perfect isolated conditions for native Colorado River cutthroat trout to thrive. The geologic isolation protects the native cutthroat's genetic purity by eliminating the possibility of hybridization by rainbow trout invading from downstream. Consequently, Northwater, Trapper, and East Middle Fork Parachute creeks all contain only Colorado River cutthroat trout. The East Fork of Parachute Creek and JQS Gulch have both cutthroats and nonnative brook trout.

The Roan Plateau provides ideal habitat for large herds of mule deer and elk. Black bears and mountain lions also frequent the area. The Roan Plateau hosts an abundance of rare and imperiled native plant communities, including cliff seeps containing rare hanging gardens. The Green River Formation, through which the plateau's valleys are cut, contains abundant fossils.

There are two primary ways to get onto the Roan Plateau. The JQS Road switchbacks up the plateau's east face. This road is impassable when wet and is best suited for four-wheel-drive vehicles. The JQS Road heads west from Highway 13 on Rifle's north side, about a third of a mile north of the Highway 325 intersection. A longer but gentler route is via Cow Creek Road. Drive north on Highway 13 from Rifle to Rio Blanco, then head west 3.3 miles on the Piceance Creek Road. The Cow Creek access road follows the canyon to the plateau's summit in about 8 miles.

CONTACT INFORMATION: Glenwood Springs Field Office, Bureau of Land Management, 50629 Hwys 6 & 24, P.O. Box 1009, Glenwood Springs, CO 81602, 970-947-2800, http://www.co.blm.gov/gsra/gshome.htm.

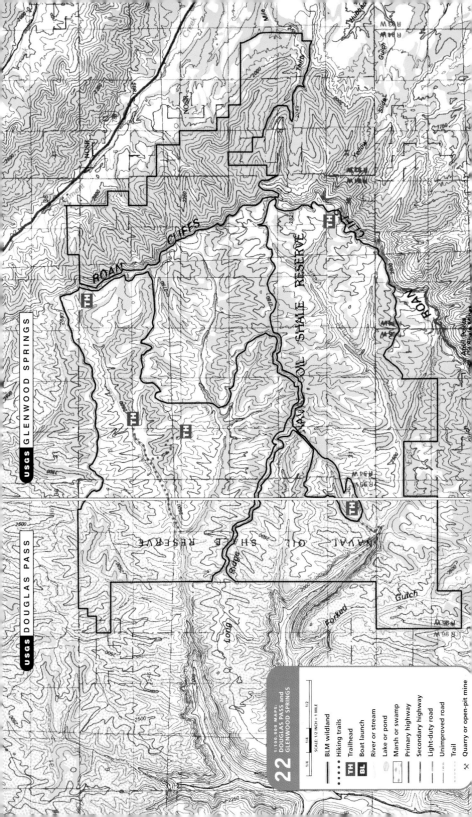

BLM wildland

Hiking trails

TH Trailhead

BL Boat launch

River or stream

Lake or pond

Marsh or swamp

Primary highway

Secondary highway

Light-duty road

Unimproved road

Trail

× Quarry or open-pit mine

22 1:100,000 MAPS:
DOUGLAS PASS and
GLENWOOD SPRINGS

SCALE: 1/2 INCH = 1 MILE

DESTINATION HIKE EAST FORK WATERFALL

ONE-WAY LENGTH: 1.5 miles
LOW AND HIGH ELEVATIONS: 7,100 and 8,100 feet
DIFFICULTY: Moderate

You can reach the 200-foot waterfall on the East Fork of Parachute Creek via Long Ridge and BLM Road 8008. This road heads west from Roan Plateau's rim about 1.7 miles north of where the JQS Road climbs onto the plateau. Drive 5.7 miles out Long Ridge on Road 8008, fork left at Road 8011 for 1 mile, and then fork left again on Road 8012 for a half mile. At this point, turn right and quickly drop down a set of switchbacks to an old cabin in about 1 mile. Park your vehicle, and then hike down the gulch following an obvious cattle trail that circles into the bottom of the East Fork. The cattle dugway traverses along the stream's south bank to the lip of the falls, offering a panoramic view before dropping steeply into the canyon below. You'll catch the best view of the falls by walking several hundred yards down the dugway, and scrambling over to the streambed where feasible. East Fork Falls leaves behind colorful, mineralized deposits on its multiple ledges.

LOOP HIKE GOLDEN CASTLE GULCH

ONE-WAY LENGTH: 3–4 miles
LOW AND HIGH ELEVATIONS: 8,600 and 9,200 feet
DIFFICULTY: Easy

The two tributaries creating the East Fork's headwaters provide an easy route for enjoying the aspen glades and meadows of Roan Plateau's upper end. From the intersection of the JQS Road atop the plateau's east rim, drive about 1.5 miles south on BLM Road 8014 and park at the head of Golden Castle Gulch. The gulch begins in an open meadow, descending quickly into an isolated gully cloaked with aspen. Weeping alcoves with larkspur and bluebells offer occasional surprises. Golden Castle joins with JQS Gulch in a shallow canyon cut into the Green River Formation's golden-hued sandstone and shale. You can either follow JQS Gulch up to the road and walk the road back to your vehicle, or cut directly south across the low ridge.

LOOP HIKE   TRAPPER/NORTHWATER CREEKS

ONE-WAY LENGTH: 5 miles
LOW AND HIGH ELEVATIONS: 7,700 and 8,700 feet
DIFFICULTY: Easy to moderate

The confluence of Trapper and Northwater Creeks occurs in a secluded canyon where cutthroat trout cluster in shallow pools. The hike begins at the western end of Cook Ridge along BLM Road 8004. From Rim Road 8000, head west on BLM Road 8004 for 4.3 miles, at which point you will note two vehicle tracks leaving either side of the road. Park here and hike north down the faint track about 1 mile into Trapper Creek. The valley is broad and shallow, with grass, sagebrush, and willows lining the stream. The last half mile before the confluence cuts a narrow gorge about 40 feet deep through beds of sandstone and shale. Blue spruce, Douglas fir, and Engelmann spruce intermixed with pockets of aspen cover the valley's north-facing slopes, while the south-facing slopes are open and drier with sagebrush and exposed rock. At the confluence, follow Northwater Creek upstream about 2 miles, and then head uphill and connect with the vehicle track that climbs the open hillside back to your vehicle.

SHUTTLE HIKE   TRAPPER CREEK

ONE-WAY LENGTH: 6 miles
LOW AND HIGH ELEVATIONS: 7,700 and 8,900 feet
DIFFICULTY: Easy to moderate

Trapper Creek's open, broad character makes traversing its entire length easy to accomplish. The valley bottom consists of grassy meadows and willows, while north-facing slopes are densely forested with spruce and aspen. Leave one vehicle at the head of Trapper Creek along Rim Road 8000 and hike down the gentle grade of Trapper Creek. Leave your second vehicle at the end of Cook Ridge along BLM Road 8004. A reasonable pickup point is at the four-wheel-drive spur 5.5 miles out BLM Road 8004. It's worthwhile to hike downstream, past this pickup point, an extra half mile to the confluence with Northwater Creek. Then, backtrack to the jeep trail and hike up to the ridge where your vehicle awaits.

You can shorten this hike, but lengthen the vehicle shuttle, by dropping into Trapper Creek at its midpoint via Road 8001, which departs Rim Road 8000 on the north side of the drainage. This effectively cuts the hike in half, whether hiking upstream or downstream.

John Fielder

15 miles west of Montrose	**LOCATION**
5,300–9,600 feet	**ELEVATION RANGE**
Riparian forest, piñon-juniper woodlands, aspen groves, ponderosa pine, spruce-fir forest	**ECOSYSTEMS**
19,650 acres	**SIZE**
Not proposed for wilderness by BLM	**WILDERNESS STATUS**
Perennial stream, cottonwoods, longest wild canyon on the Uncompahgre Plateau	**SPECIAL FEATURES**
Antone Spring, Camel Back, Davis Point, Moore Mesa	**TOPOGRAPHIC MAPS**

Roubideau Creek carves one of Colorado's most unusual canyons. Named for French fur trapper Antoine Robidoux, the canyon originates in subalpine spruce and aspen forests high on the Uncompahgre Plateau. From its origin, Roubideau Creek flows 20 miles north to the Gunnison River.

As it flows northward, Roubideau Creek cuts down into Mesozoic sandstone draped over the dome of the Uncompahgre

Uplift. Dakota, Morrison, Entrada, Wingate, and Chinle strata form cliffs of warm colors that tower over the lush montane riparian ecosystem in the canyon bottom. This stretch of the Roubideau is rich in wildlife, such as black bears, mule deer, bobcats, cougars, and golden eagles. A great number of birds nest in the canyon, including cliff swallows, white-throated swifts, Cooper's hawks, titmice, warblers, and many more.

As you move down out of the spruce and aspen forests onto BLM lands, the canyon regime becomes more arid with rock buttresses, free-standing hoodoos, piñon-juniper woodlands, and a meandering stream lined with cottonwoods. This striking lower desert canyon, with its brilliant red bands of Entrada sandstone, comprises the BLM's Camel Back Wilderness Study Area, so named for the large, isolated mesa between Roubideau Creek and Criswell Creek.

Approximately two-thirds of the roadless area lies in the Uncompahgre National Forest and one-third on BLM land. A number of trails lead into the Forest Service portion, but the hikes described here are located primarily in the downstream, more arid, BLM-managed section.

Roubideau has a mixed wilderness status. The upper 13 miles of the canyon, which reside on National Forest lands, are protected from any development activities, but the lower 9 miles remain under wilderness consideration as the Camel Back Wilderness Study Area. As with the nearby Tabeguache area, upper Roubideau Creek was not granted official wilderness designation in the 1993 Colorado Wilderness Act. Instead, because of fears about the impact of downstream wilderness on potential upstream water users (in this case, two small developed springs on the rim of the canyon), Congress gave the upper portion of Roubideau all the land-use protections that typically accompany wilderness designation without the instream flow requirements. Logging, mining, and motorized vehicles are thus restricted from upper Roubideau, but upstream water developments are not.

CONTACT INFORMATION: Uncompahgre Field Office, Bureau of Land Management, 2505 S. Townsend Ave., Montrose, CO 81401, 970-240-5300, http://www.co.blm.gov/ubra/ubra.html.

DAY HIKE — BEN LOWE'S CABIN

ONE-WAY LENGTH: 2 miles
LOW AND HIGH ELEVATIONS: 5,800 and 6,900 feet
DIFFICULTY: Moderate

One of two trails that leads into lower Roubideau Canyon from the east canyon rim, this primitive trail drops into the canyon near Ben Lowe's historic rock cabin and homestead (situated on a parcel of private land). The Transfer Road (Forest Road 508) leads directly from the Uncompahgre Valley to the canyon rim. Take Highway 348 west from Olathe (north of Montrose) and turn south on County Road 5550 in 4 miles. Drive 3 miles, jog right on Hickory Road at a T intersection, and turn left immediately onto Transfer Road. As the road nears the National Forest boundary, turn north onto BLM Road 3583, follow it about 3 miles north, and then take BLM Road 3579 to the west and north until you cross the National Forest boundary. A rough sign marks the trail's start just north of the forest boundary. In the canyon bottom, the vegetation thins as you hike downstream. Roubideau Creek is a perennial stream with substantial spring runoff.

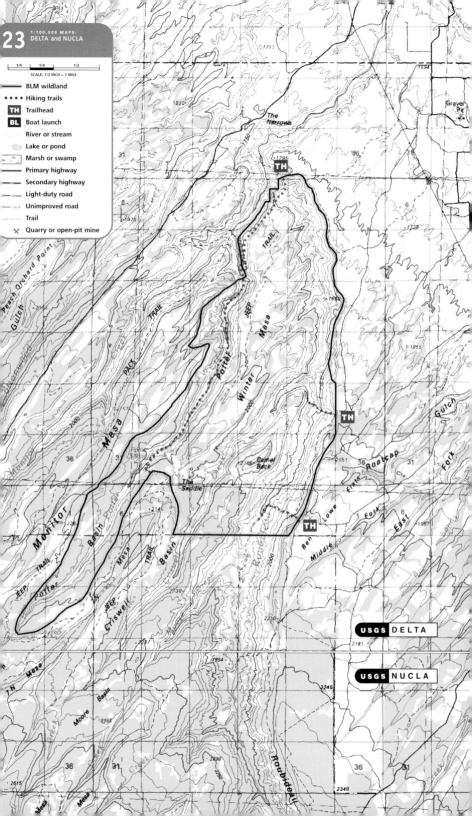

1/4 1/4 1/2

SCALE: 1/2 INCH = 1 MILE

——— BLM wildland
• • • • Hiking trails
TH Trailhead
BL Boat launch
——— River or stream
Lake or pond
Marsh or swamp
——— Primary highway
——— Secondary highway
– – – Light-duty road
‑ ‑ ‑ Unimproved road
· · · · Trail
✕ Quarry or open-pit mine

The Narrows

Peach Orchard Point

Gulch

PACK

TRAIL

Porter

JEEP

Mesa

Winter

Mesa

Camel
Back

The
Saddle

Monitor

Mesa

Basin

Porter

Mesa

TRAIL

Basin

JEEP

TRAIL

Porter

JEEP

Criswell

TRAIL

Basin

Monitor

Roatcap

Flats

Lowe

Ben

Middle

Fork

Fork

Gulch

East

Fork

USGS **DELTA**

USGS **NUCLA**

Roubideau

DAY HIKE ▶ CAMEL BACK

ONE-WAY LENGTH: 2 miles
LOW AND HIGH ELEVATIONS: 5,600 and 6,400 feet
DIFFICULTY: Moderate

The second trail that descends into the canyon from the east rim is an old stock trail. Follow the directions to the Ben Lowe Cabin trail (page 134), but proceed north another 3 or 4 miles along the rim (BLM Road 3576). The road, although not steep, is extremely rocky and may require a high-clearance vehicle. The stock trail drops into the canyon at a point just above the confluence of Roubideau and Criswell Creeks. The trail climbs out of the canyon onto the north end of Camel Back Mesa. At this point the canyon bottom is characterized by sparse vegetation and scattered cottonwoods, and it is easy to travel up or down the canyon at your leisure. A 30-foot-tall hoodoo composed of multicolored sediments sits a short distance up the west slope of the canyon.

DAY HIKE ▶ POTTER CREEK

ONE-WAY LENGTH: 7 miles
LOW AND HIGH ELEVATIONS: 5,100 and 6,600 feet
DIFFICULTY: Moderate

A county road leads into the mouth of Roubideau Canyon at the north end of the roadless area, offering an access point for hikes up either Roubideau Canyon or Potter Creek. To reach the canyon's mouth, follow the National Forest access sign to the Twenty-Five Mesa Road from the center of Delta. Just after crossing Roubideau Creek, a dirt road branches south and up the canyon. The road ends at the confluence with Potter Creek in about 5 miles. Potter Creek offers excellent hiking along a now-closed jeep road (closed to protect bighorn sheep and riparian habitat). Dense willows and thick cottonwoods line trickling Potter Creek below sandstone cliffs.

SHUTTLE HIKE ▶ BEN LOWE'S CABIN TO CANYON MOUTH

ONE-WAY LENGTH: 9 miles
LOW AND HIGH ELEVATIONS: 5,100 and 6,900 feet
DIFFICULTY: Moderate

Walking the length of the canyon offers an obviously appealing trip. You can do the shuttle hike that begins at the Ben Lowe trail (described on page 134) and ends at the mouth of the canyon (see the Potter Creek hike description above for access directions) in a long day or as a pleasant overnight exploration. The canyon bottom is broad, and Roubideau Creek provides a dependable source of water year-round.

Sewemup Mesa 24

Mark Pearson

15 miles south of Gateway	**LOCATION**
4,900–7,500 feet	**ELEVATION RANGE**
Piñon-juniper woodlands, ponderosa pine, mountain mahogany	**ECOSYSTEM**
29,840 acres	**SIZE**
18,835 acres proposed for wilderness by BLM	**WILDERNESS STATUS**
Sinbad Valley cliffs, Roc Creek Canyon, ponderosa pine forest, La Sal Mountain views	**SPECIAL FEATURES**
Buckeye Reservoir, Dolores Point South, Juanita Arch, Roc Creek	**TOPOGRAPHIC MAPS**

Sewemup Mesa is one of the most ecologically pristine areas in Colorado, owing to the isolation imposed by its almost impassable belt of encircling sandstone cliffs. Perhaps the greatest single wilderness value of Sewemup Mesa is the fact that it has been left ungrazed by domestic livestock, providing an example of an ecosystem largely undisturbed by human activities.

A striking feature of Sewemup Mesa is its band of 1,000-foot-high cliffs of Wingate sandstone enclosing more than three-quarters of the area. To the east, these cliffs rise out of the sheer slickrock gorge of the Dolores River, and to the west they tower above Sinbad Valley, the remnants of a collapsed salt dome. Domes of pink banded Entrada sandstone dot the top of the mesa, breaking the sloping landscape of piñon-juniper woodlands. Many huge ponderosa pines line the canyons of the mesa top, and grow directly from sandstone terraces along the mesa's western cliffs. Few places offer more exhilarating solitude than that obtained from the edge of Sewemup Mesa's boundless cliffs.

In contrast to the towering heights of Sewemup Mesa, adjacent Roc Creek Canyon plummets 1,000 feet in the opposite direction—straight down, forming an imposing cleft between Sinbad and Carpenter Ridges. Roc Creek forms the largest canyon draining east from the La Sal Mountains. Its brilliant red walls are framed by green forests of Douglas fir and ponderosa pine along the canyon rims. Roc Creek itself is a large, roaring creek lined again by huge ponderosas. However, the mouth of Roc Creek is in privately owned land and permission is required to hike up Roc Creek Canyon.

Sewemup Mesa derives its name from the cattle rustling exploits of the McCarty Gang, who allegedly sequestered stolen cattle on the mesa, cut out the brands, and "sewed 'em up" again. Adjacent Roc Creek, Sinbad Ridge, and Sinbad Valley are named for Sinbad the Sailor and the giant bird, the legendary roc, as chronicled in *A Thousand and One Arabian Nights.*

CONTACT INFORMATION: Grand Junction Field Office, Bureau of Land Management, 2815 H Rd., Grand Junction, CO 81506, 970-244-3000, http://www.co.blm.gov/gjra/sewemupwsa.htm.

DESTINATION HIKE SEWEMUP MESA VIA CANYON

ONE-WAY LENGTH: 4 miles
LOW AND HIGH ELEVATIONS: 4,900 and 7,200 feet
DIFFICULTY: Moderate to strenuous

Several routes from Highway 141 lead into Sewemup Mesa. Take the highway approximately 15 miles south from Gateway; immediately beyond the Montrose-Mesa county line a large canyon meets the highway. This canyon is very rugged hiking the first mile or so, but once a low alcove is passed, it is possible to climb out of the canyon to easier traveling through piñon-juniper and ponderosa pine forests. The mesa dips significantly from west to east, so it is a continuous upward climb 3 miles across the width of the mesa to the top of the 2,000-foot cliffs that define the western perimeter of the mesa. Small potholes dot the mesa top, providing an occasional source of water, and you may encounter running streams in the shallow canyons that crisscross the mesa.

DESTINATION HIKE SEWEMUP MESA VIA HIGHWAY SPRING

ONE-WAY LENGTH: 4 miles
LOW AND HIGH ELEVATIONS: 4,900 and 7,200 feet
DIFFICULTY: Moderate

Despite a tradition that Sewemup Mesa was never grazed, an old horse and cattle trail once led onto the mesa from a point just north of the developed spring along Highway 141. From a point about 0.3 mile north of the spring near mile marker 92, you can spy the rock and log cribbing just above the cliff's edge that marks the remains of this trail. Decades ago, blasting for construction of the highway obliterated the first 15 feet of the trail, leaving it to start at the top of a short cliff. You can access this old cattle trail by driving another one-tenth or two-tenths of a mile up the highway to find a suitable place to get up the low cliff, and then work your way back to the cattle trail. The cliff-forming Wingate sandstone is the key obstacle to surmounting Sewemup Mesa; this trail begins near the Wingate's lowest height. Once past the Wingate cliffs, you are home free in terms of exploring Sewemup's vast extent. The Wingate is but 20 feet high along here, rather than the typical hundreds of feet elsewhere along Sewemup Mesa's flanks. Once above the cliffs, it's a long and leisurely exploration to the mesa's spectacular west rim.

DESTINATION HIKE SEWEMUP MESA VIA ROC CREEK

ONE-WAY LENGTH: 4 miles
LOW AND HIGH ELEVATIONS: 4,900 and 7,200 feet
DIFFICULTY: Moderate

The easiest point to scale Sewemup Mesa is just north of Roc Creek, at about mile marker 89 along Highway 141. Here, the Wingate sandstone dips entirely below the ground, eliminating the barrier cliffs that surround most of the mesa. Instead, it's just a steep scramble up the broken ledges and talus of Kayenta sandstone for quick access above the Entrada Formation onto the mesa. From here, just strike out west toward the mesa rim, still miles distant and more than 1,000 feet higher.

DESTINATION HIKE SINBAD RIDGE

ONE-WAY LENGTH: 3 miles
LOW AND HIGH ELEVATIONS: 5,900 and 7,200 feet
DIFFICULTY: Easy

The easy, backdoor way onto Sewemup Mesa is from its southwestern corner at Sinbad Ridge. This saddle is reached most easily through Sinbad Valley. Most of Sinbad Valley is privately owned, and you may need permission to use this route. From Highway 141, drive west along Salt Creek (County Road 7.2) on Sewemup Mesa's northern edge into Sinbad Valley. Follow jeep trails to the valley's south end, and then park. An old trail gently eases up to the saddle between Sinbad Ridge and Sewemup Mesa. From here, it's an easy walk up onto Sewemup Mesa's cliffs.

October snowfall, Sewemup Mesa Wilderness Study Area.

John Fielder

25 South Shale Ridge

Mark Pearson

LOCATION	18 miles northeast of Grand Junction
ELEVATION RANGE	5,200–8,100 feet
ECOSYSTEM	Piñon-juniper woodlands, ponderosa, Douglas fir
SIZE	31,391 acres
WILDERNESS STATUS	Not proposed for wilderness by BLM
SPECIAL FEATURES	Hoodoos (Goblin Valley), colorful badlands, sweeping vistas
TOPOGRAPHIC MAPS	Corcoran Peak, Wagon Track Ridge, Winter Flats

Portions of South Shale Ridge might easily be called Colorado's Bryce Canyon. The south face of the ridge is a steep, multi-colored escarpment of vivid purples, oranges, and reds. Towering Douglas firs grace the landscape at the west end of the area, providing a refreshing highlight to the stark terrain of the ridge itself.

South Shale Ridge is a highly eroded feature of the colorful Wasatch Formation, ranging in elevation from 5,200 feet at its eastern base to 8,076 feet on the summit of Corcoran Peak. More than 40 miles of twisting arroyos carve through this rugged and colorful landscape, often opening into secluded parks at their sources.

A number of outstanding special features complement the area's rugged beauty. Goblin Valley is a ghostly collection of white and gray hoodoos guarding the western flank of the ridge. Many rare and endangered plants grow in or near South Shale Ridge. The threatened Uinta Basin hookless cactus *(Sclerocactus glaucus)* exists within the unit, and the rare DeBeque phacelia *(Phacelia submutica)* also occurs. The area's shale soils provide the critical habitat needed by many unique plant species, making the area a favorite for native plant specialists searching for rare species such as the DeBeque milkvetch *(Astragalus debequaeus)* and the Naturita milkvetch *(Astragalus naturitensis)*. Pyramid Rock Research Natural Area, which is just across the road from South Shale Ridge, was designated to protect more of the rare Uinta Basin hookless cactus.

Hikers enjoy sweeping vistas of the Grand Mesa, the San Juan Mountains, the La Sal Mountains, and the scenic ridgelines of the Roan Cliffs from the crest of South Shale Ridge. Raptors soar on air currents swirling above the ridge, and mule deer frequent the slopes and valleys of the area.

There are no trails in South Shale Ridge and the open nature of its badlands topography allows for easy cross-country travel anywhere along its length. The south-draining arroyos offer many routes to the ridgetop and contain fantastic colors and shapes. If you follow the road the entire length of the ridge to its western extent, it ultimately gains elevation and cuts through a forest of Douglas firs scattered across colorful badlands.

CONTACT INFORMATION: Grand Junction Field Office, Bureau of Land Management, 2815 H Rd., Grand Junction, CO 81506, 970-244-3000, http://www.co.blm.gov/gjra/gjra.html.

DAY HIKE GOBLIN VALLEY

ONE-WAY LENGTH: 1 mile
LOW AND HIGH ELEVATIONS: 6,900 feet
DIFFICULTY: Easy

To reach South Shale Ridge, exit I-70 at the town of DeBeque, approximately 30 miles east of Grand Junction. Turn left on Fourth Street and drive to the southwest corner of town, where the Winter Flats Road begins. This road heads directly west for a couple miles before skirting the south flank of South Shale Ridge. Goblin Valley lies along the road on the extreme western boundary of the roadless area, about 27 road miles and just west of Corcoran Peak. Shortly before reaching Goblin Valley, the road gains elevation and passes through a magical forest of stately Douglas firs scattered across red, pink, and orange badlands—the most Bryce Canyon–like portion of the area.

DAY HIKE CORCORAN PEAK

ONE-WAY LENGTH: 1 mile
LOW AND HIGH ELEVATIONS: 6,900 feet and 8,076 feet
DIFFICULTY: Moderate

You can scale Corcoran Peak, the high point on South Shale Ridge at 8,076 feet, from the western terminus of the ridge near Goblin Valley. Drive a mile farther north past Goblin Valley, and then either walk or drive along the jeep trail that hugs the ridge's northern slopes. Head for Corcoran Peak's summit anywhere it's convenient.

DAY HIKE COON HOLLOW

ONE-WAY LENGTH: 9 miles
LOW AND HIGH ELEVATIONS: 5,600 and 7,300 feet
DIFFICULTY: Moderate

Coon Hollow drains the eastern end of South Shale Ridge. An old gas exploration road has deteriorated into a four-wheel-drive road that provides access. Drive through DeBeque to the Winter Flats Road described on page 143 and follow it approximately 4 miles west of town. Turn west near Pyramid Rock, and drive several miles until the four-wheel-drive road becomes impassable. At this point, strike out on foot. One mile west, an old jeep track heads south and west up a shoulder to South Shale Ridge. You can follow this track around the head of the hollow, and return down a northern tributary to your starting point.

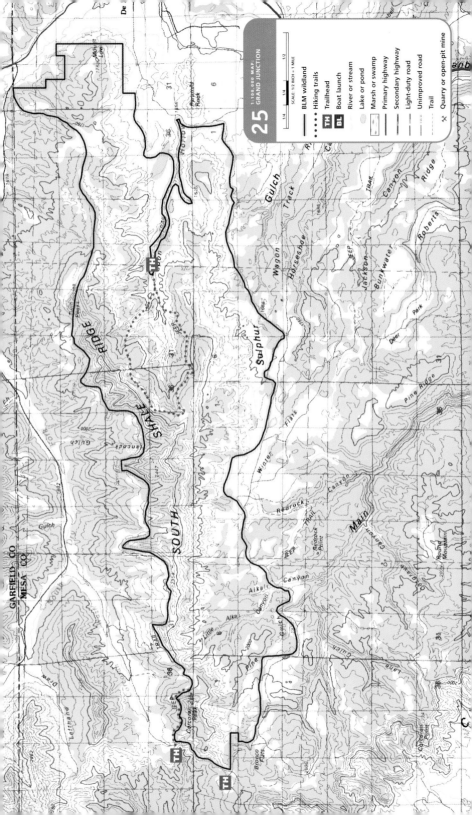

BLM wildland
Hiking trails
TH Trailhead
BL Boat launch
River or stream
Lake or pond
Marsh or swamp
Primary highway
Secondary highway
Light-duty road
Unimproved road
Trail
Quarry or open-pit mine

SCALE 1/2 INCH = 1 MILE

1/4   1/4   1/2

GARFIELD CO
MESA CO

SHALE   RIDGE

SOUTH

Sulphur

Gulch   Track

Wagon   Horseshoe

Jackson   Canyon

Bunkwater

Roberts   Ridge

Pine   Ridge

Main

Winter   Flats

Redrock   Canyon

JEEP

Redrock
Point

Alkali   Canyon

Little   Pine   Gulch

Large   Gulch

Deer   Park

Hancock   Gulch

Leithand   Draw

Bronco   Flats

Corcoran
Peak

JEEP

26 Ute Creek

Mark Pearson

LOCATION	6 miles northeast of Gateway
ELEVATION RANGE	5,600–9,400 feet
ECOSYSTEM	Piñon-juniper woodlands, oakbrush, ponderosa pine, aspen
SIZE	44,000 acres
WILDERNESS STATUS	Not proposed for wilderness by BLM
SPECIAL FEATURES	Aspen forests, panoramic vistas
TOPOGRAPHIC MAPS	Casto Reservoir, Fish Creek, Pine Mountain

Ute Creek consists of the steep granite cliffs of Unaweep Canyon, 1,000-foot-deep Ute Creek Canyon, and surrounding gently sloping mesa tops at the north end of the Uncompahgre Plateau. The area is highly representative of southwestern Colorado's scenic canyons, piñon-juniper woodlands, and groves of aspen and spruce. The roadless area includes 9,000 acres of BLM lands and approximately 35,000 acres of National Forest lands.

The roadless area includes the deepest and most dramatic portions of Unaweep Canyon, reaching depths of 2,000 to 3,300 feet. A number of steep canyons, such as Ute Creek, drain the Uncompahgre Plateau as they cut through the area. A piñon-juniper forest blankets much of this rugged terrain, and thick riparian growth characterizes the drainage bottoms, ranging from willows and cottonwoods to ponderosa pine, Douglas fir, and oakbrush. The rolling mesa tops above the rugged canyons are covered by large aspen forests broken by sagebrush flats and ringed by lush spruce forests on northern and western slopes.

Because of its location on the northwestern point of the Uncompahgre Plateau, the area offers panoramic vistas of colorful Dolores River Canyon and the distinctive La Sal Mountains in nearby Utah. The area's ubiquitous aspen and oakbrush stands make early October a particularly colorful month to visit.

CONTACT INFORMATION: Grand Junction Field Office, Bureau of Land Management, 2815 H Rd., Grand Junction, CO 81506, 970-244-3000, http://www.co.blm.gov/gjra/gjra.html or Uncompahgre National Forest, 2250 Hwy 50, Delta, CO 81416, 970-874-7691, http://www.fs.fed.us/r2/gmug.

DAY HIKE | UTE CREEK

ONE-WAY LENGTH: 3 miles
LOW AND HIGH ELEVATIONS: 6,600 and 7,700 feet
DIFFICULTY: Moderate

The Uranium Road (County Road 6.3) up Casto Draw offers access to the western portions of the area and a route into Ute Creek. Approximately 5 miles east of Gateway, turn off Highway 141 onto County Road 6.3 and follow the road as it climbs across the face of Pine Mountain. During this climb, the vegetation changes abruptly from saltbush desert to ponderosa pine forest. A couple miles after cresting Pine Mountain, a jeep track (Forest Road 607) turns east into the broad valley of Ute Creek. In about 2 miles, a faint trail that parallels Ute Creek downstream takes off from this track. You can hike 3 miles downhill to a spring, or hike farther if you like.

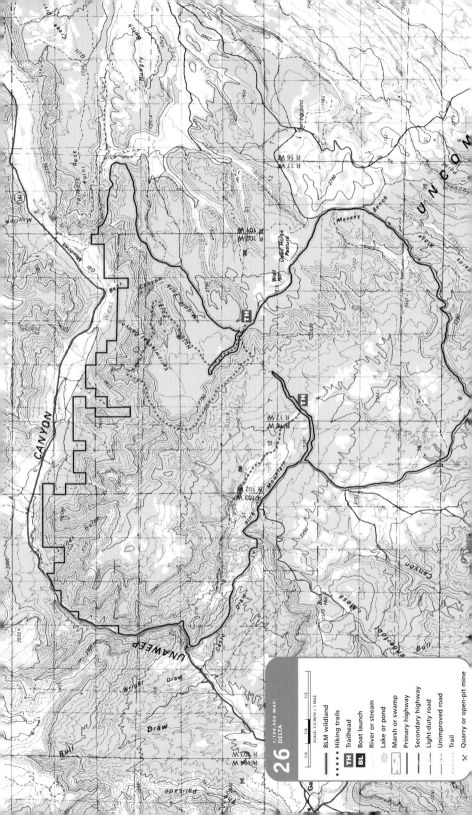

SCALE 1/2 INCH = 1 MILE

1/4   1/4   1/2   1/2

BLM wildland
Hiking trails
Trailhead
Boat launch
River or stream
Lake or pond
Marsh or swamp
Primary highway
Secondary highway
Light-duty road
Unimproved road
Trail
Quarry or open-pit mine

LOOP HIKE   UNAWEEP TRAIL

ONE-WAY LENGTH: 10 miles
LOW AND HIGH ELEVATIONS: 8,200 and 9,200 feet
DIFFICULTY: Moderate

The Unaweep Trail skirts the high point of the roadless area, just below the plateau's rim. This trail is open to motorcycles during the months of July and August, but otherwise is closed to motorized use to protect deer and elk. The Rim Trail jeep road provides access to the Unaweep Trail's starting point. Take Highway 141 southwest from Whitewater to the Divide Road, the primary Forest Service access road to the Uncompahgre Plateau. Follow the Divide Road to Divide Fork campground, and then turn west on Forest Road 404 approximately 3 miles to Forest Road 416 (or the Rim Trail, a rough jeep road). The Unaweep Trail departs the Rim Trail about 4 miles distant. You can circle around the plateau's point from here, and take one of several routes along Yellowjacket Canyon, or along the North Fork or Middle Fork of Bear Canyon, back to the starting point. The Unaweep Trail affords spectacular views of the La Sal Mountains, Lone Cone Peak, the Abajo Mountains, The Palisade, and Unaweep Canyon and passes through a number of the vast aspen glades that characterize the area.

27 Black Mountain and Windy Gulch

Windy Gulch.

LOCATION	12 miles west of Meeker
ELEVATION RANGE	6,100–7,205 feet
ECOSYSTEM	Sagebrush, piñon-juniper woodlands, oakbrush, Douglas fir
SIZE	22,206 acres
WILDERNESS STATUS	Not proposed for wilderness by BLM
SPECIAL FEATURES	Big game herds, White River frontage, raptors
TOPOGRAPHIC MAPS	Buckskin Point, White River City, White Rock

Black Mountain and Windy Gulch are two contiguous road-less areas just north of the White River and Highway 64 near Meeker. The areas consist of high ridgetops and steep-sided valleys with rugged walls graced by stately Douglas firs. The southerly slopes of the areas are covered by dense piñon-juniper woodlands, scrub oak, and serviceberry.

Both areas provide crucial wildlife habitat immediately adjacent to the Piceance Basin. All of Black Mountain, for exam-ple, sits within prime mule deer habitat, and several thousand

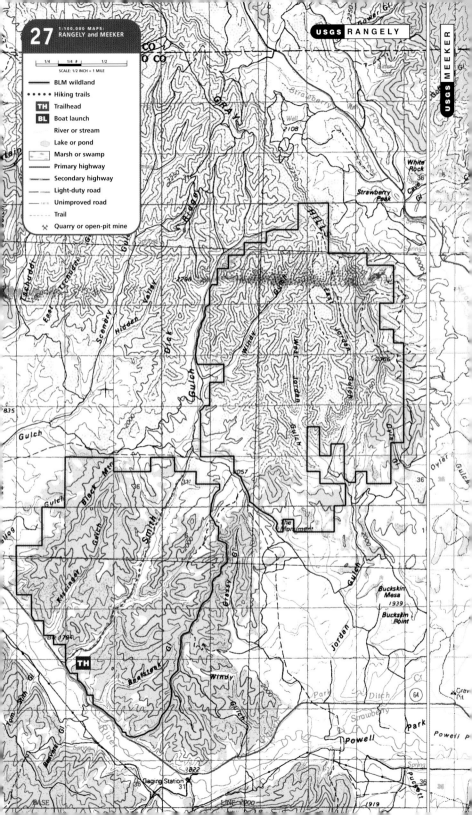

27 1:100,000 MAPS:
RANGELY and MEEKER

SCALE: 1/2 INCH = 1 MILE

———	BLM wildland
• • • •	Hiking trails
TH	Trailhead
BL	Boat launch
	River or stream
	Lake or pond
	Marsh or swamp
	Primary highway
	Secondary highway
	Light-duty road
	Unimproved road
	Trail
✕	Quarry or open-pit mine

Strawberry
Peak

White
Rock

Strawberry Peak

HILLS

Windy Gulch

West Jordan Gulch

Jordan Gulch

East Jordan Gulch

Ryan Gulch

Oyler Gulch

Scenery Valley

Hidden Valley

Dick Gulch

Gulch

Ridge

Gulch

The Monument

Buckskin
Mesa
1939

Buckskin
Point

Black Mtn.

Smith Gulch

Kissinger Gulch

Gulch

Beartrack Gl.

Ryan Gulch

Windy Gulch

Jordan Gulch

Park Ditch

Strawberry Park

Powell Park

Powell P.

Gaging Station

BASE LINE 2000

64

Gravel
Pit

TH

acres are considered critical winter range for as many as 3,000 mule deer. A major mule deer migration corridor crosses Black Mountain, with up to 8,000 animals using it annually. The areas are also winter range for elk and year-round habitat for a small population of mountain lions.

All the drainages in the two areas have sagebrush-covered valley floors and contain sandstone cliffs set in dense forests of piñon-juniper. The cliffs offer prime nesting sites for raptors, and in fact, three active golden eagle nests exist within the Black Mountain roadless area. Bald eagles wintering in cottonwoods along the White River also frequently visit Black Mountain and Windy Gulch on hunting excursions.

CONTACT INFORMATION: White River Field Office, Bureau of Land Management, 73544 Hwy 64, Meeker, CO 81641, 970-878-3601, http://www.co.blm.gov/wrra/wrraindex.htm.

DAY HIKE SMITH GULCH AND WINDY GULCH

ONE-WAY LENGTH: 4 miles
LOW AND HIGH ELEVATIONS: 5,900 and 6,400 feet
DIFFICULTY: Easy

The boundary of Black Mountain follows the White River along Highway 64 for approximately 4 miles. Several parallel drainages provide natural hiking routes within the area. The largest of these is Smith Gulch, which is marked by a small highway bridge and a dirt road on the west side of the gulch about 12 miles west of Meeker. A sign on the gate to this road notes that it provides legal public access to the BLM lands beyond. Park at the gate, and hike along an old jeep track through Smith Gulch for about 4 miles, traversing the entire width of the area. Approximately halfway up the canyon, a large tributary canyon branches to the east and offers additional hiking opportunities. There is no water in these drainages, so bring your own.

The Smith Gulch drainage offers the best legal public access to Windy Gulch since private land blocks access to much of the area. The Windy Gulch roadless area lies immediately north of Black Mountain, and Windy Gulch is itself a tributary of Smith Gulch. You can follow Smith Gulch 6 miles to its confluence with Windy Gulch and hike up Windy Gulch to its source, or you can traverse east over a ridge to West or East Jordan Gulches.

Dave Cooper

Willow Creek.

1 mile north of the town of Dinosaur	LOCATION
5,600–8,200 feet	ELEVATION RANGE
Piñon-juniper woodlands, sagebrush	VEGETATION
44,800 acres	SIZE
40,655 acres proposed for wilderness by BLM	WILDERNESS STATUS
Slickrock canyons, raptors, ancient piñon pine forests, Dominguez-Escalante Trail	SPECIAL FEATURES
Lazy Y Point, Plug Hat Rock, Skull Creek, Snake John Reef	TOPOGRAPHIC MAPS

Bull Canyon, Willow Creek, and Skull Creek are three contiguous roadless areas between Highway 40 and Dinosaur National Monument. They lie along the southern flanks of Blue Mountain, an uplifted and faulted plateau at the far southeast end of the massive Uinta Mountains. Travelers on Highway 40 who gaze through gaps in the hogback ridge just north of the road will catch a glimpse of the wild topography beyond. White sandstone flatirons stand in rows, reflecting the fierce summer sun. Colored slopes, green and purple Morrison shales, and deep vermillion Triassic shales and sandstones rise beyond the flatirons. Massive pale pink outcrops of the Weber sandstone lie above them, the same rock through which the Yampa River cuts its fantastic canyon just a few miles north in Dinosaur National Monument.

The areas provide important habitat for abundant wildlife populations. Raptor populations are perhaps most significant, including 11 active golden eagle nests, great horned owls, red-tailed hawks, and marsh hawks. BLM has identified the areas as potential peregrine falcon habitat for the falcons that frequent the National Monument.

Bull Canyon, Willow Creek, and Skull Creek possess several uncommon features that make them all the more interesting to explore. A documented campsite of the 1776 expedition of Dominguez and Escalante is located within the Bull Canyon roadless area, and the National Park Service has proposed the Dominguez-Escalante Trail for designation as a National Historic Trail. The areas are also home to ancient piñon pine forests that BLM believes to be among the oldest on the North American continent, dating to the 12th century. Scientists have used the results of tree-ring studies in these forests to determine climatic variability in North America.

CONTACT INFORMATION: White River Field Office, Bureau of Land Management, 73544 Hwy 64, Meeker, CO 81641, 970-878-3601, http://www.co.blm.gov/wrra/wrraindex.htm.

LOOP HIKE BULL CANYON/BUCKWATER DRAW

ONE-WAY LENGTH: 9–11 miles
LOW AND HIGH ELEVATIONS: 5,800 and 7,400 feet
DIFFICULTY: Moderate

Bull Canyon, the westernmost of the three areas, straddles the Colorado-Utah state line. The National Park Service access road to Harpers Corner forms the eastern boundary of Bull Canyon and leads past the Plug Hat Rock picnic area, overlooking the brilliant white walls of Bull Canyon 3.5 miles north of the Monument headquarters. From the picnic area, it is possible to descend a steep slope and work your way around the southern rim of the canyon to its floor. Bull Canyon often contains a trickle of water to tickle your toes en route to the broad, open reaches of the lower canyon. Swinging north across this open valley will take you to Buckwater Draw and an eroded jeep trail. You can follow the trail east, back up to the forested benchlands, where it ultimately intersects the Park Service access road several miles beyond the picnic area. Alternatively, it is possible to travel cross-country across these benchlands and intervening drainages directly south back to the picnic area.

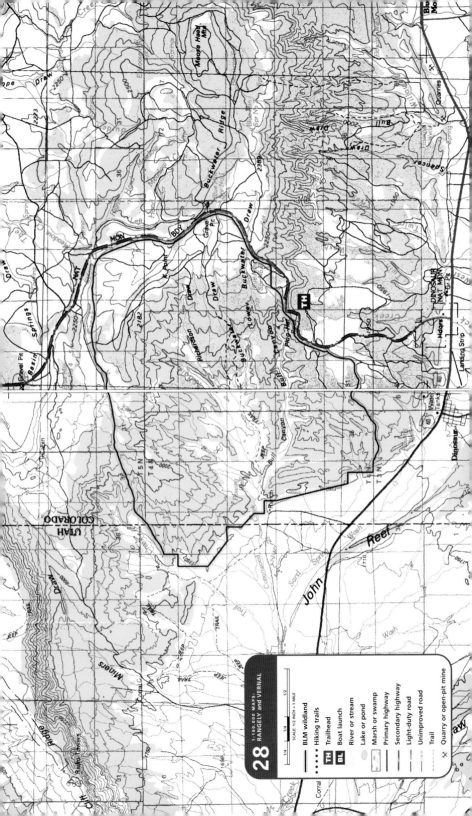

28

1:100,000 MAPS
RANGELY and VERNAL

SCALE: 1/2 INCH = 1 MILE

1/4   1/4   1/2   1 MILE

- BLM wildland
- Hiking trails
- Trailhead / **TH** **BL**
- Boat launch
- River or stream
- Lake or pond
- Marsh or swamp
- Primary highway
- Secondary highway
- Light-duty road
- Unimproved road
- Trail
- Quarry or open-pit mine

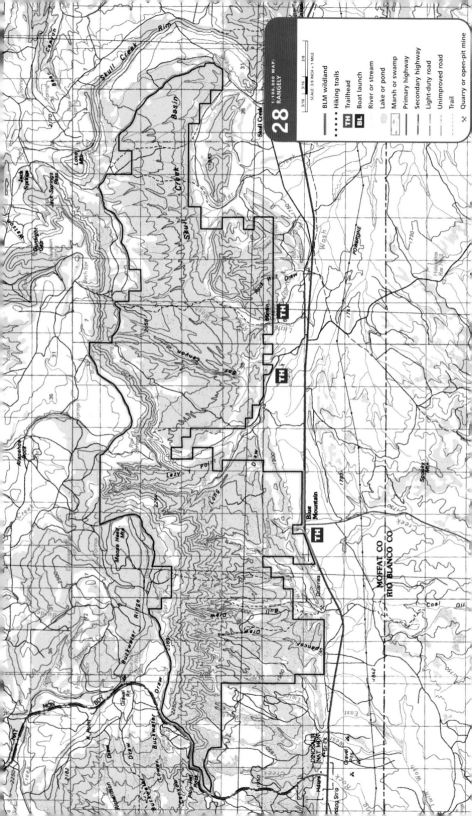

BLM wildland
Hiking trails
Trailhead
Boat launch
River or stream
Lake or pond
Marsh or swamp
Primary highway
Secondary highway
Light-duty road
Unimproved road
Trail
Quarry or open-pit mine

DAY HIKE   WILLOW CREEK

ONE-WAY LENGTH: 3 miles
LOW AND HIGH ELEVATIONS: 5,900 and 7,400 feet
DIFFICULTY: Moderate

The Willow Creek roadless area lies immediately across the Monument access road to the east of Bull Canyon. The watercourses here run north-south rather than east-west as in Bull Canyon, and the best access is from Highway 40. A hike up Willow Creek itself offers a representative glimpse of the area. Park along Highway 40 just half a mile west of the hamlet of Blue Mountain, and hike through the gap in the hogback north to the Willow Creek drainage. Willow Creek is a flat valley framed by low sandstone cliffs. As you follow the creek upward, the walls close in and short slot canyons begin to branch. A high pour-over and waterfall ultimately requires that you scramble to continue to the higher benches north of the roadless area. Hikers can take a different route back to the highway, traveling cross-country through the piñon-juniper woodlands down the sloping fronts of the hogbacks.

DAY HIKE   BOX CANYON

ONE-WAY LENGTH: 3 miles
LOW AND HIGH ELEVATIONS: 5,900 and 6,900 feet
DIFFICULTY: Moderate

The Skull Creek roadless area is not physically separated from Willow Creek by any feature other than an abandoned jeep trail; thus BLM has proposed the two areas be designated wilderness as one combined unit. Cutting into red sandstone, smooth green shale, and finally hard white sandstone, the slot canyon of Box Canyon offers an alluring introduction to the wonders of the Skull Creek roadless area. Hiking in Box Canyon, you'll often encounter places where the canyon walls are less than 6 feet apart, while in other places the walls vault upward more than 600 feet. The entrance to Box Canyon is about 5 miles east of Blue Mountain on Highway 40, and 1.5 miles north along County Road 165. The county road takes you within 1 mile of the canyon mouth. Box Canyon is only a couple miles in length, but includes several tributary canyons.

DAY HIKE ▸ MARTIN GAP

ONE-WAY LENGTH: 4 miles
LOW AND HIGH ELEVATIONS: 5,900 and 7,100 feet
DIFFICULTY: Moderate

Just 1 mile east of Box Canyon is Martin Gap and Little Red Wash. Martin Gap, a dramatic cleft in the southern hogback, creates an imposing gateway into the roadless area. Martin Gap is three-quarters of a mile off Highway 40, and is approached via County Roads 165 and 104 (a segment of the old highway). Beyond Martin Gap, the creekbed follows the sweeping curve of the exposed Skull Creek anticline. You can walk along an old jeep track several miles to the benches north of the Skull Creek Basin. The Skull Creek Basin, eroded like a giant bite from the dome of the plateau, forms a spectacular 7-mile crater ringed by cliffs and hogbacks. Incised into the sides and bottom of the basin, but discernible from above only with effort and a map, are numerous slot canyons. The same brilliant reds, whites, and greens of Box Canyon are also exposed here. Rather than follow the jeep trail, it's also worthwhile to climb east onto the high point with panoramic views across the Skull Creek anticline.

Bull Canyon, Bull Canyon Wilderness Study Area.

Mark Pearson

North of Browns Park National Wildlife Refuge, 100 miles west of Craig	**LOCATION**
5,800–8,600 feet	**ELEVATION RANGE**
Piñon-juniper woodlands, sagebrush meadows, aspen, Douglas fir	**ECOSYSTEM**
54,542 acres	**SIZE**
Not proposed for wilderness by BLM	**WILDERNESS STATUS**
Big game herds, dramatic views, trout fishery	**SPECIAL FEATURES**
Beaver Basin, Big Joe Basin, Irish Canyon, Lodore School, Willow Creek Butte	**TOPOGRAPHIC MAPS**

Cold Spring Mountain, the tail end of the Uinta Mountain uplift, forms the northern ridge of Browns Park in extreme northwest Colorado. Rising gently from Browns Park, the mountain has a dense mantle of piñon-juniper woodlands. This forest gradually succumbs to sagebrush meadows and intermittent stands of aspen along the crest of the mountain. Numerous springs, from which the mountain gets its name, surface on top and support large numbers of elk, deer, and pronghorn. The mountain offers many dramatic views of Browns Park, the Gates of Lodore in Dinosaur National Monument, the snow-covered Uintas, and the abrupt slopes of Diamond Breaks immediately across the Green River.

Limestone Ridge dominates the eastern end of the mountain. At an elevation of 8,636 feet, Limestone Ridge offers magnificent vistas, fossils, flowers, rare plant communities, and an endangered plant species, *Parthenium ligulatum*. Limestone Ridge drops into spectacular Irish Canyon, where 12 geological formations representing more than 600 million years of geological history are exposed.

Beaver Creek, a permanent stream that supports a population of endangered cutthroat trout, cuts a dramatic canyon in the west end of the mountain. The mouth of the canyon is the Beaver Creek unit of the Colorado Division of Wildlife's Browns Park State Wildlife Area.

Browns Park National Wildlife Refuge offers outstanding camping in a couple of primitive campgrounds. These provide good base camps for day hikes into Cold Spring Mountain or Diamond Breaks to the south.

CONTACT INFORMATION: Little Snake Field Office, Bureau of Land Management, 455 Emerson St., Craig, CO 81625, 970-826-5000, http://www.co.blm.gov/lsra/lsraindex.htm.

DAY HIKE BEAVER CREEK

ONE-WAY LENGTH: 5 miles
LOW AND HIGH ELEVATIONS: 5,900 and 7,400 feet
DIFFICULTY: Moderate

Hikers gain access to Beaver Creek from Highway 318, directly across from the Browns Park National Wildlife Refuge headquarters. A locked gate prevents vehicular travel on the road in the lower end of Beaver Creek. A cattle trail provides the hiking route through the canyon. You may spot bighorn sheep along Beaver Creek.

DAY HIKE MATT TRAIL

ONE-WAY LENGTH: 5 miles
LOW AND HIGH ELEVATIONS: 5,600 and 8,400 feet
DIFFICULTY: Moderate

The Matt Trail climbs from the valley floor straight up the mountain's gently sloping face, winding through dense piñon-juniper woodlands and old burns to the mountain crest. The Matt Trail is unmarked, but begins approximately 4.5 miles west of the Browns Park store at a gate along Highway 318. The gate is marked by a sign prohibiting vehicular travel, and the trail is an obvious scar through the forest. The Matt Trail reaches the summit of the mountain in about 4 miles, and leads to a primitive BLM campground atop the mountain. Road access to this campground is via County Road 10N through Irish Canyon, and then west on County Road 72 to the Diamond Peak area. Cold Spring Mountain's summit is marked by wide meadows of wildflowers and sparse aspen stands.

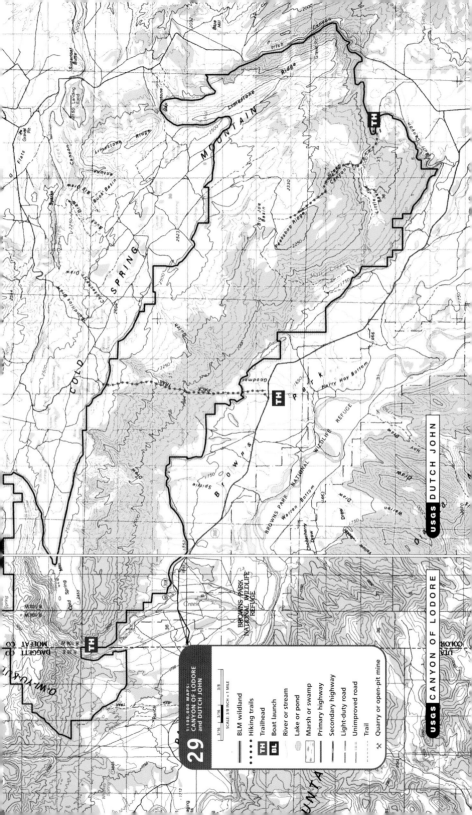

DAY HIKE PEEKABOO RIDGE

ONE-WAY LENGTH: 5 miles
LOW AND HIGH ELEVATIONS: 6,200 and 7,600 feet
DIFFICULTY: Moderate

Cold Spring Mountain's eastern end, including Limestone Ridge, is wide-open country. Hikers can pioneer routes just about anywhere they please, but one hike follows an old jeep trail to Peekaboo Ridge. From Highway 318, drive 3 miles north toward Irish Canyon on County Road 10N, and turn west on a jeep track that angles west to the base of the mountain in about 1 mile. Park where convenient, and start walking along the jeep trail into Green Canyon and Little Joe Basin. Peekaboo Ridge makes a worthwhile destination with its expansive views of Browns Park and the Gates of Lodore.

Cross Mountain 30

John Fielder

45 miles west of Craig	LOCATION
5,600–7,800 feet	ELEVATION RANGE
Sagebrush, piñon-juniper woodlands	ECOSYSTEM
18,580 acres	SIZE
14,581 acres proposed for wilderness by BLM	WILDERNESS STATUS
Cross Mountain Gorge, Yampa River, bighorn sheep, raptors	SPECIAL FEATURES
Cross Mountain Canyon, Lone Mountain, Peck Mesa, Twelvemile Mesa	TOPOGRAPHIC MAPS

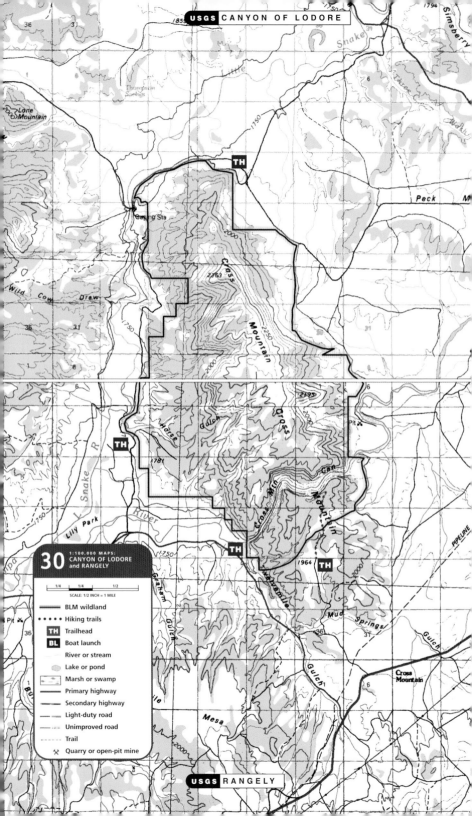

TH

Gaging Sta

Peck M

Cross

Mountain

2363

2250

2195

Cross

2000

Pit ✕

Horse

Gulch

TH

1781

Can

Mtn

Mountain

Cross

Graham

L. Snake R.

Lily Park

River

1750

TH

1964 TH

30 1:100,000 MAPS:
CANYON OF LODORE
and RANGELY

| 1/4 | 1/4 | 1/2 |

SCALE: 1/2 INCH = 1 MILE

———— BLM wildland

• • • • Hiking trails

TH Trailhead

BL Boat launch

———— River or stream

🔵 Lake or pond

〰️ Marsh or swamp

———— Primary highway

———— Secondary highway

- - - - Light-duty road

······ Unimproved road

– · – · Trail

✕ Quarry or open-pit mine

Lavandile

Mud

Springs

Gulch

Cross
Mountain

Mesa

Gulch

PIPELINE

Pit ✕

Lone
Mountain

Wild Cow Draw

1750

Cross Mountain is a magnificent example of high desert wilderness. Home to nearly all the major big game animal species in Colorado—elk, mule deer, pronghorns, bighorn sheep, black bears, and mountain lions—and to a handful of endangered species, Cross Mountain's gorge and crest offer unmatched scenic panoramas. Other features include abundant archaeological sites, numerous and varied recreational opportunities ranging from Class V kayaking to caving and hunting, and scientifically important landforms and strata.

Cross Mountain is a dominant feature of the landscape, an oblong flat-topped mountain trending north and south that rises 2,200 feet above the floodplains of the Yampa and Little Snake Rivers. This 4-mile-wide, 9-mile-long anticlinal mountain is cleft toward its southern end by the Yampa River, resulting in a 1,200-foot-deep, sheer-walled limestone canyon.

Cross Mountain Gorge provides one of the most challenging white-water boating experiences in the country during spring runoff, and offers an ideal setting for novice kayakers in late-summer low water. Four species of rare, endangered fish inhabit the Yampa River through the gorge—pikeminnow, humpback chub, razorback sucker, and bonytail chub. Other canyon inhabitants include bighorn sheep, bald and golden eagles, and peregrine falcons.

In the 1970s, the Colorado River Water Conservation District proposed a dam for the western end of the canyon, and evidence of some of the exploratory work is still visible just inside the mouth of the gorge. Plans for the hydroelectric dam were dropped in 1983 when it became apparent that the project was not economically feasible. Cross Mountain fills an interesting niche in the saga of Echo Park and the 1950s debate about whether to flood Dinosaur National Monument with a dam at the confluence of the Green and Yampa Rivers. One of our country's greatest environmental battles was finally resolved in 1954 when Congress dropped plans to build a dam inside a unit of the National Park system. At one point in the debate, the Sierra Club's David Brower suggested building a dam at Cross Mountain rather than Echo Park. Twenty-five years later, a new generation of canyon lovers fought the Cross Mountain dam to a standstill, and in the 1980s BLM ultimately proposed the gorge for wilderness protection rather than inundation.

CONTACT INFORMATION: Little Snake Field Office, Bureau of Land Management, 455 Emerson St., Craig, CO 81625, 970-826-5000, http://www.co.blm.gov/lsra/lsraindex.htm.

DAY HIKE ⟩ SOUTH RIM

ONE-WAY LENGTH: 1 mile
LOW AND HIGH ELEVATIONS: 6,400 and 6,700 feet
DIFFICULTY: Easy

Both canyon rims offer truly spectacular views of the canyon and river. A short hike leads to the south rim from a four-wheel-drive road that climbs up the mountain's south flank. Take the National Park Service access road to Deerlodge Park approximately 2 miles from Highway 40, and turn east onto a dirt road. In about a half mile, take a left fork and wind another mile or so up the slope. The rim of the canyon is about another mile's walk beyond the road's end through the piñon-juniper woodlands.

DAY HIKE · CROSS MOUNTAIN GORGE

ONE-WAY LENGTH: 4 miles
LOW AND HIGH ELEVATIONS: 5,700 and 5,900 feet
DIFFICULTY: Difficult

Though only 3.5 miles long, the gorge is a full day of hiking along its rugged north river bank, the only bank passable to hikers during low water. You can reach Cross Mountain Gorge from the National Park Service access road to Deerlodge Park, which leaves Highway 40 about 7 or 8 miles east of Elk Springs. The access road drops down to the Yampa River, and intersects Moffat County Road 125 at a bridge near the confluence with the Little Snake. Travel north on CR 125 about 1 mile, and then take a dirt track a couple miles back east to the mouth of Cross Mountain Gorge on the north side of the Yampa River (this track is on private land and you should obtain permission from the ranch near the intersection). Alternatively, you can park at the mouth of the gorge in the Park Service parking lot on the south bank, and then wade across the river at low water to reach the same starting point. The entrance to the gorge provides an immediate challenge, as you must scale a short wall to get around the entrance cliffs and into the canyon. A rope might be of assistance in surmounting this 8- to 10-foot obstacle. The route through the gorge is a rugged scramble across talus below the limestone cliffs of the gorge. The riverbank can be followed throughout almost the entire length of the canyon, but to exit the eastern end of the gorge requires that you climb the first row of cliffs before reaching an impassable wall at river level.

SHUTTLE HIKE · CROSS MOUNTAIN CREST

ONE-WAY LENGTH: 8 miles
LOW AND HIGH ELEVATIONS: 5,900 and 7,800 feet
DIFFICULTY: Moderate

The crest of Cross Mountain provides sweeping vistas of northwest Colorado, and you will likely see elk, pronghorn, mule deer, and perhaps wild horses. No established trails exist to the top of the mountain, but its gentle slopes allow access along its entire length on both east and west. A pleasant way to explore the entire mountain is a shuttle hike. You can park one vehicle at the mountain's north end along County Road 10, and leave a second vehicle at the mouth of Horse Gulch along County Road 125 on the mountain's western side. The summit, only 7,800 feet, is a surprising landscape of knee-high grasses and pockets of piñon-juniper woodlands, though water sources are scarce.

Diamond Breaks 31

Mark Pearson

On the Colorado-Utah state line adjacent to Dinosaur National Monument	**LOCATION**
5,400–8,700 feet	**ELEVATION RANGE**
Piñon-juniper woodlands, mountain mahogany, oakbrush	**ECOSYSTEM**
42,450 acres	**SIZE**
36,430 acres proposed for wilderness by BLM	**WILDERNESS STATUS**
Views into Dinosaur National Monument and Browns Park, wildlife	**SPECIAL FEATURES**
Canyon of Lodore North, Hoy Mountain, Lodore School, Swallow Canyon	**TOPOGRAPHIC MAPS**

Diamond Breaks takes its name from the breaks in Diamond Mountain carved by Hoy, Chokecherry, Davis, and other creeks as they drain into the Green River. Local tradition has it that Diamond Mountain (either this one or another several miles north) was named after the exploits of a shyster in the late 1800s who salted diamonds on the mountain and lured unsuspecting Eastern investors into parting with their money in a get-rich-quick diamond mining

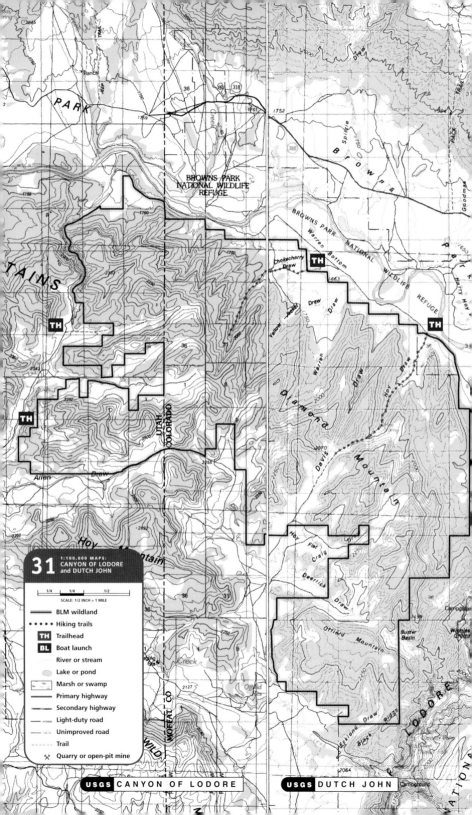

PARK

BROWNS PARK
NATIONAL WILDLIFE
REFUGE

BROWNS PARK NATIONAL WILDLIFE REFUGE

TAINS

Chokecherry Draw

Warren Bottom

Yellow Draw

Warren Draw

Diamond Mountain

Davis Draw

Hoy Draw

Allen Draw

UTAH
COLORADO

Hoy Mountain

Hoy Flat

Craig Draw

Deerlick Draw

Otfield Mountain

Buster Basin

31 1:100,000 MAPS:
**CANYON OF LODORE
and DUTCH JOHN**

| 1/4 | 1/4 | 1/2 |

SCALE: 1/2 INCH = 1 MILE

────	BLM wildland
• • • •	Hiking trails
TH	Trailhead
BL	Boat launch
	River or stream
	Lake or pond
	Marsh or swamp
	Primary highway
	Secondary highway
	Light-duty road
	Unimproved road
	Trail
✕	Quarry or open-pit mine

Otfield

Creek

MOFFAT CO

WILD

N

Westland Draw

Black Ridge

LODORE

USGS CANYON OF LODORE   **USGS DUTCH JOHN**

scheme. Of course, the shyster departed the region soon after, with money in hand and nary a diamond to be found in the barren geology of "Diamond Mountain."

Diamond Breaks is distinctive for its variety of topography and vegetation. Piñon-juniper-covered ridges and peaks rise to 8,700 feet, a startling contrast to the gentle, sagebrush-covered plain of Browns Park. The rugged mountains of Diamond Breaks are broken by open draws and stands of aspen, providing a complement to the Green River's mighty Canyon of Lodore in adjacent Dinosaur National Monument. The semiarid, dissected mountains of Diamond Breaks extend the canyon ecosystems of Dinosaur National Monument; together they offer recreational opportunities from whitewater boating deep within Dinosaur's canyons to rock climbing and ridge hiking high above in Diamond Breaks.

The ridges and peaks of Diamond Breaks afford spectacular panoramic views of features in Utah, Wyoming, and Colorado: the Green River plain, the mighty Canyon of Lodore, gentle Cold Spring Mountain, and the snowcapped peaks of the Uintas, Flat Tops, and Zirkel Range. A majestic, gnarled ponderosa-pine forest covers the southern edge of the area, growing out of bare rock in many places. Open draws and hillsides create a rainbow of color in early spring as flowers of every conceivable hue burst forth among the sagebrush.

Diamond Breaks has a high potential for significant archaeological finds. Granaries, petroglyphs, and widespread lithic scatter dating to the Fremont era 1,000 years past have been recorded in the area. There are rumors of wickyups as well.

The area is also rich in wildlife including mule deer, elk, black bears, and mountain lions. Diamond Breaks provides critical deer winter range, and encompasses a major portion of the range for a herd of 250 to 300 elk. Pronghorn roam the lower valleys near the wildlife refuge.

CONTACT INFORMATION: Little Snake Field Office, Bureau of Land Management, 455 Emerson St., Craig, CO 81625, 970-826-5000, http://www.co.blm.gov/lsra/lsraindex.htm.

DAY HIKE ▶ CHOKECHERRY DRAW

ONE-WAY LENGTH: 2 miles
LOW AND HIGH ELEVATIONS: 5,800 and 6,400 feet
DIFFICULTY: Easy

Several good hikes exist along the northern edge of Diamond Breaks up the draws that create the breaks. Beginning at the Swinging Bridge across the Green River in the far western reaches of Browns Park National Wildlife Refuge (Moffat County Road 83), follow the jeep track east along the south bank of the river. This track skirts the edge of the BLM Wilderness Study Area and ultimately leads to the western half of the Gates of Lodore within the National Monument. The first major tributary reached along this track is Chokecherry Draw. An abandoned jeep trail that now provides an ideal hiking trail leads a couple short miles up Chokecherry Draw to a long-forgotten homestead. The homestead includes the foundations of several structures, a cool spring, wild roses, and fruit trees gone wild, all in a setting of lush greenery amidst a desert forest of piñon-juniper.

DAY HIKE HOY DRAW

ONE-WAY LENGTH: 6 miles
LOW AND HIGH ELEVATIONS: 5,600 and 6,900 feet
DIFFICULTY: Moderate

Hoy Draw, the easternmost tributary in Diamond Breaks, intersects the afore-mentioned jeep track about 8 miles from the Swinging Bridge. You can follow an old trail several miles up Hoy Draw to Hoy Spring, where a cold, clear stream of water pours out of a small opening in the hillside. Shortly past the spring, the drainage reaches a low saddle, beyond which is the headwaters of Davis Draw. Davis Draw is a broad valley that you can follow south to private land marking the southern boundary of the Diamond Breaks Wilderness Study Area. Alternatively, hikers can turn north and bushwhack down Davis Draw through thick brush back to Browns Park and end up a mile west of where they started up Hoy Draw.

DAY HIKE PITT DRAW

ONE-WAY LENGTH: 3 miles
LOW AND HIGH ELEVATIONS: 6,700 and 7,400 feet
DIFFICULTY: Moderate

There is excellent access to the western boundary of Diamond Breaks from the Crouse Canyon road in Utah. From the Swinging Bridge, Moffat County Road 83 heads west into Utah, and soon thereafter enters the rugged and narrow con-fines of Crouse Canyon. The road breaks out of Crouse Canyon after several miles, and a major drainage, Pitt Draw, enters from the east. A jeep trail provides the route for a hike up the short length of Pitt Draw.

DAY HIKE CROUSE CANYON TRIBUTARY

ONE-WAY LENGTH: 3.5 miles
LOW AND HIGH ELEVATIONS: 6,800 and 8,300 feet
DIFFICULTY: Moderate

Approximately 3 miles south of Pitt Draw, an unnamed drainage intersects Crouse Creek. This 3.5-mile drainage consists of lush, flower-covered meadows and dense thickets, surrounded by ridges capped with rock outcrops that afford unrestricted views of the three-state region. Douglas fir and aspen hug the north slopes of the ridges and create unexpected forest glens. Again, an old vehicle track provides the easiest hiking route along the valley bottom and ultimately leads to a short scramble to a saddle that offers views of Cold Spring Mountain and other area features.

The Crouse Canyon road ultimately leads to Vernal, Utah. To reach Diamond Breaks starting from Vernal, follow the signs to Diamond Mountain that depart from Highway 191 a couple blocks north of the center of town.

Sawmill Canyon.

North boundary of Dinosaur National Monument, 25 miles northeast of the town of Dinosaur	LOCATION
5,800–8,000 feet	ELEVATION RANGE
Ponderosa pine, piñon-juniper woodlands, sagebrush	VEGETATION
32,414 acres	SIZE
Not proposed for wilderness by BLM	WILDERNESS STATUS
Views into Dinosaur National Monument, access to Yampa River Canyon	SPECIAL FEATURES
Canyon of Lodore South, Greystone, Jones Hole, Indian Water Canyon, Limestone Hill, Lone Mountain, Twelvemile Mesa, Zenobia Peak	TOPOGRAPHIC MAPS

Six contiguous roadless areas extend all the way to the north boundary of Dinosaur National Monument. Together, the eastern five areas encompass the southern slopes and drainages of Douglas Mountain. Rolling ridges covered by piñon-juniper woodlands, broken by sagebrush and grass parks, are typical of the areas. Deer, elk, and mountain lion inhabit the areas. Peregrine falcons, which nest nearby in the cliffs of the Yampa River Canyon, use the areas for hunting. Wild Mountain is the sixth area west of the Canyon of Lodore along the Colorado–Utah state line.

Ant Hills, Chew Winter Camp, and Petersen Draw are in truth one contiguous roadless area. Mapping errors by BLM during its wilderness inventory in 1980 resulted in the current distinction, but there are no vehicle routes of any kind in Big Joe Draw and Warm Springs Draw. The three areas are nestled in the L shape on the remote north side of Dinosaur National Monument. Along with the Tepee Draw roadless area to their east, the areas share almost 20 miles of boundary with Dinosaur National Monument. You can reach the areas via the Douglas Mountain road, Moffat County Road 116, which ultimately terminates at the Zenobia Peak fire lookout.

CONTACT INFORMATION: Little Snake Field Office, Bureau of Land Management, 455 Emerson St., Craig, CO 81625, 970-826-5000, http://www.co.blm.gov/lsra/lsraindex.htm.

DAY HIKE ▸ PETERSEN DRAW

ONE-WAY LENGTH: 7 miles
LOW AND HIGH ELEVATIONS: 5,200 and 7,400 feet
DIFFICULTY: Strenuous

Follow State Highway 318 west from Maybell to County Road 12 (the turnoff to Greystone); head south from Greystone several miles up onto Douglas Mountain on County Road 116. Douglas Mountain is covered with stands of stately ponderosa pine. The roadless areas generally begin in the fringes of this pine forest, and descend south into the desert tributary canyons of the Yampa River. To reach Petersen Draw, take County Road 119, which departs from County Road 116 soon after gaining the crest of Douglas Mountain. Take the road until you intersect Petersen Draw, and then you can walk down the draw approximately 4 miles to its confluence with Five Springs Draw, and from there walk another 2 or 3 miles to the Yampa River. The last several miles are inside Dinosaur National Monument.

DAY HIKE ▸ WARM SPRINGS DRAW

ONE-WAY LENGTH: 5 miles
LOW AND HIGH ELEVATIONS: 5,100 and 7,400 feet
DIFFICULTY: Moderate to strenuous

You can reach Ant Hills and Chew Winter Camp from BLM Road 166, which heads down Five Springs Draw from County Road 116 about 8 miles across Douglas Mountain. The road deteriorates into a jeep trail that parallels the monument boundary west to Big Joe Draw. The road generally defines the boundaries of Ant Hills and Chew Winter Camp roadless areas. The major feature in Ant Hills is the upper few miles of Warm Springs Draw. From a parking point in Big Joe Draw, hike west across the Ant Hills and into the headwaters of Warm Springs Draw. Following Warm Springs Draw downstream takes you to the rapid and river campsite of the same name on the Yampa River inside the Monument.

DAY HIKE TEPEE DRAW

ONE-WAY LENGTH: 5 miles
LOW AND HIGH ELEVATIONS: 5,500 and 7,000 feet
DIFFICULTY: Moderate

To get to Tepee Draw roadless area, take one of the several rough jeep trails that branch off County Roads 60 and 119 south of the mountain crest. One jeep trail leaves County Road 60 and winds across the east portion of Douglas Mountain to the top of Tepee Draw and Corral Springs Draw. A 5-mile hike takes you down Tepee Draw to the Yampa River and Tepee Rapid.

DAY HIKE WILD MOUNTAIN

ONE-WAY LENGTH: 3 miles
LOW AND HIGH ELEVATIONS: 6,600 and 8,300 feet
DIFFICULTY: Moderate

Wild Mountain lies astride the Colorado–Utah state line on the northwest boundary of Dinosaur National Monument. Wild Mountain, a prominent landmark dominating the viewshed from the Echo Park and Harpers Corner overlooks within Dinosaur National Monument, forms the steep, northern backdrop to Jones Hole. The access to Wild Mountain is from Vernal, Utah. Take Highway 191 north and turn right a couple blocks from the town center at the sign to Diamond Mountain and Jones Hole. Take the Diamond Mountain road to the Jones Hole National Fish Hatchery, following the signs to Jones Hole all the way. Just before dropping down into the valley and fish hatchery, an old jeep trail branches off to the north. This trail leads in a steep walk to the top of Wild Mountain. Wild Mountain affords spectacular views of the Canyon of Lodore, the Yampa Canyon, and the Uinta Mountains.

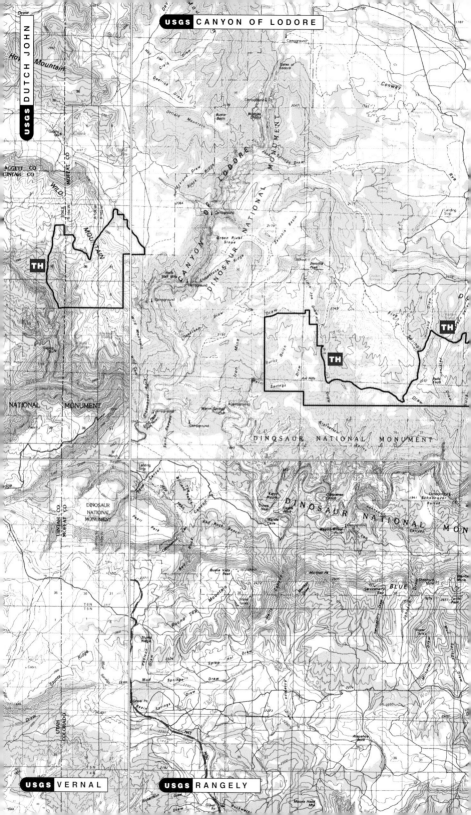

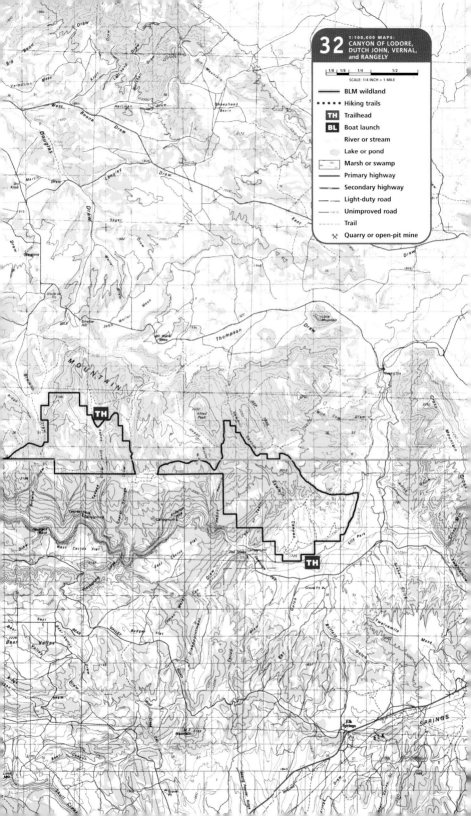

SCALE: 1/4 INCH = 1 MILE

BLM wildland
Hiking trails
TH Trailhead
BL Boat launch
River or stream
Lake or pond
Marsh or swamp
Primary highway
Secondary highway
Light-duty road
Unimproved road
Trail
Quarry or open-pit mine

LOOP HIKE VALE OF TEARS

ONE-WAY LENGTH: 8 miles
LOW AND HIGH ELEVATIONS: 5,700 and 6,600 feet
DIFFICULTY: Moderate

The largest of the six roadless areas is Vale of Tears at Dinosaur National Monument's extreme eastern end, directly across from the Deerlodge Park campground and boat launch on the Yampa River. The Vale of Tears is an extremely scenic drainage of red, yellow, tan, and brown badlands near the confluence with the Yampa River. At its higher elevations, piñon-juniper appear as well as ponderosa pine. You reach Vale of Tears either by one of several very rough jeep roads from the top of Douglas Mountain, or more easily from the valleys of the Yampa and Little Snake Rivers. Take County Road 125 north from the National Park Service Deerlodge Park access road for approximately 3 miles. At this point, a road turns west and crosses the Little Snake River. Once across the Little Snake, the road winds its way south to the Yampa River. The road terminates at the mouth of the Vale of Tears, which makes a fine starting point for hikes, as do any of several jeep trails that branch off prior to it. One looping route is to hike up the mouth of Sawmill Canyon approximately 3 miles, traverse west across a broad saddle, and return down the colorful Vale of Tears to the Yampa River. It's a 2-mile walk back to your starting point from here.

Dave Cooper

25 miles south of Rangely	LOCATION
6,000–8,550 feet	ELEVATION RANGE
Sagebrush, piñon-juniper woodlands, Douglas fir, mountain mahogany, oakbrush	VEGETATION
18,510 acres	SIZE
Not proposed for wilderness by BLM	WILDERNESS STATUS
Wildlife habitat, petroglyphs	SPECIAL FEATURES
Big Foundation Creek, East Evacuation Creek, Texas Creek, Texas Mountain	TOPOGRAPHIC MAPS

Oil Spring Mountain, an isolated remnant of wild country in the oil and gas country around Rangely in far western Colorado, might be described as an oasis in a sea of development. Because this forested mesa has thus far escaped extensive development, it is an important haven for wildlife herds north of Douglas Pass.

The northern slopes of Oil Spring Mountain rise through dense conifer forest to small stands of aspen shaded beneath sandstone cliffs. On southern exposures, mountain mahogany, oakbrush, piñon, and juniper prevail. The numerous vegetation types result in a diversity of wildlife using the area. Oil Spring Mountain is a black bear concentration area, unique for lands in the lower White River drainage in western Colorado. An important mule deer migration route is located on the northeast side of Oil Spring Mountain. Mule deer summer on the upper slopes of the mountain and use the lower elevations for winter range. Elk use the upper elevations on a year-round basis, and an elk winter concentration area is located around Red Cedar Spring. Mountain lions also frequent the area.

Oil Spring Mountain holds secrets in the form of numerous cultural sites—for example, artifacts and petroglyph panels commonly occur in alcoves carved into the mountain's sandstone cliffs. Artifact dating indicates the area has been occupied from approximately 7,000 years ago to the late 1870s.

CONTACT INFORMATION: White River Field Office, Bureau of Land Management, 73544 Hwy 64, Meeker, CO 81641, 970-878-3601, http://www.co.blm.gov/wrra/wrraindex.htm.

DAY HIKE ❯ OIL SPRING MOUNTAIN

ONE-WAY LENGTH: 2 miles
LOW AND HIGH ELEVATIONS: 8,000 and 8,600 feet
DIFFICULTY: Moderate

State Highway 139, the Douglas Pass road from Grand Junction to Rangely, provides access to Oil Spring Mountain. Oil Spring Mountain is approached via the road in West Creek, which branches west from the highway approximately 11 miles north of Douglas Pass. After several miles, a road forks right from West Creek and climbs in a switchback to a low pass. This saddle marks the southeast corner of the roadless area, and several grassy meadows provide pleasant camping spots along here. From the saddle, a hiker can bushwhack through dense brush up the ridge to the highest point of the mountain, though the mountaintop is also heavily forested and you'll obtain the best vantage points by maneuvering to one of the rims of the summit plateau. You can circumnavigate the flat top of the mountain, following the rim or some game trails. There is actually a small spring on Oil Spring Mountain on its south side.

DAY HIKE ❯ MISSOURI CREEK

ONE-WAY LENGTH: 5 miles
LOW AND HIGH ELEVATIONS: 6,400 and 7,100 feet
DIFFICULTY: Moderate

Continuing over the saddle described above, the road drops into Missouri Creek and veers northwest, forming the western boundary of the roadless area. Several tributary canyons in the lower segments of the drainage offer routes into the roadless area, and are drier and consequently more open than the mountaintop. Cultural sites such as artifacts and petroglyph panels are most common in this portion of the area, where several alcoves are carved into sandstone cliffs. One large canyon system begins along the road approximately 11 miles from the saddle. The forked canyon system provides a 5-mile bushwhack loop.

33

1:100,000 MAPS:
DOUGLAS PASS
and RANGELY

SCALE 1/2 INCH = 1 MILE

BLM wildland
Hiking trails
TH Trailhead
BL Boat launch
River or stream
Lake or pond
Marsh or swamp
Primary highway
Secondary highway
Light-duty road
Unimproved road
Trail
× Quarry or open-pit mine

University of Colorado Wilderness Study Group

LOCATION	30 miles northwest of Meeker
ELEVATION RANGE	5,600–7,400 feet
ECOSYSTEM	Piñon-juniper woodlands, sagebrush
SIZE	20,100 acres
WILDERNESS STATUS	Not proposed for wilderness by BLM
SPECIAL FEATURES	Scenic vistas, White River frontage
TOPOGRAPHIC MAPS	Elk Springs, Rough Gulch, Smizer Gulch, Wapiti Peak

Piñon Ridge consists of rolling hills immediately north of the White River. These hills overlook a broad basin of high mesas and deep arroyos from a sheer and abrupt bluff. Sweeping scenic vistas of the White River valley, the Danforth Hills, and the mesas of the Rangely Basin are obtained from Piñon Ridge. Piñon Ridge is one of the very few undeveloped areas of the lower White River drainage.

Piñon Ridge is an arid area, cut by numerous seasonal streams that create a spiderweb of isolated drainages. Sagebrush, grasses,

34

SCALE: 1/2 INCH = 1 MILE

══════	BLM wildland
• • • • •	Hiking trails
TH	Trailhead
BL	Boat launch
	River or stream
	Lake or pond
	Marsh or swamp
	Primary highway
	Secondary highway
	Light-duty road
	Unimproved road
	Trail
✕	Quarry or open-pit mine

RIDGE

SPRINGS

ELK

2162

2100

PINYON

RIDGE

Sagebrush Creek

Nipple Valley Gl

Cool

Elk Spri

Fork

1802

988

1874

1850

1960

WEST

TR

Gulch

Draw

1758

Crooked Gu

1725

1750

Baugh

Gulch

Mc Andrews

TH

Gulch

Stedman Mesa

Gravel Pit

36

31

Blair

Colorow

36

31

1718

Gravel Pit

Gaging Sta

Mesa

Gravel Pit

Smizer Gu

Radio Tower

1750

and cacti cover the lower elevations, and piñon-juniper woodlands blanket the hills and ridges. A wide variety of wildlife exists within the area, including eagles and other raptors that build nests along ridge outcrops and prey on extensive prairie dog populations. Larger mammals such as mule deer, coyotes, and mountain lions inhabit the forested slopes.

Piñon Ridge is particularly suited for hiking, owing to its outstanding scenic qualities and the presence of overgrown jeep trails that provide excellent foot and horse trails for exploration. Steep canyons and mesas in the western sections of Piñon Ridge offer challenging hikes and climbs for the more adventurous.

CONTACT INFORMATION: White River Field Office, Bureau of Land Management, 73544 Hwy 64, Meeker, CO 81641, 970-878-3601, http://www.co.blm.gov/wrra/wrraindex.htm.

DAY HIKE ▶ PIÑON RIDGE

ONE-WAY LENGTH: 3 miles
LOW AND HIGH ELEVATIONS: 5,800 and 6,800 feet
DIFFICULTY: Moderate

A new road, recently constructed by BLM, is the easiest way to reach Piñon Ridge roadless area. The road generally forms the eastern boundary of the roadless area along McAndrews Gulch and connects Highways 40 and 64. From Highway 40, turn south on BLM Road 1509 about 4 miles east of Elk Springs. The road heads south along the east side of Piñon Ridge and eventually connects with Rio Blanco County Road 77, which leads directly to Highway 64 across the White River. All these roads may require four-wheel-drive vehicles in inclement weather, and many of them are deeply rutted from hunter traffic during the fall. Any of several overgrown jeep trails from BLM Road 1509 offer enticing hiking routes to Piñon Ridge itself. One possibility is the route up Rough Gulch on the area's south end. You can follow one trail up the gulch, and return on another along the ridgeline. At the area's north end, another route to Piñon Ridge heads off west from the road near Sagebrush Draw.

John Fielder

80 miles west of Craig, 20 miles north of Dinosaur National Monument	LOCATION
5,700–8,120 feet	ELEVATION RANGE
Piñon-juniper woodlands, saltbush desert	VEGETATION
88,340 acres	SIZE
Not proposed for wilderness by BLM	WILDERNESS STATUS
Colorful badlands, petroglyphs, spectacular vistas, rare plants	SPECIAL FEATURES
Coffee Pot Spring, G Spring, Hiawatha, Irish Canyon, Sheepherder Springs, Vermillion Mesa	TOPOGRAPHIC MAPS

Vermillion Basin consists of vividly colored badlands and is host to a large number of very rare plants and plant communities. The area includes all or parts of five areas identified by the Colorado Natural Areas Program as potential Research Natural Areas for protection of rare plants. In addition, an array of geologic formations, petroglyphs, seashell fossil beds, soft-rock canyons, and varying topography make this area a delight for hikers.

The central Vermillion Basin, including the Dry Creek area, is a stunning desert canyon, with a few sandstone layers shaping, coloring, and breaking the soft sediments. Standing on one peninsula of the plateau, with a rich green canyon bottom lying below, you have the sensation of standing next to a small Grand Canyon. All around lie beautiful and delicate badlands.

Vermillion Creek contains one of the most spectacular collections of petroglyphs found in Colorado. At least eight panels, four of them with dozens of petroglyphs, line the canyon walls. One petroglyph rises over 6 feet high on a ledge 40 feet above the canyon floor. Other petroglyphs feature bow hunting, religious figures, coyotes, elk, deer, and footprints. The canyon itself is similarly spectacular, with desert varnish, sculpted sandstone, and a steep, crumbling cliff rising more than 1,000 feet.

Vermillion's western boundary is defined by Irish Canyon. The canyon exhibits the most complete record of geologic history in the Uinta Mountains, of which it is the easternmost extent.

Vermillion's wildlife includes pronghorn, mule deer, elk, golden and bald eagles, sage grouse, and game birds. A variety of desert wildflowers flourish, including Indian paintbrush, scarlet gilia, lupine, larkspur, and phlox.

CONTACT INFORMATION: Little Snake Field Office, Bureau of Land Management, 455 Emerson St., Craig, CO 81625, 970-826-5000, http://www.co.blm.gov/lsra/lsraindex.htm.

DAY HIKE ▶ VERMILLION CREEK PETROGLYPHS

ONE-WAY LENGTH: 2 miles
LOW AND HIGH ELEVATIONS: 6,100 and 6,300 feet
DIFFICULTY: Moderate

You can reach the mouth of Vermillion Canyon via Highway 318 and Moffat County Road 10N. Approximately 3 miles north on 10N, County Road 169 branches east. Follow CR 169, 1 mile or so, until you reach a two-track road that veers north toward the base of the uplifted ridge (the main road curves right and descends a steep hill to a ranch on private land). Follow the two-track as far as you like and park your vehicle. Find a route down a reddish dirt slope to the bottom of Vermillion Creek and follow the creek upstream. The canyon itself is relatively short, consisting of only 1 mile of stream meander incised into the limestone beds. Beyond this ridge, the stream course breaks out into an open, shallow basin defined by brilliantly colored badlands. The petroglyphs are on the west cliff beginning 10 to 20 feet above the stream in the middle of the short chasm.

DAY HIKE LOOKOUT MOUNTAIN

ONE-WAY LENGTH: 3 miles
LOW AND HIGH ELEVATIONS: 6,600 and 8,100 feet
DIFFICULTY: Moderate

This hike begins atop Lookout Mountain in the northeastern section of the area. You reach Lookout Mountain most easily via a network of dirt roads, beginning with the Sand Wash Road (County Road 67) that leaves Highway 318 a couple miles past the Little Snake River bridge. Follow CR 67 approximately 25 miles north to BLM Road 2058, and turn southwest for several miles to Lookout Mountain. The Vermillion Bluffs create a dramatic escarpment rising more than 1,700 feet from the wash below to the summit of Lookout Mountain. Hikers can pick a route down through the colorful badlands, earthflows, slumps, and mud caves along an abandoned jeep trail that switchbacks from the mountain's radio tower. For plant lovers, Lookout Mountain contains four plant taxa listed by the Colorado Natural Areas Program of state concern, including the only known occurrences in Colorado of two plant species, the hairy townsendia and the capitate chicken sate.

DAY HIKE DRY CREEK

ONE-WAY LENGTH: 3 miles
LOW AND HIGH ELEVATIONS: 6,100 and 6,300 feet
DIFFICULTY: Easy

A third access takes hikers into the middle of the Vermillion Basin roadless area. Again leaving Highway 318 at the Sand Wash Road, take County Road 48 west approximately 5 miles north of the highway and follow it and County Roads 46 and 52, 20 miles or more west to G Gap. A Research Natural Area at G Gap includes two plant associations of state concern and the best-condition occurrence of the regional endemic plant *Cymopterus duchesnensis* (Duchesne biscuitroot). From G Gap, descend west to Dry Creek. The road crosses Dry Creek at this point, and cuts the roadless area into two units. Several hikes are possible upstream and downstream from here, following abandoned jeep trails, cattle trails, or the creek bed. Upstream, hikers skirt the base of the orange, pink, white, and purple Vermillion Bluffs. Downstream lies a broad valley flanked by jagged, razor-edged spires of assorted fantastic shapes and colors.

DAY HIKE BEARS EARS

ONE-WAY LENGTH: 2 miles
LOW AND HIGH ELEVATIONS: 6,800 and 7,600 feet
DIFFICULTY: Moderate

This hike leads into the patchwork of old-growth piñon-juniper woodlands and open burned meadows around the Bears Ears. These low summits offer panoramic views of northwest Colorado and provide a pleasant introduction into the chattering life of a piñon-juniper forest. Follow County Roads 46 and 52 from Highway 318 to their curve north just east of the Bears Ears, and then strike out across sagebrush meadows for the nearby summits.

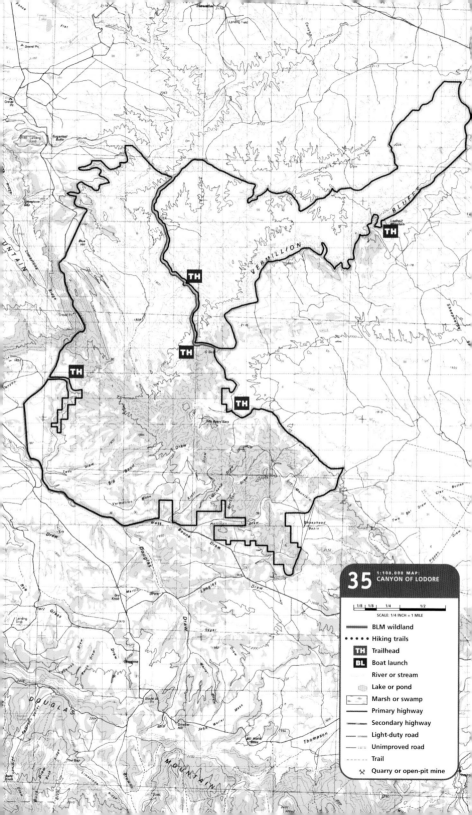

35 1:100,000 MAP:
CANYON OF LODORE

SCALE: 1/4 INCH = 1 MILE

BLM wildland
Hiking trails
TH Trailhead
BL Boat launch
River or stream
Lake or pond
Marsh or swamp
Primary highway
Secondary highway
Light-duty road
Unimproved road
Trail
Quarry or open-pit mine

SHUTTLE HIKE STROMATOLITES/PETROGLYPHS

ONE-WAY LENGTH: 9 miles
LOW AND HIGH ELEVATIONS: 6,100 and 6,800 feet
DIFFICULTY: Moderate

A fascinating destination near G Gap is the stromatolites at Sanders Draw. Stromatolites are beach-ball-sized fossilized mudballs of blue-green algae 65 million years old. Follow BLM Road 2058 approximately 1 mile downhill (west) from G Gap (see Dry Creek access description, page 185), and then park at the two-track. Walk southwest 2 miles across the open benchland to the track's end on the bluff above Sanders Draw. The stromatolites are eroding out of the bluff's rim, and look like a collection of massive bowling balls strewn across the slope. From the stromatolites, strike out down the draw toward Vermillion Creek, then turn downstream into the slot canyon of Vermillion Creek to the petroglyphs. Your shuttle vehicle should be parked at the description for the petroglyphs day hike.

Vermillion Bluffs.

Mark Pearson

36 | Yampa River

John Fielder

LOCATION	15 miles southwest of Craig
ELEVATION RANGE	6,200–7,000 feet
ECOSYSTEM	Piñon-juniper woodlands, cottonwood riparian zone
SIZE	15,960 acres
WILDERNESS STATUS	Not proposed for wilderness by BLM
SPECIAL FEATURES	10 miles of Yampa River, big game herds, eagles
TOPOGRAPHIC MAPS	Axial, Horse Gulch, Round Bottom

The Yampa River is usually considered the least impacted of Colorado's mighty rivers. Downstream portions of the river are protected within Dinosaur National Monument, while the river's headwaters are protected within the Flat Tops Wilderness. A third sample of the Yampa ecosystem—described in this section—exists in a segment of the river midway along its course through the rangelands of northwest Colorado.

The Yampa River roadless area includes the stretch of the Yampa west of Milk Creek, where the river slices through Duffy

Mountain. BLM manages the main body of the area as the Little Yampa–Juniper Canyon Special Recreation Management Area (SRMA) for recreational rafting, canoeing, camping, and hunting. As an SRMA, the area receives more frequent patrolling, special management for protecting its visual qualities, and additional consideration for public access.

The Yampa River is one of Colorado's premier wintering grounds for bald eagles. Sage grouse rearing grounds exist in the area's southwestern portion, and hikers and boaters often spy pronghorn in the open grasslands. Visitors will likely see extensive evidence of the large numbers of deer and elk that winter in the area.

The roadless area encompasses more than 10 miles of the Yampa River and includes a portion of the river that would have been inundated by the Juniper Mountain dam once proposed by the Colorado River Water Conservation District. The dam proposal is largely defunct owing to the presence of several endangered species of fish in the river (including the pikeminnow and the humpback chub, which would be negatively affected by dam construction) and to the poor economics surrounding the project.

CONTACT INFORMATION: Little Snake Field Office, Bureau of Land Management, 455 Emerson St., Craig, CO 81625, 970-826-5000, http://www.co.blm.gov/lsra/lsraindex.htm.

DAY HIKE DUFFY MOUNTAIN

ONE-WAY LENGTH: 4 miles
LOW AND HIGH ELEVATIONS: 6,100 and 6,900 feet
DIFFICULTY: Easy

County Road 17 grants hiking access to Duffy Mountain. This road connects Highways 40 and 13, approximately 19 miles west of Craig on Highway 40, or 26 miles south of Craig on Highway 13. From County Road 17, BLM Road 1596 heads east toward Duffy Mountain south of the river. From atop Duffy Mountain, a visitor has views northeast to Craig and west toward Juniper Canyon. Duffy Mountain and the other ridges and valleys surrounding the Yampa River are gently rolling, sage-covered hills and provide innumerable opportunities for adventurous route-finding. The obvious hike is to follow a north-trending draw a couple miles down to the Yampa River. After topping out on Duffy Mountain, hike northwesterly along the main jeep trail to the one large draw, and pick your way down to the river.

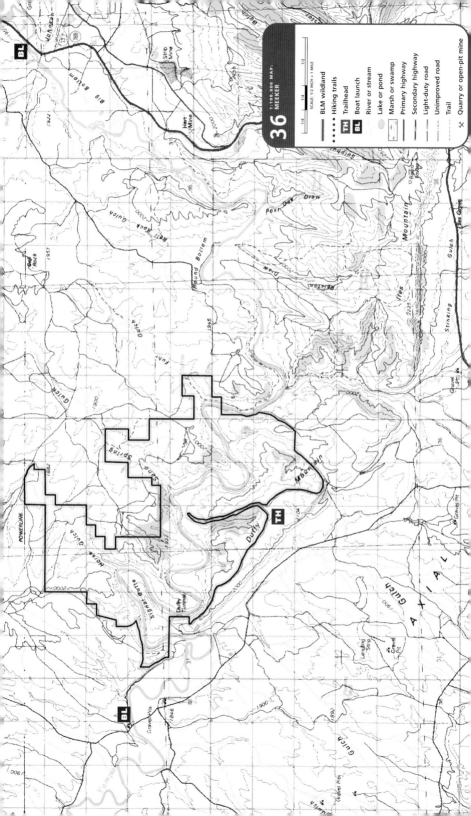

RIVER TRIP YAMPA RIVER

ONE-WAY LENGTH: 25 miles
LOW AND HIGH ELEVATIONS: 6,100 and 6,300 feet
DIFFICULTY: Class I and II

River travel is a popular means of exploring the Yampa River's wilderness values. A largely unaltered riparian ecosystem lines the riverbanks; the cottonwoods that populate several large parks offer inviting campsites to boaters. The launch point for river trips is a boat ramp and parking area at the Highway 13 bridge across the Yampa several miles south of Craig. The river cuts wide meanders through private land for the first few miles, and then enters public land a mile below the Williams Fork confluence. There are scattered tracts of private land along the river for the next 25 miles until the Yampa exits Duffy Mountain into irrigated pastures. The roadless area begins approximately 10 miles downriver at the Milk Creek confluence. Canoeists might consider leaving the river at the highway bridges at Moffat County Roads 17 and 53 to avoid the significant rapids downstream in Juniper Canyon.

Yampa River.

John Fielder

37 Beaver Creek

LOCATION	23 miles northeast of Cañon City
ELEVATION RANGE	6,000–10,000 feet
ECOSYSTEM	Piñon-juniper woodlands, ponderosa pine, Douglas fir
SIZE	27,724 acres
WILDERNESS STATUS	20,750 acres proposed for wilderness by BLM
SPECIAL FEATURES	Trout fishery, granite canyons, bighorn sheep
TOPOGRAPHIC MAPS	Big Bull Mountain, Mt. Big Chief, Mt. Pittsburgh, Phantom Canyon

Beaver Creek is composed of extremely scenic and rugged terrain on the dramatic south slope of the Pikes Peak massif. The canyons and tributaries of Beaver Creek, which form the heart of the area, are deeply sculpted in granite reminiscent of the spectacular sandstone canyons of the Colorado Plateau, and are highlighted by groves of ponderosa pine. Beaver Creek is a sizable stream year-round, and its headwaters reach to the very top of Pikes Peak.

In the Beaver Creek area, life zones range from the upper Sonoran to the montane, from desert species of plants to verdant pine-spruce-fir forests and meadows. Beaver Creek is a renowned coldwater fishery, featuring a variety of trout, including cutthroat. One of the highlights of any trip through Beaver Creek is a sighting of one of the 50 or so bighorn sheep that are residents of the area. Other terrestrial animals include mule deer, occasional elk, numerous black bears, mountain lions, and, of course, beavers. Golden eagles and endangered peregrine falcons have also been sighted.

The Colorado Division of Wildlife owns and manages 870 acres of the streambed of East and West Beaver Creeks and the main stem for several miles below their confluence. A cooperative management agreement currently exists between the Division of Wildlife and the BLM to ensure that this critical inholding retains its wilderness values.

CONTACT INFORMATION: Royal Gorge Field Office, Bureau of Land Management, 3170 E. Main St., Cañon City, CO 81212, 719-269-8500, http://www.co.blm.gov/ccdo/canon.htm.

DAY HIKE   BEAVER CREEK

ONE-WAY LENGTH: 2.5 miles
LOW AND HIGH ELEVATIONS: 6,300 and 6,900 feet
DIFFICULTY: Easy

Several trails depart from Division of Wildlife lands at the mouth of Beaver Creek Canyon. You can reach the trailhead at Beaver Creek State Wildlife Area from either U.S. Highway 50 between Pueblo and Cañon City, or state Highway 115 south of Colorado Springs. From Highway 50, turn north on the Phantom Canyon road (State Highway 67), drive several miles, turn east on County Road 123, and then turn onto County Road 132. From Highway 115, drive directly to County Road 123 at the curve north of Penrose, and then to County Road 132. Hikers can leave their cars at the corral parking area, about 1 mile past the bridge at the wildlife area. There is camping at the wildlife area (no facilities) or at a private campground at Indian Springs in Phantom Canyon, approximately a 25-minute drive from the wildlife area.

A well-maintained trail heads north up Beaver Creek from the parking area. The trail climbs the hillside and generally parallels the course of the streambed several hundred feet uphill to the confluence of East and West Beaver Creeks, 2.5 miles from the parking lot. It is also possible to follow the creek itself, though this requires several stream crossings and some bushwhacking. Keep a sharp eye out for poison ivy and rattlesnakes in addition to bighorn sheep.

DAY HIKE   TRAIL GULCH

ONE-WAY LENGTH: 5 miles
LOW AND HIGH ELEVATIONS: 6,300 and 8,500 feet
DIFFICULTY: Moderate

A second trail branches from the main Beaver Creek Trail at Trail Gulch and winds its way approximately 5 miles north across rugged country, where it connects with East Beaver Creek. Trail Gulch is a dry hike that offers a good introduction to the rugged pine forests that characterize much of the Front Range.

LOOP HIKE   TRAIL GULCH/BEAVER CREEK

ONE-WAY LENGTH: 5 miles
LOW AND HIGH ELEVATIONS: 6,300 and 7,200 feet
DIFFICULTY: Moderate

A pleasant loop hike beckons by connecting Trail Gulch and Beaver Creek. Follow the Trail Gulch route (as described above) upstream to a signed left turn that leads over a ridge to the confluence of East and West Beaver Creeks. Above the confluence, the streams become particularly wild with cascades, small waterfalls, and narrowing canyon walls. From the confluence, follow the Beaver Creek Trail back to the trailhead.

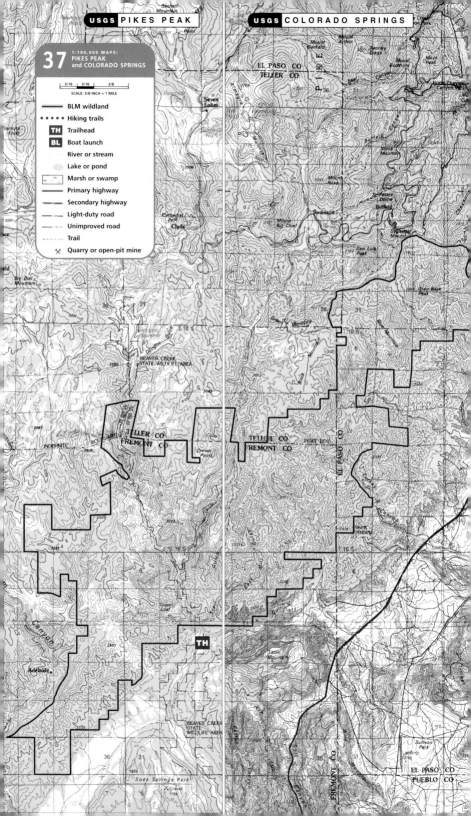

37 1:100,000 MAPS:
PIKES PEAK
and COLORADO SPRINGS

3/16   3/16   3/8

SCALE: 3/8 INCH = 1 MILE

BLM wildland

• • • • Hiking trails

TH Trailhead

BL Boat launch

River or stream

Lake or pond

Marsh or swamp

Primary highway

Secondary highway

Light-duty road

Unimproved road

Trail

⚒ Quarry or open-pit mine

Looking down the West Fork of Beaver Creek, Beaver Creek Wilderness Study Area.

38 Browns Canyon

John Fielder

LOCATION	6 miles southeast of Buena Vista
ELEVATION RANGE	7,500–10,300 feet
ECOSYSTEM	Piñon-juniper woodlands, cottonwood, ponderosa pine, aspen
SIZE	21,350 acres
WILDERNESS STATUS	6,614 acres proposed for wilderness by BLM
SPECIAL FEATURES	Arkansas River, rugged isolation, scenic vistas
TOPOGRAPHIC MAPS	Cameron Mountain, Nathrop, Salida East, Salida West

Browns Canyon of the Arkansas River is widely known among whitewater boating enthusiasts. The busiest stretch of the Arkansas, Browns Canyon totals 85,000 visitor user days annually, according to figures compiled by BLM. However, the vast majority of these visitors never set foot within the rugged and isolated slopes and gulches that climb steeply east of the river, culminating on Aspen Ridge approximately 5 miles from the river.

The Browns Canyon roadless area consists of both BLM land adjacent to the Arkansas River and portions of the San Isabel

National Forest. The BLM lands nearer to the river are characterized by rocky, broken slopes dissected by a half-dozen rugged drainages. Forests of piñon pine and juniper gradually give way to stands of ponderosa pine and, finally, aspen at the crest of the ridge. Rocky outcrops throughout the area provide expansive views of the Sawatch Range and the Collegiate Peaks. Many species of wildlife prize the area's isolation, and more than 100 bighorn sheep call the area home. This block of land is without trails, and the forbidding topography dissuades many potential visitors from venturing deep within it.

Hiking choices include skirting along high ridges to obtain bird's-eye views of the Collegiate Peaks, or trekking down tributaries to the river's edge. Chaffee County Road 185 parallels the higher, eastern boundary of the area and is the most direct access for hikes. From Salida, follow Chaffee County Road 175 to County Road 185, which is a passable though occasionally rough two-wheel-drive route. From the north, turn on County Road 310 from U.S. Highways 24 and 285, and then follow County Road 187 to 185.

CONTACT INFORMATION: Royal Gorge Field Office, Bureau of Land Management, 3170 E. Main St., Cañon City, CO 81212, 719-269-8500, http://www.co.blm.gov/ccdo/canon.htm.

DAY HIKE ASPEN RIDGE

ONE-WAY LENGTH: 1–2 miles
LOW AND HIGH ELEVATIONS: 10,000 and 10,300 feet
DIFFICULTY: Easy to moderate

A short hike across meadows and through groves of aspen takes hikers to the crest of Aspen Ridge and the high point at the south end of the area. Follow County Road 185 to the watershed divide at the top of Green Gulch, and then strike out cross-country along the fenceline toward the ridge less than 1 mile to the west. From the ridge, intrepid hikers can drop down Sawmill Gulch or Green Gulch to the river.

DAY HIKE COTTONWOOD CREEK

ONE-WAY LENGTH: 7 miles
LOW AND HIGH ELEVATIONS: 7,500 and 9,400 feet
DIFFICULTY: Moderate to strenuous

The longest drainage off Aspen Ridge is main Cottonwood Creek. This drainage offers a wild route to the river through winding, rocky arroyos and scattered stands of aspen and ponderosa pine. Park along County Road 185, at one of the branches of Cottonwood Creek in Bassam Park or Coons Park, and follow the creekbed 7 miles cross-country to the Arkansas River. Return the same way, or climb uphill along one of the many rocky ridges back over the crest of Aspen Ridge to your starting point.

LOOP HIKE — MIDDLE COTTONWOOD/LITTLE COTTONWOOD CREEKS

ONE-WAY LENGTH: 15 miles
LOW AND HIGH ELEVATIONS: 7,500 and 9,700 feet
DIFFICULTY: Moderate to strenuous

Middle Cottonwood Creek, a substantial stream, offers one of the best routes to the river. The route follows a jeep trail where it leaves County Road 185 in Bassam Park, and soon heads down the streambed of Middle Cottonwood, reaching the river in about 7 miles. Little Cottonwood Creek is found about 1 mile north along the riverbank. Turn back east and hike up Little Cottonwood, crossing an old jeep trail in about 3 miles, leading back to Bassam Park.

Alternatively, you can turn this into a shuttle hike by leaving one vehicle at the Ruby Mountain recreation site on the Bald Mountain Road. The Bald Mountain Road forms the northern boundary of the area and leaves County Road 187 1 or 2 miles south of Highways 24 and 285. Drop down the slope to the river near Ruby Mountain and park a shuttle vehicle just north of the Little Cottonwood Creek drainage.

RIVER TRIP — BROWNS CANYON

ONE-WAY LENGTH: 10 miles
LOW AND HIGH ELEVATIONS: 7,400 and 7,700 feet
DIFFICULTY: Class III and IV

Floating the Arkansas River is easily the most popular means of exploring Browns Canyon. Many thousands of private and commercial boaters enjoy this thrilling stretch of scenic whitewater every year. The launch site for this segment is typically at Fisherman's Bridge (junction of County Road 301 and Highway 285) several miles south of Buena Vista, and the take-out is the Hecla Junction boat ramp at the end of County Road 194. The river offers choice opportunities to hike up Little Cottonwood, Middle Cottonwood, or main Cottonwood Creeks. This stretch of river offers challenging whitewater and should be approached with caution.

USGS PIKES PEAK   USGS GUNNISON

39 Bull Gulch

John Fielder

LOCATION	13 miles north of Eagle
ELEVATION RANGE	6,400–9,700 feet
ECOSYSTEM	Piñon-juniper woodlands, sagebrush, Douglas fir, aspen, spruce fir
SIZE	15,004 acres
WILDERNESS STATUS	10,415 acres proposed for wilderness by BLM
SPECIAL FEATURES	Colorado River, colorful geology, scenic vistas
TOPOGRAPHIC MAPS	Burns South, Gypsum

Bull Gulch is one of the few roadless areas along the mid-elevation reaches of the Colorado River. Bull Gulch creates a scenic carved basin amidst the forested redrock country of the Colorado River drainage above the Eagle River confluence. It encompasses a remarkable ecological transition point between the alpine birthplace of the Colorado and the famous desert canyon country through which the river travels on its way to the sea.

Dropping precipitously from a forested rim at 9,700 feet, Bull Gulch erodes the deep red formations of Maroon Bells fame as it drains into the Colorado River. The entrance to Bull Gulch is a labyrinth of twisting corridors and sculpted bowls carved through maroon sandstone. The roar of the river is immediately left behind, replaced by the silence of the canyon, broken only by the tinkle of dripping seeps that line the canyon walls.

The lower reaches of Bull Gulch are covered by dense piñon-juniper woodlands, which give way at higher elevations to stands of aspen, Douglas fir, blue spruce, and ponderosa pine. Bull Gulch is a bouquet of color in the fall owing to brilliant golden aspen that highlight an already spectacular blend of vivid red sandstone, dark green spruce and fir, and majestic blue sky, all capped by towering cliffs of blinding white sandstone.

Bull Gulch provides important deer and elk winter range, and supports predator populations of mountain lions, bobcats, and coyotes. Prairie falcons nest here, and hunting perches for endangered bald eagles have been identified as well.

The most obvious overland access to Bull Gulch is via the Eby Creek road, which parallels the eastern rim of Bull Gulch. This road connects I-70 at Eagle with the Colorado River near Burns, but unfortunately the road is closed to the public from the south end about 4 miles north of the Eagle exit on I-70.

CONTACT INFORMATION: Glenwood Springs Field Office, Bureau of Land Management, 50629 Hwys 6 & 24, P.O. Box 1009, Glenwood Springs, CO 81602, 970-947-2800, http://www.co.blm.gov/gsra/gshome.htm.

DAY HIKE | BULL GULCH

ONE-WAY LENGTH: 5 miles
LOW AND HIGH ELEVATIONS: 6,400 and 8,600 feet
DIFFICULTY: Moderate

The Colorado River road between McCoy and Dotsero offers access to the Bull Gulch roadless area. Take the river road to the summit of Blue Hill about 3 miles east of Burns. Turn south onto the westernmost of the two dirt roads (BLM Road 8540) at this intersection and follow the road about 3.5 miles to a four-wheel-drive trail that heads west toward Black Mountain. (The main road is closed at a gate another half-mile down the road). This jeep trail ends in a mile or so and offers good access along game trails into the headwaters of Bull Gulch. Several good primitive camping sites exist along this trail amid scattered stands of ponderosa pine. The Bull Gulch basin consists of open, sagebrush-covered hillsides ringed by aspen and spruce-fir forests below the basin rim. You can descend the basin into Bull Gulch all the way to the Colorado River. The last half mile or so is through a maroon, slickrock canyon.

RIVER TRIP ▸ BULL GULCH VIA COLORADO RIVER

ONE-WAY LENGTH: 13.5 miles
LOW AND HIGH ELEVATIONS: 6,400 and 6,500 feet
DIFFICULTY: Class II and III

The mouth of Bull Gulch is best approached via the Colorado River. From the river, Bull Gulch has incised a short, slickrock canyon that opens into the wide basin described on page 201. A short loop hike of 5 or 6 miles is possible by climbing out of Bull Gulch north into the adjacent unnamed drainage and returning down it to the river, and thence to Bull Gulch.

The Colorado River along this stretch includes several Class II rapids and a couple of bridge pilings that are serious river hazards. The nearest river launch sites above Bull Gulch are at the BLM's Pinball Recreation Site (about 1.5 miles upstream of Bull Gulch) or at Burns. Pinball Rapid can pose a hazard because of a railroad bridge just below Bull Gulch. At Twin Bridges (another bridge hazard) or Cottonwood Island, about 3 miles below Bull Gulch, there are informal take-out sites that may require permission from private landowners. Developed recreation sites with boat take-outs are located at Lions Gulch (12 river miles downstream of Bull Gulch) and at Sheep Gulch (5 miles farther downstream from Lions Gulch). Jacks Flat offers a good campsite a couple miles below Bull Gulch on river left for boaters wishing to make an overnight trip.

The BLM has published a river map for the Colorado River between Kremmling and Dotsero. To float the river segment along Bull Gulch, contact the BLM office in Kremmling or Glenwood Springs for a copy of this map.

Burns

WESTERN

Derby
Junction

BL

TH

Big Red
Hill

Greenhorn

Greenhorn
Gulch

Greenhorn

39 1:100,000 MAP:
VAIL

| 1/4 | 1/4 | 1/2 |

SCALE: 1/2 INCH = 1 MILE

BLM wildland
• • • • Hiking trails
TH Trailhead
BL Boat launch
River or stream
Lake or pond
Marsh or swamp
Primary highway
Secondary highway
Light-duty road
Unimproved road
Trail
Quarry or open-pit mine

40 Castle Peak

John Fielder

LOCATION	8 miles north of Eagle
ELEVATION RANGE	8,400–11,275 feet
ECOSYSTEM	Sagebrush, oakbrush, aspen, spruce-fir forest
SIZE	16,180 acres
WILDERNESS STATUS	Not proposed for wilderness by BLM
SPECIAL FEATURES	Craggy Castle Peak, scenic vistas, beaver ponds
TOPOGRAPHIC MAPS	Castle Peak, Eagle

Castle Peak is a distinctive, and aptly named, promontory readily apparent from I-70 between Wolcott and Eagle. The roadless area spans mid-level elevations from 8,000 to 11,000 feet, generally below the level of most designated Forest Service wilderness areas and well above the more typical desert canyon and plateau lands of the BLM. Castle Peak supports a large range of plant and animal habitat, from mixed sagebrush and grasslands on its extreme east side, through meadowlike openings intermixed with aspen groves, to spruce-fir forests with trees of substantial size.

Castle Peak offers a delightful variety of hiking opportunities. Dense spruce-fir timber and chest-high grasses dominate the slopes north and west of the peak, and bushwhacking in these areas can be tiresome. The lower, and more accessible, eastern and southern slopes consist of rolling meadows crossed by several old vehicle ways that provide ready hiking routes to spectacular view points such as Picture Lake. Most of the area is open enough to allow a view of the surrounding countryside, but with enough trees of one sort or another to allow a considerable feeling of solitude. Even during hunting season, people rarely venture into the interior of the area.

Castle Peak itself is not only a visual reference point for the whole area, but interesting in its own right as an outlier of volcanic rock similar in age and origin to expanses of volcanic strata underlying the Flat Tops. Situated between the Flat Tops, Gore Range, and Sawatch Range, Castle Peak provides sweeping vistas of much of Colorado's most dramatic mountain scenery. There is also good fishing for brook trout in the area's many creeks and ponds.

CONTACT INFORMATION: Glenwood Springs Field Office, Bureau of Land Management, 50629 Hwys 6 & 24, P.O. Box 1009, Glenwood Springs, CO 81602, 970-947-2800, http://www.co.blm.gov/gsra/gshome.htm.

DAY HIKE ▶ CASTLE CREEK

ONE-WAY LENGTH: 6 miles
LOW AND HIGH ELEVATIONS: 8,200 and 10,400 feet
DIFFICULTY: Easy to moderate

The Colorado River Road between McCoy and Dotsero provides legal access to Castle Peak from the north. About 3 miles east of Burns, turn south at the crest of Blue Hill after you climb high above the river canyon. Follow BLM Road 8540 for 3 miles south, and take a left spur that leads to an obvious parking area. From here, hike along an obvious trail for a mile or so toward Winter Ridge, after which the trail fades away. Many old bulldozer trails crisscross the forest on Winter Ridge and offer hiking routes. You can hike 3 miles south into the headwaters of Castle Creek, and loop back east a short distance to find another trail returning to your starting point that parallels the first one about a half mile east.

From a map, it may appear that a more direct route is found by taking the Eagle exit on I-70 and driving north, but this road is closed to the public 4 miles beyond its start.

DAY HIKE CASTLE PEAK

ONE-WAY LENGTH: 4 miles
LOW AND HIGH ELEVATIONS: 9,200 and 11,275 feet
DIFFICULTY: Moderate

Legal access to Castle Peak is best attained from the Milk Creek Road on the east side. Take State Highway 131 north from I-70 at the Wolcott exit. The Milk Creek Road (County Road 54) leaves Highway 131 in approximately 3 miles, and winds its way onto the eastern slopes of the roadless area. If the Milk Creek Road is wet, a four-wheel-drive vehicle is advisable. Take the right branch of the road about 1.5 miles after leaving the highway and follow it about 6 miles around the west side of Horse Mountain. At this point, leave the road and hike along a faded jeep trail westward through the area's many small ponds toward Castle Peak, and approach the peak from the southeast.

John Fielder

Castle Peak reflects on beaver pond, Castle Peak Wilderness Study Area.

41 Deep Creek

LOCATION	15 miles northeast of Glenwood Springs
ELEVATION RANGE	6,200–10,460 feet
ECOSYSTEM	Piñon-juniper woodlands, aspen, spruce-fir forest
SIZE	8,000 acres
WILDERNESS STATUS	Not proposed for wilderness by BLM
SPECIAL FEATURES	Limestone canyon, numerous caves
TOPOGRAPHIC MAPS	Broken Rib Creek, Dotsero

Deep Creek carves an extremely rugged and remote limestone canyon and in the process has created one of Colorado's most pristine wilderness retreats. Beginning at Deep Lake near the Flat Tops Wilderness Area, Deep Creek plunges more than 4,500 feet in a span of only 15 miles before it reaches the Colorado River near Dotsero. The many extraordinary features of Deep Creek have prompted the BLM and Forest Service to evaluate the potential for protecting the canyon under the auspices of the Wild and Scenic Rivers Act.

The limestone strata of Deep Creek have created ideal conditions for the formation of caves, and Deep Creek is blessed with more than 40 known caves. These include many of the state's most outstanding caves, including Groaning Cave, Colorado's longest at 10,000 feet; Big A Disappointment Cave, with the largest opening of any in the state; and 20-pound Tick Cave, accessible only with scuba gear. These and many other caves in Deep Creek are described in Lloyd E. Parris's 1973 book, *Caves of Colorado,* and in *Colorado Caves* by Richard Rhinehart (2001).

The higher reaches of Deep Creek are covered with forests of aspen, spruce, and fir, interspersed with grassy meadows. As the creek drops closer to its confluence with the Colorado River, the landscape becomes more arid and vegetation turns toward piñon-juniper woodlands and sagebrush. The combination of dense vegetation and rugged terrain creates ideal hiding habitat for black bears, elk, and mountain lions. At its lower end, Deep Creek is a cold, clear, roaring stream lined by mature cottonwoods in a narrow, limestone canyon with colorful hoodoos dotting its steep slopes.

There are a few faint trails in the area, but the primary route for hikers wishing to explore the length of Deep Creek is the streambed itself. Hiking the upper end of Deep Creek is extremely arduous and in sections requires slithering down waterfalls, groping along cliffs, and ducking under fallen logs.

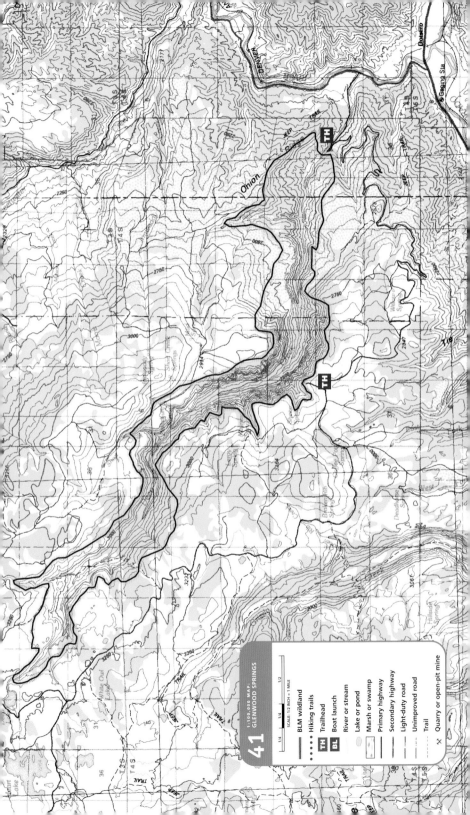

BLM wildland

Hiking trails

TH Trailhead

BL Boat launch

River or stream

Lake or pond

Marsh or swamp

Primary highway

Secondary highway

Light-duty road

Unimproved road

Trail

× Quarry or open-pit mine

SCALE: 1/2 INCH = 1 MILE

1/4   1/4   1/2

DAY HIKE DEEP CREEK

ONE-WAY LENGTH: 4 miles
LOW AND HIGH ELEVATIONS: 6,600 and 7,600 feet
DIFFICULTY: Moderate

To get to Deep Creek, take the Dotsero exit on I-70 east of Glenwood Springs. Take the Colorado River road 2 miles north from Dotsero, and turn west onto the Coffee Pot Road. A primitive trail follows the creek's south bank beginning at a picnic area at the first switchback, approximately 1.7 miles up the road. From here, the first 3 or 4 miles are on a gentle grade and a decent trail before entering the White River National Forest. The creek runs for another 10 miles through the National Forest to Deep Lake.

Looking down Deep Creek toward the Colorado River.

DAY HIKE — DEEP CREEK OVERLOOK

ONE-WAY LENGTH: 0.25 mile
LOW AND HIGH ELEVATIONS: 9,900 feet
DIFFICULTY: Easy

The Deep Creek Overlook along the Coffee Pot Road offers superb views into the canyon from its south rim. The turnoff to the overlook and picnic area is a few miles into the White River National Forest after climbing numerous switchbacks out of the Colorado River valley.

42 Grape Creek

John Fielder

LOCATION	10 miles southwest of Cañon City
ELEVATION RANGE	6,400–9,500 feet
ECOSYSTEM	Piñon-juniper woodlands, cottonwood, ponderosa pine, aspen
SIZE	42,690 acres
WILDERNESS STATUS	Not proposed for wilderness by BLM
SPECIAL FEATURES	Grape Creek Canyon, perennial stream, large ponderosa pines, scenic vistas
TOPOGRAPHIC MAPS	Curley Peak, Iron Mountain, Mount Tyndall, Rockvale, Westcliffe

Most of the canyons along Colorado's Front Range were developed in one fashion or another during the last century. Highways, towns, mines, and power lines exist separately or in combination. Grape Creek remains an exception to this general rule. Though a narrow-gauge railroad traveled the canyon in the 1880s, it has long since disappeared and its bed now forms the basis of an easy hiking route.

The Grape Creek roadless area includes almost 20 miles of Grape Creek and its lush riparian zone. Grape Creek has carved a rugged and scenic canyon through the metamorphic strata of the northern Wet Mountains. This canyon, which traverses the entire length of the roadless area, forms the primary travel route for hikers wishing to explore Grape Creek.

Life zones that range from the upper Sonoran to the montane offer a fascinating array of vegetative types including sagebrush, rabbit brush, cactus, and yucca through piñon-juniper woodlands and into pine-spruce-fir forest intermixed with montane meadows and aspen at the highest elevations around Tanner Peak.

Predator populations, including high concentrations of mountain lions, indicate an abundance of prey species. Mule deer, elk, black bears, and many smaller mammals are found here, as are wild turkeys. The expansive cliffs house nesting and roosting birds of prey, including eagles. The Colorado Division of Wildlife has identified possible nesting sites for peregrine falcons. Grape Creek is a large perennial stream that supports a significant brown and rainbow trout fishery.

The Grape Creek roadless area actually consists of three distinct administrative units: the BLM's Upper and Lower Grape Creek Wilderness Study Areas and the 18,000-acre San Isabel National Forest Tanner Peak roadless area, which is contiguous to the eastern edge of Lower Grape Creek. The combination of units creates a diversity of recreational opportunities that range from canyon hiking to ascents of 9,500-foot peaks in the Wet Mountains.

CONTACT INFORMATION: Royal Gorge Field Office, Bureau of Land Management, 3170 E. Main St., Cañon City, CO 81212, 719-269-8500, http://www.co.blm.gov/ccdo/canon.htm.

DESTINATION HIKE   GRAPE CREEK

ONE-WAY LENGTH: Up to 20 miles
LOW AND HIGH ELEVATIONS: 5,900 and 7,400 feet
DIFFICULTY: Easy to moderate

Hikes into the mouth of Grape Creek begin at Temple Canyon City Park. Turn south on Fremont County Road 3 about 10 miles west of Cañon City (this is also the road to the south entrance of the Royal Gorge). Follow the county road approximately 7 miles to Temple Canyon City Park. Leave your vehicle at the park and follow the creek or the abandoned railroad grade upstream as far as you like. It is about 20 miles to the upper end of the roadless area. Grape Creek lies downstream from DeWeese Reservoir and drains much of the Wet Mountain Valley; hikers should be cautious and treat any water used for human consumption.

DESTINATION HIKE TANNER PEAK

ONE-WAY LENGTH: 8 miles
LOW AND HIGH ELEVATIONS: 7,400 and 9,600 feet
DIFFICULTY: Moderate

To reach the higher elevation portions of the area around Tanner Peak, take the Oak Creek Grade Road (Fremont County Road 143) in the San Isabel National Forest. To connect with this road, turn south from Highway 50 in Cañon City at the Fourth Street Viaduct, and then turn south again in Prospect Heights onto Fremont County Road 143. The Tanner Trail takes off about 11 miles down the road, and heads in a westerly direction to Curley Peak (3 miles) and Tanner Peak (8 miles). The trail climbs sharply up Bear Gulch past forest giants to a summit ridge. Grassy parks and a spacious forest of stately ponderosa pine, aspen, and spruce trees define the ridge. Curley and Tanner Peaks are rocky outcrops that provide sweeping views of the Sangres, Pikes Peak, and into Grape Creek Canyon.

SHUTTLE HIKE BEAR GULCH/GRAPE CREEK

ONE-WAY LENGTH: 10 miles
LOW AND HIGH ELEVATIONS: 6,900 and 9,600 feet
DIFFICULTY: Easy to moderate

The middle of Grape Creek Canyon is accessible via Bear Gulch from County Road 143. Follow the road west about 3 miles beyond the Tanner Peak trailhead, and turn north at a BLM sign announcing public access to Grape Creek via Bear Gulch. This road is closed to vehicular traffic a half mile or so before it reaches the creek, about 2 miles from County Road 143. Hike the short distance to Grape Creek, and then proceed down the canyon to its mouth at Temple Canyon City Park where your other vehicle awaits.

SHUTTLE HIKE STULTZ TRAIL/TANNER TRAIL

ONE-WAY LENGTH: 8 miles
LOW AND HIGH ELEVATIONS: 6,900 and 9,600 feet
DIFFICULTY: Moderate

A second Forest Service trail accesses Tanner Peak. The Stultz Trail also begins from Fremont County Road 143, about 3 miles north of the Tanner Trail, and a fine 8-mile circuit hike is possible if you combine the two trails. The car shuttle is a short 3 miles along County Road 143, which can almost as easily be done as a loop hike.

John Fielder

Grape Creek winds its way through the Wet Mountains,
Lower Grape Creek Wilderness Study Area.

John Fielder

20 miles northeast of Glenwood Springs	**LOCATION**
7,600–11,000 feet	**ELEVATION RANGE**
Transition from piñon-juniper woodlands to aspen, spruce-fir forest	**VEGETATION**
9,120 acres	**SIZE**
10 acres proposed for wilderness by BLM	**WILDERNESS STATUS**
Ecological transition, access to Flat Tops Wilderness, spectacular vistas, Hack Lake	**SPECIAL FEATURES**
Sweetwater Lake	**TOPOGRAPHIC MAPS**

The Flat Tops Wilderness is one of Colorado's most distinctive wilderness areas. It encompasses the vast expanse of the White River Plateau and is characterized by undulating tundra broken by pockets of spruce-fir forests and sparkling lakes tucked at the bases of volcanic cliffs.

Hack Lake lies on the southern edge of the Flat Tops and offers hikers a dramatic approach to the wilderness. One major, well-maintained trail (the Ute Trail) traverses the Hack Lake Wilderness Study Area and eventually joins with the network of forest trails that lace the Flat Tops.

The lower elevations, and southern exposures, of Hack Lake are covered by sparse piñon-juniper woodlands typical of the Colorado Plateau, but surprising amidst the lush forests of the Flat Tops. The Ute Trail winds across these exposed slopes, providing dramatic views of the Sawatch Range, and eventually turns the corner of the ridge to unveil an abrupt transition to groves of cool aspen with lush undergrowth.

CONTACT INFORMATION: Glenwood Springs Field Office, Bureau of Land Management, 50629 Hwys 6 & 24, P.O. Box 1009, Glenwood Springs, CO 81602, 970-947-2800, http://www.co.blm.gov/gsra/gshome.htm.

DESTINATION HIKE ▶ HACK LAKE

ONE-WAY LENGTH: 4 miles
LOW AND HIGH ELEVATIONS: 7,700 and 9,900 feet
DIFFICULTY: Easy

To get to Hack Lake, follow the Colorado River Road north from I-70 at Dotsero approximately 6.5 miles to the Sweetwater Lake Road. The Ute Trail begins immediately across the road from the Sweetwater Lake Resort (ask at the lodge if you can't find it) and is so named because it was a historic route of the Ute Indians. The trail splits just before reaching the bench on which Hack Lake sits, and the right branch goes on to connect with the W Mountain Trail that crosses the Flat Tops. Hack Creek pours out of a hillside, draining underground from Hack Lake on the shelf above. As the path tops out onto this bench area, it enters a spruce-fir forest that opens to reveal the blue-green mirror of the small lake. Hack Lake is a spring-fed pond, so that no surface stream enters or leaves. Beyond, across a mountain meadow, graced by a picturesque and historic log cabin, the forest rolls up to summit cliffs. With each gain in elevation, the view unfolds a greater panorama, taking in the Gore Range and the northern Sawatch Range to the east and the massive peaks of the Elk Range to the south. Several outfitters around Sweetwater Lake offer guided packhorse trips to Hack Lake.

DESTINATION HIKE ▶ SHEEP CREEK TO HACK LAKE

ONE-WAY LENGTH: 6 miles
LOW AND HIGH ELEVATIONS: 9,200 and 10,200 feet
DIFFICULTY: Moderate

The four-wheel-drive trail in Sheep Creek offers a rougher, more remote approach to Hack Lake. Turn north onto the four-wheel-drive road approximately 8 miles up the Sweetwater Lake Road from the Colorado River. The road heads north toward Dotsero State Wildlife Area. Take the left branch, and follow the road to its end in about 3.5 to 4 miles at an undeveloped camping area. From there, a trail leads 1 or 2 miles up Sheep Creek until it eventually connects with the Ute Trail and the W Mountain Trail, which you can follow around to Hack Lake. The vegetation is rolling sagebrush-filled meadows that give way to aspen and spruce fir.

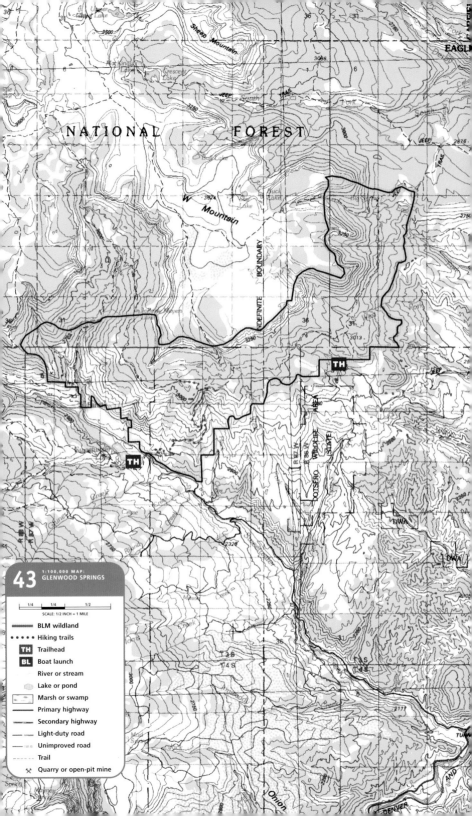

NATIONAL FOREST

43 1:100,000 MAP:
GLENWOOD SPRINGS

SCALE: 1/2 INCH = 1 MILE

1/4	1/4	1/2

▬▬	BLM wildland
• • • •	Hiking trails
TH	Trailhead
BL	Boat launch
	River or stream
🛆	Lake or pond
	Marsh or swamp
▬▬	Primary highway
▬▬	Secondary highway
▬▬	Light-duty road
▬▬	Unimproved road
----	Trail
✕	Quarry or open-pit mine

44 McIntyre Hills

John Fielder

LOCATION	12 miles west of Cañon City
ELEVATION RANGE	5,900–8,100 feet
ECOSYSTEM	Piñon-juniper woodlands, ponderosa pine, Douglas fir
SIZE	17,310 acres
WILDERNESS STATUS	Not proposed for wilderness by BLM
SPECIAL FEATURES	Scenic vistas, rugged topography, Arkansas River views
TOPOGRAPHIC MAPS	Echo, Hillside, McIntyre Hills

Rolling, piñon-juniper forested hills and steep rugged drainages range upward to the 8,100-foot elevation of the McIntyre Hills along the Arkansas River's south bank. Ponderosa pine and Douglas fir occur at higher elevations, and springs and pools in the major drainages provide a fairly reliable water source for wildlife and recreation.

Rugged topography and dense vegetation combine as excellent habitat for mule deer, black bears, turkeys, and small mammals. Golden eagles and prairie falcons nest here, and the

BLM wildland
Hiking trails
TH Trailhead
BL Boat launch
River or stream
Lake or pond
Marsh or swamp
Primary highway
Secondary highway
Light-duty road
Unimproved road
Trail
× Quarry or open-pit mine

SCALE: 1/2 INCH = 1 MILE
1/4   1/4   1/2

area represents a sizable portion of one of the densest populations of mountain lions in the western United States. The Colorado Division of Wildlife considers McIntyre Hills to be a top priority for transplanting bighorn sheep.

McIntyre Hills is generally without snow, so it offers year-round hiking opportunities for the numerous residents of the nearby Front Range. Extremely rugged topography and a lack of trails almost assure total solitude for visitors. The most immediate access to McIntyre Hills is from U.S. Highway 50. The roadless area begins along the highway approximately 2.5 miles east of Texas Creek and the junction with state Highway 69. From this point for another 7 miles, the highway forms the area's northern boundary. Short, steep hikes up one of the gulches or directly to the ridge are possible in infinite combination, and the adjacent highway offers many possibilities for one-way hikes with car shuttles. From the ridgecrest, wave after wave of wild country unfolds, offering uncommon views of the Arkansas River gorge and the length of the Sangre de Cristo Range.

CONTACT INFORMATION: Royal Gorge Field Office, Bureau of Land Management, 3170 E. Main St., Cañon City, CO 81212, 719-269-8500, http://www.co.blm.gov/ccdo/canon.htm.

DAY HIKE ⟩ FIVE POINT GULCH

ONE-WAY LENGTH: 6 miles
LOW AND HIGH ELEVATIONS: 6,100 and 7,400 feet
DIFFICULTY: Moderate

Five Point Gulch is the longest drainage, stretching almost 6 miles into the heart of the roadless area. The drainage intersects Highway 50 approximately 4 miles east of Texas Creek, and hikes begin at the Colorado State Parks' Five Point Recreation Site. The stream course is lined by giant cottonwoods, and the many rocky outcrops that dot adjacent ridges give vantage points for scanning jumbled terrain for new routes into seemingly unexplored tributaries. Exploring Five Points Gulch will undoubtedly result in a good day's exercise.

John Fielder

10 miles east of Antonito	**LOCATION**
7,000–8,700 feet	**ELEVATION RANGE**
Rabbitbrush, piñon-juniper woodlands	**VEGETATION**
16,100 acres	**SIZE**
Not proposed for wilderness by BLM	**WILDERNESS STATUS**
Rio Grande Gorge, raptors, scenic vistas	**SPECIAL FEATURES**
Kiowa Hill, La Segita Peaks NE, Sky Valley Ranch, Ute Mountain	**TOPOGRAPHIC MAPS**

The most dramatic feature of this area is the approximately 8 miles of Rio Grande corridor. BLM studied this segment of the river for inclusion in the National Wild and Scenic Rivers system because of its remarkable raptor population and outstanding recreational opportunities. The river cuts a steep-sided canyon lined with riparian vegetation. The cliffs and the adjacent food sources from the river draw raptors by the hundreds during the peak of migration, among them red-tailed and rough-legged hawks, prairie falcons, kestrels, harriers, and golden and bald eagles. The bald eagle, for example, is a common winter resident of the area, and as many as 300 eagles have been counted along the Rio Grande corridor during winter.

Recreational activities include float boating, raptor viewing, fishing, hiking, camping, and general wilderness solitude experiences. BLM estimates that approximately 500 float trips launch annually from the Lobatos bridge south into New Mexico. Because of these attributes, BLM has designated this stretch of river as part of the longer Rio Grande Corridor Special Recreation Management Area.

The area west of the river consists of an interesting and varied landscape of vast desert grasslands intersected by hills and ridges. Dominant vegetation types include western wheatgrass, Indian rice grass, saltbush, and rabbitbrush.

Elevation within the Rio Grande roadless area ranges from 7,000 feet along the river to 8,700 feet on the highest point in the area, Punchas Peak. Vantage points such as this offer spectacular panoramic views of the San Luis Valley, the Rio Grande corridor, the Sangre de Cristo Range, the San Juan Mountains, and two impressive landmarks known as the Twin Peaks—Ute Mountain and San Antonio Peak.

The Rio Grande area offers year-round habitat for pronghorn and mule deer. The Colorado Natural Areas Program has conducted field studies of the area looking for a rare and endangered plant species, *Astragalus ripleyi* (Ripley's milkvetch), which is known to favor rocky outcroppings and side canyons.

CONTACT INFORMATION: La Jara Field Office, Bureau of Land Management, 15571 County Rd. T5, La Jara, CO 81140, 719-274-8971, http://www.co.blm.gov/ccdo/canon.htm.

DAY HIKE PUNCHAS PEAK

ONE-WAY LENGTH: 2 miles
LOW AND HIGH ELEVATIONS: 7,700 and 8,740 feet
DIFFICULTY: Easy

From Antonito, head east on the Kiowa Hill Road (County Road G) to a fork approximately 9 miles out of town. The north fork defines the northern boundary of the roadless area and skirts several low hills. To climb Punchas Peak, park along the road 3 or 4 miles beyond the fork, and head south cross-country approximately 1.5 miles to the summit.

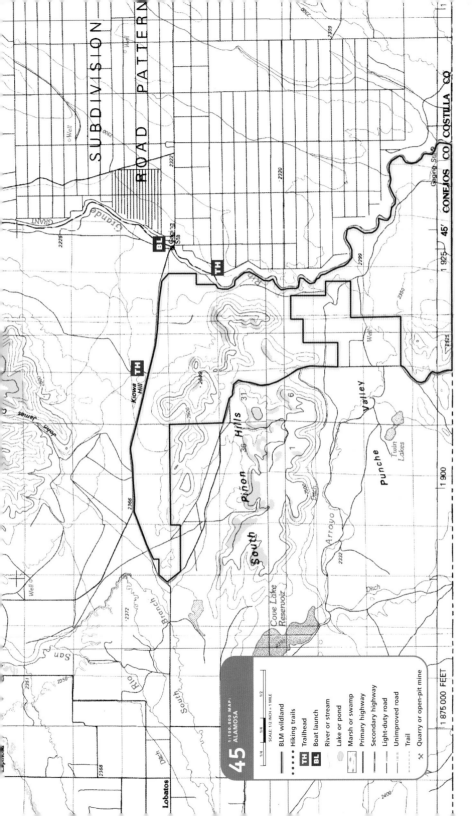

SUBDIVISION

ROAD PATTERN

CONEJOS CO COSTILLA CO

45'

1 925

1 900

1 875 000 FEET

11

Well

Well

Grande

Grant

Rio

Gaging Sta

2225

2200

2300

2322

2220

2299

2350

2425

2449

Kiowa Hill

South

Piñon Hills

36

31

6

1

Punche Valley

Twin Lakes

2500

2366

2332

Arroyo

2372

San James Wash

Well

Well

2251

2350

2368

2400

South

Branch

San

Ditch

Lobatos

Cove Lake Reservoir

Ditch

2299

Gaging Sta

BL

TH

TH

45

1:100,000 MAP: ALAMOSA

SCALE 1/2 INCH = 1 MILE

1/4   1/2   3/4   1 MILE

BLM wildland

• • • • • Hiking trails

TH Trailhead

BL Boat launch

River or stream

Lake or pond

Marsh or swamp

Primary highway

Secondary highway

Light-duty road

Unimproved road

Trail

× Quarry or open-pit mine

DAY HIKE) RIO GRANDE CORRIDOR

ONE-WAY LENGTH: Up to 10 miles
LOW AND HIGH ELEVATIONS: 7,700 and 8,740 feet
DIFFICULTY: Easy to moderate

The best hike in the area is along the Rio Grande corridor. One can either hike in the canyon itself or along the rim. To hike in the canyon, begin at Lobatos Bridge where the Kiowa Hill Road crosses the Rio Grande. You can walk a short distance along the west bank at high water before an overhanging cliff blocks the way. At low water, which is most of the year, you can probably hike for miles if you don't mind crossing the river as needed. Occasional breaks in the river cliffs offer opportunities to climb out of the canyon for a rim view. The intimate gorge provides complete silence, broken only by the sound of the river, raptor calls, and deer crashing through the brush.

You can easily hike along the canyon's west rim past outcrops of volcanic rock and sparse desert vegetation. The canyon rim offers outstanding views into the gorge and of the surrounding hills and peaks. Breaks in the canyon rim may require short detours away from the rim. At Punche Arroyo, a slot canyon and plunge pool near the river offer inviting exploration. A rock cairn marks the New Mexico border. The rim hike begins about 1 mile south of Lobatos Bridge, at the slump that marks a good stopping point along a dirt road that follows the river's west bank.

RIVER TRIP) RIO GRANDE

ONE-WAY LENGTH: 23 miles
LOW AND HIGH ELEVATIONS: 7,200 and 7,300 feet
DIFFICULTY: Class I and II

The Kiowa Hill Road (County Road G) takes you to the Lobatos bridge and an access point for Rio Grande float trips along the area's eastern edge. Floating the river provides the best chance for glimpsing some of the numerous raptors in the area, although the river is closed to recreational use during nesting season. The float is a flatwater trip suitable for any kind of watercraft if you take out before reaching the Taos Box. The take-out is at Lee Trail, 23 miles downstream, and requires an arduous 500-yard haul uphill. Continuing downstream, you will run into the wild whitewater of the Taos Box. Contact the BLM's Taos Resource Area office in New Mexico for more information about floating the Rio Grande.

John Fielder

25 miles south of Alamosa	**LOCATION**
7,700–9,500 feet	**ELEVATION RANGE**
Fescue-mountain muhly-prairie, piñon-juniper woodlands	**VEGETATION**
20,364 acres	**SIZE**
Not proposed for wilderness by BLM	**WILDERNESS STATUS**
Scenic vistas, high desert biome	**SPECIAL FEATURES**
Kiowa, Manassa, Manassa NE	**TOPOGRAPHIC MAPS**

The San Luis Hills are a prominent and geologically unique landform of the southern San Luis Valley. Rising more than 1,000 feet above the valley floor, the San Luis Hills are an erosional remnant of the vast volcanic deposits that form the San Juan Mountains and underlay the depositional soils of the valley. The area remained stable while the surrounding basin subsided along the faults of the Rio Grand Rift. The eastern flank of the area is the western fault along which the subsidence occurred, forming the present-day Rio Grande Valley. The San Luis Hills remain a physical anomaly within the San Luis Valley, still standing high after thousands of years of erosion have softened their features.

You can see the volcanic layers underlaying the San Luis Hills in steep rock faces on the hills' northern side. Steep-sided ridges are interspersed with rocky crags and out-croppings, covered with colorful lichen and offering shade from the sun. Small stands of piñon pine and juniper are present, mostly on the southern and eastern portions of the mesa tops. You'll catch sweeping vistas of the San Luis Valley and surrounding mountain ranges from the unnamed summits in the area. This bird's-eye view provides a perspective of the valley's river systems and landforms found nowhere else.

Wildlife species that inhabit the San Luis Hills include mule deer, pronghorn, various small mammal and rodent species, piñon jay, and raptors. Water limits deer populations, as there are no perennial streams within the area. However, the San Luis Hills provide an important island of coniferous cover and winter range to deer and pronghorn amidst the agricultural lands of Conejos County.

Fall, winter, and spring are the best times to visit the San Luis Hills. At a time when foothill areas at equal elevation may be snowed in, the physical isolation and southern exposure of the San Luis Hills combine to provide ideal conditions for winter hiking and horseback riding. Scattered archaeological sites, geologic features, and potential raptor sightings are of particular interest to visitors. There are no water sources, so bring your own water.

The San Luis Hills consist of two units separated by Highway 142. The southern unit goes by BLM's name for the wilderness study area, San Luis Hills, while the northern unit is called Flat Top Mesa.

CONTACT INFORMATION: La Jara Field Office, Bureau of Land Management, 15571 County Rd. T5, La Jara, CO 81140, 719-274-8971, http://www.co.blm.gov/ccdo/canon.htm.

DAY HIKE ❯ SAN LUIS HILLS

ONE-WAY LENGTH: 2 miles
LOW AND HIGH ELEVATIONS: 7,900 and 9,500 feet
DIFFICULTY: Easy

To reach San Luis Hills, travel south from Alamosa on U.S. Highway 285 and turn east on Highway 142. Approximately 4 miles east of Manassa, a couple of dirt roads head south from the highway to the northern edge of the San Luis Hills. Park anywhere along the dirt road that forms the area's northern boundary, and pick a route through the open sagebrush and scattered piñon-juniper woodlands for the 1,500-foot climb to the crest of the hills.

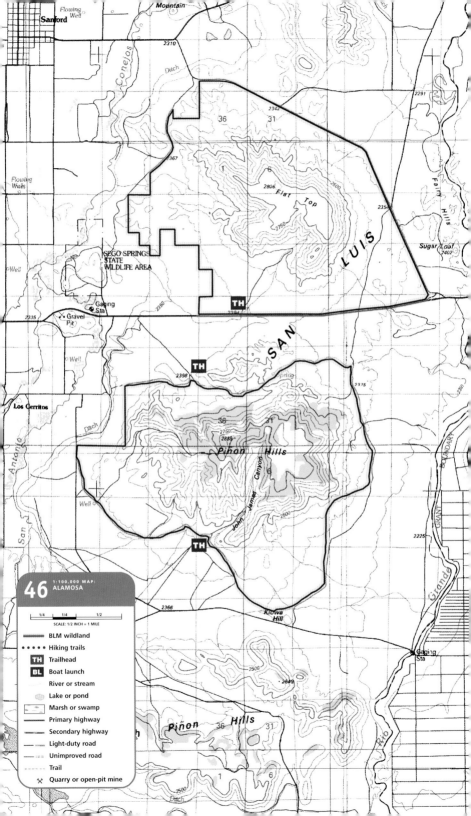

Sanford

Flowing
Well

Mountain

2310

Ditch

Conejos

2291

2342

36   31

367

1

6

2806   Flat   Top   2500

2359

Flowing
Wells

2760

Sugar Loaf
2402

SEGO SPRINGS
STATE
WILDLIFE AREA

LUIS

Farm

Hills

Well

2350

Gaging
Sta

2335   Gravel
Pit

2384

TH

SAN

2375

2398

TH

2230

Spring

Los Cerritos

36   31

2550

Piñon   Hills

2885

John   James   Canyon

San

Well

Antonio

Ditch

2500

6

2500

2225

TH

GRANT   BOUNDARY

2366

Kiowa
Hill

1/4   1/4   1/2

SCALE: 1/2 INCH = 1 MILE

Gaging
Sta

——— BLM wildland

Rio

Grande

TH   Trailhead

BL   Boat launch

2500   2649

River or stream

Lake or pond

Marsh or swamp

——— Primary highway

— — Secondary highway

— — Light-duty road

——— Unimproved road

Piñon   Hills

36   31

········· Trail

× Quarry or open-pit mine

1   6

Ditch

2500

DAY HIKE JOHN JAMES CANYON

ONE-WAY LENGTH: 6 miles
LOW AND HIGH ELEVATIONS: 7,900 and 9,500 feet
DIFFICULTY: Moderate

The southern side of San Luis Hills and the main drainage, John James Canyon, is also accessed via Highway 142. Turn south 2 miles east of Manassa, and angle southeast toward the Rio Grande, following the network of roads approximately 6 miles to the Kiowa Hill Road. John James Canyon slices 3 miles to the heart of the San Luis Hills. A rough jeep road goes to the edge of the Wilderness Study Area where you can park, then a track continues into the canyon. A good loop hike is to follow the canyon to its head, scramble up the high hill to the west to gain the dramatic views of the Sangre de Cristo Range and the Rio Grande, and then head south down the hillside a couple miles back to your vehicle.

DAY HIKE FLAT TOP MESA

ONE-WAY LENGTH: 3 miles
LOW AND HIGH ELEVATIONS: 7,900 and 9,200 feet
DIFFICULTY: Easy

Flat Top Mesa lies directly across state Highway 142 north of San Luis Hills. The mesa top itself is unexpectedly vast, the rolling terrain hiding visitors from one another. A desert grassland, underlaid by volcanic soil and rock, is populated by sweet-smelling sagebrush interspersed with blooming prickly pear cactus. A dirt track heads northeast toward Flat Top Mesa approximately 6 miles east of Manassa on the highway. Park along this track, and hike a couple miles cross-country through sagebrush and piñon-juniper woodlands to the mesa's summit, which offers extraordinary views of the San Luis Valley and its environs. The Fairy Hills, Piñon Hills, Rio Grande, Sangre de Cristo Mountains, Great Sand Dunes, and the San Juan Mountains complete a sweeping 360-degree vista.

Rabbitbrush shines above the Rio Grande, San Luis Hills Wilderness Study Area in distance.

John Fielder

47 Thompson Creek

Kirk Koepsel

LOCATION	20 miles south of Glenwood Springs
ELEVATION RANGE	6,600–10,700 feet
ECOSYSTEM	Cottonwood, oakbrush, piñon-juniper woodlands, Douglas fir, aspen, ponderosa pine
SIZE	23,200 acres
WILDERNESS STATUS	Not proposed for wilderness by BLM
SPECIAL FEATURES	Rock formations, riparian zone
TOPOGRAPHIC MAPS	Mount Sopris, Placita, Redstone, Stony Ridge

Thompson Creek is a Western Slope "Garden of the Gods." The creek cuts a dramatic gorge through the heart of soaring, razor-thin vertical fins composed of the Maroon Formation's red sandstone and shale. Thompson Creek's spectacular red stone fins are of the same geologic era as the faulted hogbacks that give rise to the Colorado Springs phenomenon. These jumbled red sediments parallel the Crystal River and are also found on Assignation Ridge in adjacent National Forest lands.

Carbondale

Mulford

White
Hill

DENVER AND RIO GR

Landing Strip

Gravel Pit

INDEFINITE BOUNDARY

Gaging Sta

Jerome Park

Barbers

Bowled Gulch

Smith Gulch

Union Mine

Gravel Pit

TH

Stony Ridge

Assignation Ridge

RIVER

Lake Ridge

Avalanche

N   A   T   I   O   N   A   L

Mount Sopris

F   O   R

Gravel Pit
Campground

Gaging Sta

Camp

Campgrounds

TH

Redstone

The roadless area consists of two distinct landforms. One is Assignation Ridge, a long, straight ridge west of the Crystal River. Assignation Ridge is covered by dense scrub oak, aspen, and mixed conifer forests, and is managed by the White River National Forest.

The other landform consists of Thompson Creek and the beautiful gorge it carves through the ragged, broken-topped rock fins of the Maroon Formation at the area's northern end. Narrow-leaf cottonwood and Douglas fir dominate the vegetation alongside polished red, sandstone bowls sculpted by the stream. Scrub oak and piñon-juniper woodlands cover the slopes away from the creek. Together, the features create a haven for wildlife such as elk, bears, mountain lions, and wild turkeys in addition to the ubiquitous mule deer.

BLM has long recognized the beauty of the area, designating it as an Area of Critical Environmental Concern. Thompson Creek is also under consideration as a possible "Wild" or "Scenic" addition to the potential Wild and Scenic River designation of the Crystal River.

CONTACT INFORMATION: Glenwood Springs Field Office, Bureau of Land Management, 50629 Hwys 6 & 24, P.O. Box 1009, Glenwood Springs, CO 81602, 970-947-2800, http://www.co.blm.gov/gsra/gshome.htm; or Sopris Ranger District, White River National Forest, 620 Main St., Carbondale, CO 81623, 970-963-2266, http://www.fs.fed.us/r2/whiteriver.

DAY HIKE THOMPSON CREEK

ONE-WAY LENGTH: 4 miles
LOW AND HIGH ELEVATIONS: 6,600 and 7,400 feet
DIFFICULTY: Moderate

Thompson Creek joins the Crystal River about 4.5 miles south of Carbondale along Highway 133, but the mouth of the canyon at this point is on private land and public access is effectively blocked by "No Trespassing" signs. It is best to drop into Thompson Creek from BLM land to the west. From Highway 133 in Carbondale, turn west at Main Street, which quickly turns into Thompson Creek Road (County Road 108). In approximately 7.4 miles, Forest Road 305 branches left. This road crosses Thompson Creek in another 2.4 miles, at which point a trailhead denotes the route downstream. The Thompson Creek trail appears deceptively as a well-worn, maintained route the first mile or so, but it then enters the narrow confines of the deep gorge cut through surrounding rock fins. The trail vanishes and is replaced by scrambling rock-hopping through and across the stream, making the route infeasible at high water. Remnants of trestles and the long-abandoned grade of the Aspen and Western Railroad are found in the lower canyon.

DAY HIKE BRADERICH TRAIL

ONE-WAY LENGTH: 7 miles
LOW AND HIGH ELEVATIONS: 7,900 and 9,200 feet
DIFFICULTY: Easy

The southern end of the area, and the South Thompson Creek drainage, are most easily reached from the Braderich Trail in the White River National Forest. The Braderich Trail begins approximately 2.5 miles west of Redstone on the road to Coal Basin. The trail heads up Braderich Creek for about 3 miles, crosses a saddle, and drops into the headwaters of South Thompson Creek before cutting across the drainage basin and connecting with Forest Road 305. The trail offers a leisurely exploration of the higher-elevation aspen and conifer forests of South Thompson Creek's watershed.

48 Troublesome

John Fielder

LOCATION	20 miles north of Kremmling
ELEVATION RANGE	8,100–11,100 feet
ECOSYSTEM	Lodgepole pine, aspen, spruce fir
SIZE	88,865 acres
WILDERNESS STATUS	Not proposed for wilderness by BLM
SPECIAL FEATURES	Forest streams, scenic views, big game
TOPOGRAPHIC MAPS	Cabin Creek, Corral Peaks, Gunsight Pass, Hyannis Peak, Parkview Mountain, Radial Mountain

One of the last of the large, unprotected roadless areas in northern Colorado, Troublesome provides the crucial ecological connection between the vast wilderness of Rocky Mountain National Park and the distant, rugged wild areas of the Gore and Park Ranges. Twenty or so miles of the Continental Divide snake through the Troublesome roadless area and the volcanic Rabbit Ears Range, but the divide here stands in marked contrast to stereotypical ideas about it. Instead of the craggy peaks that denote the divide in the nearby Indian Peaks or in the San Juan Mountains of southern Colorado, the Continental Divide in Troublesome reaches a gentle high point of 12,296 feet. This crest separates North and Middle Parks, and the dense forests that blanket the rising land offer refuge to healthy herds of mule deer and elk. In fact, Colorado Division of Wildlife officers assert that Troublesome must be left undeveloped to ensure the continued health of these herds.

At almost 89,000 acres in size, Troublesome comprises a large, intact block of lodgepole-pine forest dissected by wide, verdant willow-filled valleys. Beavers thrive in this riparian habitat and, combined with deer and elk, create a semblance of America's native wildlife prior to settlement. Even more important, however, may be Troublesome's role as the ecological link between surrounding large wild areas. Scientists now know that wide-ranging species such as grizzly bears, wolves, and wolverines depend on isolated blocks of undeveloped land to thrive and disperse. For example, to prevent genetic inbreeding, populations require occasional infusions of new blood. If rare species such as wolves, wolverines, and lynx ever regain a foothold in the larger wild areas surrounding Rocky Mountain National Park or around Mount Zirkel, their continued genetic health depends on the ability to safely disperse from one population to another. Troublesome fills that ecological role by offering a sanctuary halfway between the Front Range and the Park and Gore Ranges. Its dense forests provide a natural secluded bridge for species needing to avoid the open environs of North and Middle Parks.

From a human recreational standpoint, Troublesome offers a refreshing contrast to the jagged peaks and alpine lakes found in so many other Colorado wilderness areas. Troublesome's gentle, wide valleys afford easy hiking and abundant campsites in close proximity to dependable water supplies. The area's trail system suggests a variety of loop hikes, though private land restricts access from the west and south. Horsepackers make frequent use of Troublesome, but there are relatively few hikers.

Troublesome is a combined BLM/Forest Service roadless area, with the BLM portion containing only about 10,000 of the 89,000 acres in the area. The BLM segment, however, includes important low-elevation riparian zones along Troublesome Creek and Rabbit Ears Creek in the southwest corner of the area.

More than 50 miles of trails provide for a variety of dispersed recreational activity, including hiking, horseback riding, backpacking, ski touring, fishing, hunting, and nature study. Unfortunately, private land blocks direct access from nearby roads to the BLM portion of Troublesome. It is possible to get into the BLM area either by traveling cross-country or in a roundabout fashion using existing Forest Service trails.

CONTACT INFORMATION: Kremmling Field Office, Bureau of Land Management, 1116 Park Ave., P.O. Box 68, Kremmling, CO 80459, 970-724-3437, http://www.co.blm.gov/kra/kraindex.htm.

DESTINATION HIKE   RABBIT EARS CREEK

ONE-WAY LENGTH: 8 miles
LOW AND HIGH ELEVATIONS: 8,500 and 10,700 feet
DIFFICULTY: Moderate

To reach the headwaters of Rabbit Ears Creek, take Forest Road 700, which leaves the east side of Highway 14 halfway between Walden and Muddy Pass. From this road, follow a jeep road east along the Continental Divide toward an electronic communication site; after a couple miles, drop into the Rabbit Ears Creek drainage. No trails exist in this drainage, so you are on your own as far as route-finding is concerned. The creek crosses into the BLM area about 4 miles downstream. You can follow Rabbit Ears Creek another 4 miles downstream to its confluence with Troublesome Creek at private land.

DESTINATION HIKE   TROUBLESOME CREEK

ONE-WAY LENGTH: 15 miles
LOW AND HIGH ELEVATIONS: 8,400 and 9,900 feet
DIFFICULTY: Moderate

You can use Forest Service trails in East Fork, Middle Fork, and Haystack Creeks to reach Troublesome Creek on BLM land. Take Highway 125 north from Windy Gap to Buffalo Creek, turn left on Forest Road 108, and drive several miles to its end. From the trailhead, follow the Troublesome Access Trail around private land and up the ridge via old jeep tracks. The trail heads north via another jeep road and descends through lodgepole-pine forest to the East Fork of Troublesome Creek. Upon reaching the creek, head downstream. In several miles, turn north along Forest Trail 57 up Middle Fork Creek. This trail ultimately leads to Matheson Reservoir, which sits on Troublesome Creek at the BLM/Forest Service boundary. The Haystack Creek Trail (Forest Trail 55) also connects with Middle Fork Creek, but enters from the north over Troublesome Pass instead of from the east. From Matheson Reservoir, you can hike a couple miles down Troublesome Creek to its confluence with Rabbit Ears Creek on private land.

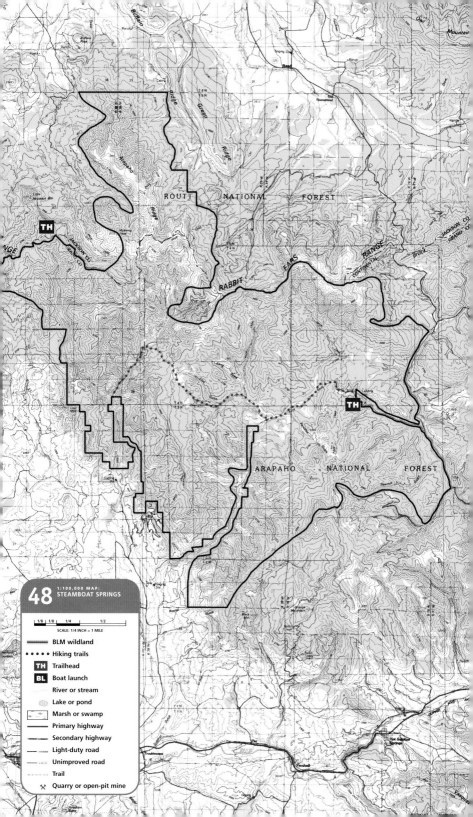

APPENDIX A:
Recommended Equipment Checklist

DAY HIKES

Lightweight daypack
Snacks or lunch
Raingear
Sweater
Hat or sun visor
Wool hat
Gloves
Binoculars
Water or purification
   system
Trail guide or maps
Headlamp
First-aid kit
Flower, bird, or other
   field guides
Compass
Sunscreen and sunglasses
Lighter or fire starter
Toilet paper
Insect repellant
Camera and film
Knife
Extra food for
   emergencies

ADDITIONAL GEAR FOR OVERNIGHT HIKES

Sturdy backpack
Sleeping bag
Ground cloth
Change of clothing
Stove and fuel
Cup and spoon
Toothbrush
Biodegradable soap
Trowel for digging
   "cat holes"
Garbage bags
Thin rope or cord
Tent or bivouac sack
Sleeping pad
Camp chair
Booties or slippers
Cooking gear
Food
Pack cover
Comb
Towel
Playing cards
Reading material
Journal

APPENDIX B:
BLM Field Offices

COLORADO STATE OFFICE
2850 Youngfield St.
Lakewood, CO 80215
303-239-3600
www.co.blm.gov

Glenwood Springs Field Office
50629 Hwys 6 & 24
P.O. Box 1009
Glenwood Springs, CO
  81602
970-947-2800
www.co.blm.gov/gsra/
  gshome.htm

Grand Junction Field Office
2815 H Road
Grand Junction, CO
  81506
970-244-3000
www.co.blm.gov/gjra/
  gjra.html

Gunnison Field Office
216 N. Colorado St.
Gunnison, CO 81230
970-641-0471
www.co.blm.gov/gra/
  gra-hmepge.htm

Kremmling Field Office
1116 Park Ave.
P.O. Box 68
Kremmling, CO 80459
970-724-3437
www.co.blm.gov/kra/
  kraindex.htm

La Jara Field Office
15571 County Road T5
La Jara, CO 81140
719-274-8971
www.co.blm.gov/ccdo/
  canon.htm

Little Snake Field Office
455 Emerson St.
Craig, CO 81625
970-826-5000
www.co.blm.gov/lsra/
  lsraindex.htm

Royal Gorge Field Office
3170 E. Main St.
Cañon City, CO 81212
719-269-8500
www.co.blm.gov/ccdo/
  canon.htm

San Juan Field Office
15 Burnett Court
Durango, CO 81301
970-247-4874
www.co.blm.gov/sjra/
  sjra.html

Uncompahgre Field Office
2505 S. Townsend Ave.
Montrose, CO 81401
970-240-5300
www.co.blm.gov/ubra/
  ubra.html

White River Field Office
73544 Hwy 64
Meeker, CO 81641
970-878-3601
www.co.blm.gov/wrra/
  wrraindex.htm

APPENDIX C:
Colorado Conservation Groups Working to Protect BLM Wildlands

Colorado Environmental Coalition
1536 Wynkoop St., #5C
Denver, CO 80202
303-534-7066
www.ourcolorado.org

Colorado Mountain Club
710 10th St., #200
Golden, CO 80401
303-279-3080
www.cmc.org

National Wildlife Federation
Rocky Mountain Natural
  Resource Center
2260 Baseline Road,
  Suite 100
Boulder, CO 80302
303-786-8001
www.nwf.org/grasslands

The Nature Conservancy
Colorado Field Office
1881 Ninth St., Suite 200
Boulder, CO 80302
303-444-2985
www.tnc.org

Sierra Club, Rocky Mountain Chapter
1410 Grant St.,
  Suite B-205
Denver, CO 80203
303-861-8819
www.sierraclub.org/
  chapters/co/

Sierra Club, Southwest Regional Office
2260 Baseline Rd.,
  Suite 105
Boulder, CO 80302
303-449-5595
www.sierraclub.org

Western Colorado Congress
P.O. Box 472
Montrose, CO 81402
970-249-1978
www.gwe.net/
  homepages/wcc/

The Wilderness Society
7475 Dakin St., Suite 410
Denver, CO 80221
303-650-5818
www.wilderness.org

APPENDIX D:
Selected References

For more information about various topics mentioned in this book, particularly with regard to natural history and additional route descriptions for some areas, consult the following titles.

Boddie, Caryn, and Peter Boddie. *The Hiker's Guide to Colorado.* Helena, Mont.: Falcon Press Publishing Co., 1991.

Borneman, Walter R., and Lyndon J. Lampert. *A Climbing Guide to Colorado's Fourteeners.* Boulder, Colo.: Pruett Publishing Co., 1990.

Cassells, E. Steve. *The Archaeology of Colorado.* Boulder, Colo.: Johnson Books, 1990.

Chronic, Halka. *Roadside Geology of Colorado.* Missoula, Mont.: Mountain Press Publishing Co., 1980.

Cockrell, David. *The Wilderness Educator: The Wilderness Education Association Curriculum Guide.* Merrillville, Ind.: ICS Books, Inc., 1991.

Hudson, Wendy, ed. *Landscape Linkages and Biodiversity.* Washington, D.C.: Island Press, 1991.

Kelsey, Michael R. *Canyon Hiking Guide to the Colorado Plateau.* Provo, Utah: Kelsey Publishing, 1991.

Kricher, John C., and Gordon Morrison. *The Peterson Field Guide Series: A Field Guide to the Ecology of Western Forests.* New York: Houghton Mifflin Company, 1993.

Parris, Lloyd E. *Caves of Colorado.* Boulder, Colo.: Pruett Publishing Co., 1973.

Rhinehart, Richard. *Colorado Caves.* Englewood, Colo.: Westcliffe Publishers, 2001.

Simer, Peter, and John Sullivan. *The National Outdoor Leadership School's Wilderness Guide.* New York: Simon and Schuster, 1983.

Wheat, Doug. *The Floater's Guide to Colorado.* Helena, Mont.: Falcon Press Publishing Co., 1983.

Zwinger, Ann. *Run, River, Run.* Tucson: The University of Arizona Press, 1975.

—. *Wind in the Rock.* Tucson: The University of Arizona Press, 1978.

INDEX

NOTE: Bold citations denote wilderness area descriptions; citations followed by the letter "m" indicate maps.

ABOUT THE AUTHOR

MARK PEARSON has been active in Colorado wilderness issues with the Sierra Club and the Colorado Environmental Coalition for more than 20 years. He first began exploring Colorado's BLM lands in 1978 with a hike into Demaree Canyon, and has since become an avid proponent of desert wilderness in Colorado.

Pearson participated as a private citizen in the planning and management decisions for many of the areas described in this book, and he has visited all of them. Pearson grew up in the Denver metropolitan area and now lives in Durango, Colorado, with his wife, Sherree Tatum. Don't be surprised to run into him in a sandy wash or on a desert river.

ABOUT THE PHOTOGRAPHER

JOHN FIELDER is a nationally renowned nature photographer, publisher, teacher, and preservationist. He is the photographer of 30 exhibit-format books and guidebooks, most about his home state of Colorado. Fielder has worked tirelessly to promote the protection of Colorado's open space and wildlands. His photography has influenced people and legislation, earning him awards from many conservation groups, including the Sierra Club's Ansel Adams Award. His most recent books include the best-selling *Colorado: 1870–2000, Photographing the Landscape: The Art of Seeing,* and *A Colorado Winter.* He lives with his family in Greenwood Village, Colorado.